The Intermittent Fasting Cookbook

Fast & Easy Recipes to Burn Fat, Build M
and Slow Down Aging

By

Olivia Cress

The information herein is offered for informational purposes solely and is universal as such. The presentation of the information is without a contract or any guarantee assurance. The trademarks used are without any consent, and the publication of the trademark is without permission or backing by the trademark owner. All trademarks and brands within this book are for clarifying purposes only and are owned by the owners themselves, not affiliated with this document.

Table of Contents

INTRODUCTION

THE BENEFITS OF FASTING

Fasting is not something that most of us ever think about – food is everywhere and, in all likelihood, right now you're within striking distance of an emergency skinny latte and a muffin. Now I love food as much as the next person, so what I find great about fasting is that it's as much about eating delicious things as it is about abstaining. And there are none of the harmful effects you get from following crazy diets or popping pills, because fasting provides a natural high, an inner boost that works with your body, not against it.

When I first learned about fasting, it was in the context of an invitation to join an intensive meditation retreat in the Himalayas. In fact, I only stumbled across meditation in a foggy, end-of-yoga-class kind of way (and usually ended up snoring!). By contrast, I'd always been fascinated by the inner poise of people who did yoga. I didn't just envy their lithe bodies – I wanted their unshakable contentment and smiling eyes. How did they manage to waft around so effortlessly and have boundless energy for eye-watering yoga moves? And they all seemed to look incredibly youthful and naturally glowing. What was their secret? Whatever it was, I had to have it. So, as you do when you are childless and too young to care about a job and responsibilities, I gave up a regular salary and sold my worldly possessions to enjoy an alternative (and rather late) gap year in an Indian ashram where I planned to study yoga and meditation. Admittedly, it was the thought of becoming supple and slender rather than discovering nirvana that sweetened the deal for me. As it happened, one of the simplest techniques I learned over those intensive months has become one of my most important life lessons for mind and body – how to fast.

Fasting is so easy; you really can't fail. In fact, it's something we all do already – breakfast, quite literally, is breaking a fast of around 12 hours. And let's not forget one of the best things of all – if you "do" fast properly (there are several techniques to choose from and by the end of the book you will discover which one suits you), you can finally give up on the endless hamster wheel of weight loss and gain that sees otherwise sane and successful people becoming slaves to whatever dieting fad happens to be the flavor of the month. I know the pain of that world because I existed in it for so long. I also know how good it feels to be free of it.

FASTING VERSUS OTHER WEIGHT-LOSS APPROACHES

It's time to stick my neck out. I'd go as far to say that I see fasting as the future of weight loss. The diet industry is just that – an industry – and a great many consumers have woken up to the fact that they have been sold a dummy. As any seasoned dieter knows, behind the hype and celebrity following, many trendy diet plans are just plain silly and impractical.

Long-term calorie restriction, the backbone of traditional weight loss, can make you prone to weight gain. Not only that, the nutritional aspects of many commercially savvy weight-loss plans are at best borderline, and at worst downright dangerous. The fact that one of the largest dieting companies in the world is owned by a confectionery company illustrates (to me at least) that the industry behind dieting and the promise of weight loss may need a bit of a shake-up.

Fundamentally, fasting for weight loss is all about nutrition. When you do eat, you must eat well. When you're fasting, there's no cutting out of major food groups such as carbohydrates or essential fats. In this book you'll find lots of information about what to eat when you adopt a fasting regime, rather than simply calculating when you don't eat. In fact, nutrition is even more important when you're fasting since you're eating less overall.

If I'm right and fasting becomes the next big thing in dieting, what will happen? Well, fasting is already rapidly gaining in popularity and when a trend begins

– particularly a global trend – newspaper headlines don't necessarily get all the facts right. And when a trend imbibes the collective consciousness, particularly in weight loss, you can guarantee that money-wasting gimmicks will follow. Therefore, as part of your induction into the world of fasting, I'll be giving you a gimmick-free tour of the scientifically backed benefits of fasting for weight loss, longevity and performance.

Every piece of advice in this book is sound and practical. In my research I've discovered that in order to achieve the best results, fasting techniques should be subtly different for women and men, and different again if you're using fasting to enhance performance. Whilst science acts as the perfect signpost, we're all unique – biologically, physically and emotionally, and ultimately it remains your job and your job alone to turn evidence into action.

Even with the greatest advances, there are certain things that science, or nutrition for that matter, can't explain fully but I will nevertheless attempt to describe how fasting may make you feel more connected and happier in yourself. Fasting, more than any other nutrition or diet approach, can help you to reset your attitude and recognize the difference between physical hunger and appetite. Slowing down your eating can make the experience as much a "mental break" as a physical boost. Indeed, fasting has been used for centuries as a method of mental and spiritual purification. It's like setting a part of you free again.

THE SCIENCE ON FASTING

The scientific studies on fasting focus largely on alternate-day fasting and on prolonged periods of fasting. Much of the scientific research is done on animals rather than on humans – mainly because it's considered unethical to starve people for no reason! However, the evidence that is out there about the benefits of fasting is just so compelling and exciting that it's worthy of a few minutes of your attention (and I'll be busting several dieting myths along the way).

The following are a few highlights from the science of fasting that we'll explore in the forthcoming chapters:

FASTING FOR WEIGHT LOSS

- It might seem counter-intuitive, but intermittent fasting could help you get your hunger under control. This is partly because of its effects on your hunger hormones, and partly because it helps you to learn the difference between physical and emotional hunger.
- Forget what you've been told about regular meals boosting metabolism – studies show that people who are overweight tend to snack more often.
- Fasting is just as effective as traditional diets for losing weight, but might be easier to stick to and less likely to slow your metabolism – perfect if you want to lose that last bit of stubborn flesh.

- If you're stressed, and troubled by weight around your middle, shorter fasts may be better at tackling belly fat than longer ones.

FASTING FOR HEALTH

- Fasting – especially in combination with eating less protein – acts like a "spring clean" for the body by switching on a cellular mechanism called autophagy and by reducing the levels of a hormone called insulin-like growth factor (IGF-1) that can send cell growth out of control.
- Regular juice fasts may deliver potent anti-ageing benefits without you having to cut out food completely.
- Whichever fasting format you choose, it's likely to reduce inflammation – good news for conditions such as eczema, asthma and arthritis.
- Contrary to the popular belief that sugary snacks are "brain food", fasting may help adults to concentrate better. It could even help to build new brain cells.

FASTING FOR WOMEN

- The effects on blood sugar control seem to be different in women and men. Studies suggest that fasting improves men's blood sugar control, but may not have a beneficial effect on women.
- Most women know that adopting any new healthy habit is generally more challenging the week before their period starts. So, my advice is

to go easy that week. Your nearest and dearest will be thankful too.

- When it comes to the overall impact of fasting on menstrual cycles, we only have animal studies to go on, and the effects aren't clear. However, any improvements in overall diet usually go some way to helping with any menstrual problems – so make sure you pay as much attention to what you do eat as you do to what you don't eat. If you notice any negative changes, or have lost weight to the point where your periods become disrupted, stop fasting.

FASTING FOR GYM BUNNIES

- Doing weight training while fasting can help your body build more muscle.
- If you favor cardio workouts, training while fasting can help your body learn to tap into its fat stores more intensively – but it's not such a good idea to run a race without eating beforehand.
- Again, there are gender differences – men tend to build muscle so long as they work out before their main meal, whereas women seem to respond better to training after a meal.

Part 1

Knowledge (The Winning Formula to Lose Weight)

Chapter One

EAT, FAST AND LOSE WEIGHT

Fasting simply means extending the time between meals when we don't eat, and is something that humans have practiced since they first walked the planet. It's only in recent times that we've had access to food 24 hours a day. Before then, we typically went for extended periods without eating. Fasting's no passing "fad" – unlike the modern trend of "grazing", the notion that we should constantly be ingesting small amounts. Interest in when and what we eat and drink has been increasing steadily and is set to continue. Nutritional knowledge helps us understand how our bodies and minds work, and nutritional intervention has a major role to play in the lives of everyone, from Olympic athletes to busy mums and people with medical conditions. No longer seen as something "alternative", nutritional therapy has now gone mainstream.

FASTING TODAY

Celebrities are usually the first to focus attention on any technique that involves the body beautiful, and fasting is no exception. So, as part of my research for this book, I went in search of some of the world's most famous celebrity personal trainers to ask them if they use fasting with their clients.

I've used intermittent fasting on many occasions – notably when people need to lose those last 2–4.5kg [5–10lb], or in order to stimulate stubborn fat loss. I have one client who fasts every Wednesday, just drinks water, green tea, some amino acids, and that's it, and that works very well for her. There are many protocols for fasting and each individual can use the one that works best for them. As with all diets though, the protocol needs to be sustainable so it can be implemented into a lifestyle."

If you still believe that fasting is just another passing diet fad – here today, gone tomorrow – think again. As I mentioned in the Introduction, I predict that fasting will not only become the next big global health trend but that it's here to stay. From a professional point of view, a technique that gets results without compromising health, that helps restore a sense of calm in the mind, and that costs nothing to do, kind of has it all.

THE TRUTH ABOUT FAT AND WEIGHT LOSS

These days, in countries where there's an abundance of food, we've become used to constant grazing – rarely sitting down for meals and simply picking at high-calorie, high-fat and high-sugar foods all day long. We've forgotten what it feels like to be really physically hungry.

The unfortunate truth is that many of us are designed to get fat. It all comes down to evolution. Back in the dim and distant past, when food shortages were common, people who had substantial fat "in storage" were more likely to survive.

Research carried out in the last century proved that extended periods of starvation are much less dangerous for people who have high levels of body fat – in fact, the heavier you are, the more likely it is that fasting will lead to substantial fat loss with muscle being spared. In contrast, the slimmer you are (and your ancestors were), the more likely it is that you'll break down muscle through extreme dieting.

People often blame their genes for a "slow metabolism" or "big bones", but it turns out things are more complicated than that. The genetic factors that helped your ancestors lay down fat stores seem to relate to a complex range of factors rather than simply affecting your metabolic rate. For example, there are subtle differences in appetite, or in the tendency to fidget.

WHY SOME PEOPLE ARE NATURALLY SLIM

Emerging research suggests that naturally slim people have genetic advantages that make it easier for them to avoid weight gain. They're not blessed with faster metabolisms, but tend to be able to regulate their appetite and burn off excess calories without even noticing it.

TO THEM, FOOD IS JUST FOOD

Naturally slim people enjoy food, but they don't have a strong emotional connection to it. Foods aren't "good" or "bad", they're just food. Therefore, slim types don't feel guilty when they tuck into a slice of cake or have a few chips with their dinner.

THEY CAN STOP AFTER JUST ONE BITE

When our naturally slim friends eat indulgent foods, they can stop after just a little, rather than polishing off the plate. Many of us are familiar with that feeling of having broken the diet rules:

"That's today ruined... I may as well finish the whole cake and start again tomorrow."

Slim people don't get that "all-or-nothing" feeling that's typical in seasoned dieters.

THEY RECOGNIZE THE DIFFERENCE BETWEEN HUNGER AND APPETITE

The mechanisms controlling our appetites are complex. Research suggests that naturally slim people may be more resistant to appetite signals that aren't linked to physiological hunger. What this means is, they eat when their body needs nourishment, not when their brain is trying to trick them into believing they're hungry. In contrast, those of us with a genetic tendency to gain weight can feel physically hungry when tempted by food, even if our bodies don't need the calories.

THEY BURN IT OFF

There's a theory that our body weight has a "set point" (a natural weight at which it tries to maintain itself). When a naturally slim person overeats, they tend to compensate by moving around more, without even thinking about it. So, as well as a few more gym sessions, they may fidget, get stuck into cleaning the house, or walk rather than taking the car. But for the majority of us, overeating is followed by a few hours relaxing on the sofa!

OTHER FACTORS INFLUENCING WEIGHT

Ultimately, weight gain comes down to the fact that we're eating more calories than we're burning off, and over time this has led to many of us gradually getting fatter. But tackling the issue is about more than simply cutting calories. The quality of what we eat is important too. The types of food that are so readily available to us – those muffins and sugary drinks – tend to be packed with sugar or refined carbohydrates (carbs) and it's very easy to eat them and not notice when we're full. Instead, try replacing those "empty" calories with nutrient-rich, lean proteins, leafy green vegetables and even healthy fats from nuts and oily fish. I promise you; these will make you feel full and you'll be much less tempted to overeat.

It's also important to detect underlying problems or habits that can be causing or contributing to a weight problem. For example, stress, emotional eating or chemical calories may have been the tipping point for your body. Unhealthy eating can mean that you're not getting enough of the vitamins, minerals and essential fats that your body needs to function well. What's more, many "fad" diets aren't nutritionally balanced, so they starve the body of the vital nutrients your body needs.

On a basic level, these problems can make it very hard for you to stick to a diet. Likewise, "crash" diets tend to drastically restrict your body's intake of calories. If your body isn't getting the nutrients it needs, the result can be irritability, depression and even lowered brain function, all of which inevitably affect your motivation to continue with the diet. And when you come off the diet, you quickly return to your previous weight and may end up gaining even more weight. This is because, when you lose weight, your metabolic rate naturally dips – more about this shortly.

STRESS AND WEIGHT GAIN

The link between stress and weight gain begins with tiny glands called adrenals. Their basic task is to rush all your body's resources into "fight or flight" mode by increasing production of adrenaline and other hormones – you may recognize this feeling with an increased heart rate, and your blood pressure may be raised.

Unlike our ancestors, who weren't distracted by mobile phones, deadlines, emails and the multi-tasking challenges of modern life, today we live under constant stress. Instead of occasional, acute demands followed by rest, we're constantly over-worked, under-nourished, exposed to environmental toxins, and plagued by worries… with no let-up.

Every challenge to the mind and body creates a demand on the adrenal glands. The result is a state of constant high alert and high levels of the hormone cortisol in the body, leading to a huge number of health problems, such as a tendency to hold on to stubborn belly fat. The other main side- effects of stress and adrenal overload are digestive problems, rapid ageing, lowered immunity and skin problems.

Sometimes it's less about the stress in our lives and more about the stress we place on ourselves with what we eat and drink. Take caffeine, for example. We're all familiar with the "buzz" that caffeine can give. Many products are marketed solely on the basis of this false energy kick, but that lively feeling is actually the sensation of adrenaline being pumped around the body as a result of the caffeine hit. The adrenal glands tire of constant stimulation and when the inevitable adrenal fatigue kicks in, it leads to a slowdown in the conversion of stored fats (and proteins and carbohydrates) into energy. We experience this failure in the energy chain as a craving for further stimulants in the form of more caffeine from another cup of tea, coffee, cola drink or caffeinated beverage. The last piece of the picture with caffeine is what usually comes with it. Remember that an average coffee these days contains a sizeable portion of milk, sugar or syrup and then there's the ubiquitous temptation of a muffin or pastry accompaniment!

INSULIN RESISTANCE AND THE EFFECTS OF ALCOHOL

When the body is overloaded with carbs (which are extremely commonplace in the average Western diet), it has to respond by making more insulin. Carbs are broken down into molecules of the sugar glucose, and insulin is the hormonal "key" that unlocks the cells to allow the glucose in. Over a period of time, excess insulin affects the cells by making them less sensitive to taking sugars into the cell and creating energy. This in turn prevents the cells from burning fat. The good news is that fasting may improve how your body handles sugar and help your body burn fat instead of storing it.

As far as your body's concerned, alcohol is chemically similar to sugar, so drinking any form of alcohol will set off the same insulin resistance seesaw that can promote weight gain. And that's before you even begin to consider the calorie content of the drink itself, which is likely to be very high and devoid of any nutritional benefit – so-called "empty calories". What's more, alcohol acts as a potent appetite booster, so more alcohol equals more food consumed!

There's yet another reason behind alcohol's "beer belly" effect. Alcohol reduces the amount of fat your body burns for energy, while preventing the absorption of many of the essential nutrients needed for successful weight loss, particularly the B vitamins and vitamin C. In one study published in the American Journal of Clinical Nutrition, eight men were given two glasses of vodka with diet lemonade, each containing just under 90 calories. For several hours after drinking the vodka, the amount of fat the men burned dropped by a massive 73 percent. Because your body uses more than one source of fuel, if alcohol is consumed then this alcohol "energy" will be used instead of fat – not good news for the waistline!

EMOTIONAL EATING

As we all know, a lot of eating is emotionally driven. Many people with weight problems fear feeling hungry. Furthermore, reaching for the sugar-fix from food or from alcohol is what helps free us, temporarily, from whatever uncomfortable emotion we might be feeling. Of course, sometimes an eating problem masks an underlying psychological problem or challenge. In such cases, expert advice, counselling or psychotherapy or psychology can really help.

Even when eating is free from emotional factors, the fact is, the longer you spend on a diet (whether for health or for weight loss), the less strict you become and the more likely it is that calories will sneak in without you noticing – a bite of this here, a nibble of that there. Fasting shakes up this model of eating altogether. Having a large section of the day when food simply isn't allowed to pass your lips prevents random snacking, and might also alert you to how often you do this normally. If you'd describe yourself as someone with limited self- control, fasting is an easier option than almost any other diet out there as you don't have to count every calorie or become a slave to food group fads – the only thing you really need to do is watch the clock.

"CHEMICAL CALORIES"

It's thought that chemicals in the environment have a blocking effect on the hormones that control weight loss. When the brain is affected by these toxins, hormone signaling can be impaired. Reducing chemicals in our homes, foods and drinks is important when looking at the overall picture of weight loss and health. As you'll discover in the "Nutritional Rules for Fasting" chapter, one of my nutrition rules as part of any fasting program me is to eat real food rather than fake food. If you can't pronounce what it says on the label, you probably shouldn't be eating it!

THYROID PROBLEMS

An underactive thyroid can cause weight gain, too. Symptoms include fatigue, cold, hormonal problems, depression and low libido as well as unexplained weight gain. The challenge is sometimes that the problem is sub- clinical, in other words, your test from the doctor may come back negative but you still have the symptoms. This can be frustrating for the sufferer as it sometimes means a re-visit in six months to a year to see if the symptoms register as qualifying for medical intervention.

A nutritious diet designed with thyroid health in mind can help. For the thyroid to work optimally, it needs nutrients such as iodine, manganese, vitamin C, methionine, magnesium, selenium, zinc, and the amino acids cysteine and L- tyrosine. These are all found in healthy foods such as fruit, vegetables, nuts, seeds and meat.

WHY TRADITIONAL DIETING MAKES YOU HUNGRY

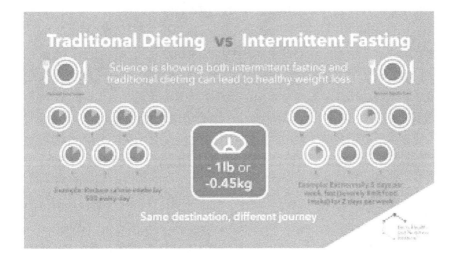

Going on a traditional diet without adequate energy intake for long periods of time can make your metabolic rate plummet and your appetite soar. Say you reduce your calories to below 1,000 a day for a number of weeks to fit into a party dress, the chances are you'll feel hungry and fed up much of the time, and as soon as the party starts, you'll dive head first into all the foods you've been avoiding, re-gaining that lost weight in no time! This, in a nutshell, sums up the seesaw of the diet industry.

The real trick is to keep your body feeling fuller for longer. I'm not talking about choosing one ready-meal over another, it's about understanding how to manage hunger so you naturally eat less most of the time. Please note, I don't say all of the time. Special events and over-indulging every now and then are good for the soul.

In tandem with a good diet overall, fasting can be used to retrain your hunger without the need for appetite suppressants or dodgy supplements. When you begin to fast, you will feel hungry at your usual meal times. However, if you choose not to eat at that time, the peaks and troughs of hunger start to level out. All this happens without a decrease in metabolic rate. It doesn't take a genius to recognize that if you feel hungry less often, you'll eat less and therefore lose weight. There's a biological explanation for this. Feelings of hunger and satiety (feeling full) are controlled by two main hormones produced within the body, ghrelin (even the word sounds hungry) and leptin. This dynamic duo of hormones has a powerful effect on how much food you eat and how much of what you've consumed you "burn off".

GHRELIN

This hormone seems pretty straightforward. When your stomach's empty, it sends out some ghrelin to tell an area of your brain, the hypothalamus, that you ought to be eating. You then feel ravenous. But research published in the American Journal of Physiology suggests that ghrelin levels also rise in anticipation of eating – you get hungry partly because you're expecting a meal, not just because you have an empty stomach.

On a traditional diet, you get a peak of ghrelin before every meal – but because you don't eat as much as you'd really like to, you never feel fully satisfied. When you're fasting, your ghrelin levels still rise, but anecdotal evidence suggests that over time your body finds this sensation easier to get used to, probably because of the changes in your meal patterns. There's also a theory that a nutritionally poor diet sends ghrelin rocketing faster than a nutrient-dense plan like the ones I recommend.

WHY MOST DIETS FAIL

This probably isn't the first book about weight loss you've ever read. I often say I've been down the diet road myself so many times that I could be a tour guide. If you're asking yourself why fasting is going to be any different, here are the facts you need to know:

• "Yo-yo" dieting is the bane of many people's lives, but even if you've lost and gained weight countless times, recent research has shown that it's possible to lose weight safely without messing up your metabolism.

• Burning off more calories than you eat is the only way to lose weight – and the simple truth is that you will lose weight if you manage to keep the number of calories you eat below the amount you burn off... boring but true.

There are hundreds of different ways to create a calorie deficit – as evidenced by the huge diet book, diet shake, diet bar and "miracle" weight-loss supplement industry. But there are two main reasons why diets never tend to live up to their expectations, especially as you get closer to your goal weight:

1   Traditional diet misrepresent the calories in/calories out equation.

We've all heard that 450g (1lb) of fat is roughly equal to 3,500 calories, so the traditional calorie-counting approach is to cut calories by 500–1,000 per day in order to lose 450–900g (1–2lb) per week. The trouble is, as you get slimmer you become lighter and that actually reduces the number of calories you burn at rest (your basal metabolic rate). So, in traditional weight-loss plans, weight loss is initially rapid but tends to slow down over time, even if you maintain that original calorie deficit. This can be very demotivating.

2   It's sticking to your chosen approach that's often the hard part.

Even if you get your calories exactly right, how boring does counting every calorie get? Demotivation – either as a result of not seeing the numbers on the scales going down as quickly as they were, or boredom – can lead to lapses, which slow down the rate of weight loss even further. When you go back to your old eating habits – surprise, surprise – you'll gain all the weight back, and a little more, as a result of the natural dip in basal metabolic rate (calorie burn) caused by your initial weight loss.

HOW FASTING MAKES A DIFFERENCE

FASTING MAY BOOST METABOLIC RATE

You're probably thinking, "If I start starving myself, won't that be worse for my metabolism?" First of all, fasting is not starving yourself, and don't worry that eating less often will damage your metabolism. Losing weight naturally slows your basal metabolic rate (the number of calories you burn at rest) in proportion to the amount of weight you lose, no matter which method you use. This is because your daily energy (calorie) needs are directly related to your age, height, gender and weight, in particular your lean body mass (muscle). It doesn't mean that eating more often will fire up your metabolism.

You'll hear over and over again that after a night of sleep, your metabolism has ground to a halt and you need to eat breakfast to stoke your metabolic fire. The idea that "breakfast boosts metabolism" is simply not true – it hasn't been backed up by research at all. The breakfast myth is based on the "thermic effect of food". Around 10 percent of our calorie burn comes from the energy that we use to digest, absorb and assimilate the nutrients in our meals. Roughly speaking, if you eat a 350-calorie breakfast, you'll burn 35 calories in the process. But notice that you've eaten 315 extra calories to burn that 35. No matter what time of day you eat, you'll burn off around 10 percent of the calories in your food through the thermic effect of food. So, whether you eat your breakfast at 7am, 10am or never, if you eat roughly the same amount and types of food overall, its effect on your metabolism will be the same.

In fact, all the research on fasting seems to show that eating less often could actually boost your metabolic rate. In one British study conducted at the University of Nottingham, a two-day fast boosted participants' resting metabolic rate by 3.6 percent. In another study by the same research group, 29 healthy men and women fasted for three days. After 12–36 hours, there was a significant increase in basal metabolic rate, which returned to normal after 72 hours. The exact mechanisms for why this happens aren't clear.

FASTING INCREASES FAT BURN

What is clear is that more of the calories you use for fuel during fasting come from your fat stores. Scientists can estimate what proportion of your energy is coming from fats and carbohydrates by measuring the amount of oxygen inhaled and the amount of carbon dioxide exhaled in your breath. The higher the proportion of oxygen to carbon dioxide, the more fat you're burning. As part of the same Nottingham study, findings proved that the proportion of energy obtained from fat rose progressively over 12–72 hours, until almost all the energy being used was coming from stored fat. This is incredible news really!

We're so often told to "breakfast like a king, lunch like a prince and dine like a pauper" with a view to becoming healthy, wealthy and wise. This is usually explained by telling us that breakfast kick-starts the metabolism – but it turns out that eating breakfast doesn't boost your fat-burning potential at all. In a small study on breakfast-eaters – published in the British Journal of Nutrition – a 700-calorie breakfast inhibited the use of fat for fuel throughout the day. Put simply, when we eat carbohydrates, we use it for fuel, and this prevents our bodies tapping into our stubborn stored fat. Constant grazing might be what's keeping fat locked away in your belly, bum or thighs – and fasting is one way to release it.

FASTING MAINTAINS LEAN MUSCLE

The more muscle you have, the more calories you burn at rest. And before you say you don't want big muscles, another way to put that is: the less muscle you lose as you drop in weight, the less your basal metabolic rate falls as you move toward your goal weight. (Remember, your basal metabolic rate is the rate at which you burn calories, so it's really important in order to make staying in shape easier in the long term.) Besides, muscle takes up less room than fat. So, a person with good lean muscle mass will take a smaller dress size or use a narrower belt notch than someone who doesn't have it.

Fasting is better than plain old calorie restriction when it comes to maintaining lean body mass. This is largely because fasting triggers the release of growth hormone (GH), which encourages your body to look for other fuel sources instead of attacking its muscle stores. This is thought to be a survival advantage – back when humans were hunter gatherers it wouldn't have made sense for our muscle mass to reduce when food was scarce – we needed strong legs and arms to hunt down our dinner!

In one study carried out by researchers at Intermountain Medical Center in the USA, participants were asked to fast for 24 hours. During this time, GH levels rose by a whopping 1,300 percent in women and 2,000 percent in men.

It's important to note that more isn't necessarily better when it comes to GH – what's key is resetting the balance between GH release (which happens in the fasted state) and insulin release (which happens in the fed state, however small your meal) in order to stimulate fat loss without losing lean muscle. You never need to fear growing giant muscles as a result of fasting – GH is released in waves and goes back to normal levels quickly as soon as your body has released enough fat to burn.

As mentioned earlier, if you're already slim, it's especially important not to overdo it when fasting. Research published in the academic journal Obesity Research shows that within just two days of complete fasting, there's a dramatic increase in the use of muscle for fuel in people who are already a healthy weight. This is because they have less fat available to burn overall. Perhaps the advice for people who are already svelte but who want to fast for health benefits is to fast little and often rather than to eat little and often.

FASTING PATTERNS GIVE YOU ENERGY WHEN YOU NEED IT

Alongside maintaining your muscle mass to reduce the dip in your metabolic rate that happens as you lose weight, fasting may help with stubborn weight in other ways.

There's a theory that the reduction in calorie burn typically seen after following a calorie-restricted diet may be related more to changes in activity level than to basal metabolic rate. When you're only eating, say, 1,200 calories day after day, it may be difficult to maintain the energy levels and motivation to exercise. But following an intermittent fasting pattern means that you can concentrate your workouts around the times when you're eating. More energy means a tougher workout – and more calorie burn overall.

COMMON QUESTIONS AND ANSWERS

Q Isn't "not eating" dangerous?

A It's very important to establish that fasting is not starvation, which, of course, is dangerous. What I'm talking about is the health benefits of increasing the gaps between meals or eating less from time to time.

Some people who are fully signed up to the merry-go-round of traditional dieting will argue that not eating is likely to induce a low-blood-sugar or "hypo" episode. Feeling faint, clammy and unable to concentrate are typical symptoms, happily offset by a visit to the vending machine or, for the health- aware, a snack such as an oatcake or nuts and seeds. I'm not suggesting that snacking should be outlawed – most of the time, I'm more than happy to tuck right in. But fasting challenges the assertion that we can't survive, or even thrive, without five mini-meals a day.

Q Won't I feel light-headed and really hungry on a fast?

A You might be worried that your blood sugar levels will dip too low between meals and that you'll feel faint and weak. But when you're not eating, other hormonal signals trigger your body to release glucose or make more. In one Swedish study by researchers at the Karolinska Institute, students who'd reported that they were sensitive to hypoglycemia (low blood sugar) felt irritable and shaky during a 24-hour fast, but there was actually no difference in their blood sugar levels – it may all have been in their minds.

Q   Hang on a minute… My trainer told me that six small meals will fire up my metabolism and stop me feeling peckish. Who's right?

A   This is one of those fitness and nutrition "truths" that has been repeated so many times, people are convinced that it's a fact. In one small study at the US National Institute on Aging, researchers found that people who ate only one meal a day did tend to feel hungrier than those who ate three. But beyond eating three meals a day, meal frequency doesn't seem to make a difference to hunger or appetite, so it comes down to what's actually easiest for you. A study published by the International Journal of Obesity showed that people who are overweight tend to snack more often.

The truth is, you will feel hungry when fasting – there's no getting away from that – but rather than a constant unsatisfied feeling, your hunger will come in waves. You'll start to recognize the difference between physical and psychological hunger. And you'll get to eat meals that are big enough to leave you feeling genuinely satisfied when you do eat.

Q   Can fasting change my shape?

A   For many women, that last bit of surplus weight is carried around the hips and thighs and it simply won't shift. To solve this problem, I suggest looking to the true body professionals.

According to noted intermittent-fasting expert Martin Berkhan, there's a good reason for this. All the cells in our body have "holes" in them known as receptors. To switch activity on and off in those cells, hormones or enzymes enter the receptors. Fat cells contain two types of receptor – beta 2 receptors, which are good at triggering fat burning, and alpha 2 receptors, which aren't. Guess which is mostly found in the fat stores of your lower body? Yes, our hips and thighs have nine times more alpha 2 receptors than beta.

Fasting is the only thing that alters alpha 2 receptor expression in adults – when we're fasting, the alpha 2 receptors are more likely to stay hidden. If you combine this with the fact that GH and catecholamines (hormones released by the adrenal glands) are particularly good at encouraging fat loss, then fasting is a way for your body to release the stubborn fat it retained while you were on traditional diets.

Q   What about belly fat?

A   All over the Internet you'll see promises that you can get rid of belly fat in a matter of days by taking supplements. We all know that this is simply not true. Stubborn fat around the middle is linked to a number of factors – including stress, alcohol, lack of exercise and a diet high in refined carbohydrates.

Stress + refined carbohydrates + alcohol = a recipe for belly fat, especially if you're unlucky enough to be genetically predisposed to weight gain around the middle.

Q   How does fasting help torch belly fat?

A   To burn belly fat, free fatty acids must first be released from your fat cells (this is called lipolysis) and moved into your bloodstream, then transferred into the mitochondria of muscle or organ cells, to be burned (a process known as beta-oxidation).

Glucagon (another pancreatic hormone that has pretty much an equal and opposite effect to insulin) rises around four to five hours after eating, once all the digested nutrients from your last meal have been stored or used up. The purpose of glucagon is to maintain a steady supply of glucose to the brain and red blood cells, which it achieves by breaking down stored carbohydrates and leftover protein fragments in the liver. It also activates hormone-sensitive lipase, which triggers the release of fat from the fat cells, allowing other cells to be fueled by fat as opposed to glucose.

Q What else can I do to help get rid of belly fat?

A Endurance exercise selectively reduces abdominal fat and aids maintenance of lean body mass, so it's great to do in combination with intermittent fasting. Choose a fasting method that will enable you to take regular exercise – gentle activity such as walking will help, but high-intensity training is even better.

Also, a very small recent study, carried out at the University of Oklahoma in the USA, found that quality protein intake was inversely associated with belly fat, so make sure you fuel up on lean proteins (which your fasting plans are rich in), when you are eating.

Q What about losing that last 4.5kg (10lb)?

A This is often the hardest weight to shift. Not only that, it tends to creep back over a matter of weeks after you've finally reached your target weight. A familiar story is the strict diet we follow to get into beach-body shape in time for a holiday: in all the years I've helped people to lose weight, I've lost count of the number of times I've heard people telling me that all their hard work was undone by two weeks of sun, sea and sangria!

Remember that losing weight is all about creating a calorie deficit. Here, fasting is acting in two different ways. First, fasting helps maintain calorie burn – so in theory you can eat more overall and still lose weight. Second, fasting might just be easier to stick to than a boring calorie-counting diet. And when it comes to beach bodies, remember that old saying "a change is as good as a rest". If you're bored of the approach you've taken to weight loss up to now, a short blast of fasting can help you achieve your goal weight without damaging your metabolism.

This is backed up by research. Most of the studies on intermittent fasting show that it can be just as effective for fat loss as traditional diets, but the studies are all designed differently so it's difficult to say exactly which fasting approach will be the most effective for you. Scientific studies on intermittent fasting have shown varying results – from an average weight loss of a few kilos in the first few days, to 8 percent of body weight within eight weeks.

During the first few days of the fast you'll generally lose weight quickly, which can feel very motivating, especially if the scales have been stuck for a while.

One thing to note is that your weight will fluctuate. At first, you'll lose water (because stored glucose holds roughly four times its weight in water, and is quickly used up during a fast), and yesterday's food should make its way through your digestive tract. Alongside this, you'll lose some body fat. But the next day, you'll gain weight via the new intake of water and food. Don't worry! Over time, your average weight will fall. That's why it's important to limit weighing yourself to once or twice a week, and to be consistent in the time and day you use the scales.

Part 2

Practice (Unlock Your Metabolism)

EAT, FAST AND LIVE LONGER

THE HEALING POWER OF FASTING

Over the last decade I've seen my clients achieve amazing results with fasting. Getting to the optimum weight for your body frame is as much about health as it is about looking and feeling good. Fasting improves health alongside helping to shift the pounds and, just as importantly, it can help heal somebody's relationship with food, which is often at the heart of the struggle with weight.

I firmly believe that what I can achieve with a client during a week of fasting would take me months or possibly years with a conventional nutrition approach. In fact, I'll stick my neck out and say that fasting can and will change how we as a society view healing – if someone told you there was a pill that could reduce the risk of diabetes, cancer and heart disease and keep you looking and feeling young, you'd be tempted to take it, wouldn't you?

Unlike medication, so long as you're sensible about it, there are no harmful side-effects of fasting. Contrast this with the side-effects of common prescription and over-the-counter drugs – even if the chance of side-effects is small, the risks are still real. One study published by the peer-reviewed British Medical Journal into the side-effects of statins (cholesterol-lowering drugs), confirmed cases of increased risk of muscle weakness, cataracts, acute kidney failure, and moderate or severe liver dysfunction. Of course, if disease has taken hold, the benefits of medication will often outweigh the risks. However, we need to be working toward a model of preventative action.

HOW FASTING PROMOTES HEALING

Nothing in the body, or mind, works in isolation, so it shouldn't come as a surprise to learn that fasting creates a healthy "ripple effect" of sorts.

The over-arching theory is that fasting helps to de-stress the body. When you fast, you give your body a break and a chance to catch up on its inner "to-do" list. We all know how good it feels to have a well-earned holiday and return rested, rejuvenated and with renewed joie de vivre. Well, fasting has a similar effect on your body.

Around 70 percent of your daily energy is spent maintaining internal functions, such as digestion and detoxification. If you're a busy, on-the-go person and don't give your body the best conditions to rest, digest and ultimately heal, ill-health will catch up with you sooner or later.

Have you ever had that sluggish feeling, much like a slow hangover that's really difficult to shake off? Just as your home or office can become dusty and dirty, so your body can become clogged up with toxins and waste matter from the environment around you (more about this later in the chapter). When your body is clean and strong, it's able to eliminate toxins efficiently, but when it becomes overloaded it can become sluggish, overweight (or underweight in some instances) and more susceptible to disease. The result is that "toxic signals", such as aches and pains, irritable bowel, skin complaints, mood swings and fatigue, start to kick in. If these signals are ignored, they allow longer-term chronic health problems to take hold.

Cue fasting. Thousands of studies or observations of both man and animals have established the fact that when the body goes without food, the tissues are called upon in an inverse order of their importance to the organism. What this means is that when you fast, fat is the first tissue to go. And, contrary to expectations, instead of food deprivation causing a debilitating loss of nutrients, in short-term fasts the body retains the majority of these.

Fasting is now considered an acceptable treatment or approach for promoting longevity, improving insulin response, reducing inflammation, boosting cardiovascular health and even for supporting cancer treatment. Fasting may deliver health benefits and more, without many of the unpleasant side-effects produced by other treatments, and, again, without an extortionate price tag.

FASTING AND ANTI-AGEING

Ageing is inevitable. Everything that keeps us alive from one day to the next can be called your metabolism, and running your body has side-effects. Those side-effects accumulate and eventually will cause problems. Welcome to the reality of ageing... But reality is ever changing and there's good reason to be optimistic. Like looking for the proverbial pot of gold, we seekers of health are all out there, trying to find the elixir of youth.

You're as young or as old as your smallest vital links – your cells. Ageing begins when your normal process of cell regeneration and rebuilding slows down. At a cellular level, the hormone insulin-like growth factor (IGF-1) has both positive and negative effects. Like insulin, it's anabolic, meaning that, in effect, it tells our cells to grow and multiply. If IGF-1 is kept high, our cells constantly divide and multiply, which is good if we're trying to build big muscles and not so good if those cells become damaged and cancerous. High levels of IGF-1 have been linked to prostate cancer and post-menopausal breast cancer. When IGF-1 levels drop, the body slows production of new cells and starts repairing old ones, and DNA damage is more likely to be permanent.

KEEPING THE HEART AND CIRCULATION HEALTHY

Inflammation is involved in cardiovascular disease, in concert with high levels of "bad" fats in the blood. Most studies on fasting show that it reduces triglyceride levels and improves the ratio of triglycerides to "good" cholesterol (that is, high-density lipoprotein [HDL] – the transport protein that helps remove excess cholesterol from the bloodstream). In animal studies, resistance to what is known as "ischemic injury" – the type of artery damage that's associated with the build-up of plaques and hardening of the arteries – has been seen.

All in all, although the findings are far from clear and lots more research is needed, fasting seems to give the body an internal tune-up and to increase resistance to age-related illnesses.

Going back to those scary statistics from the beginning of this chapter – cardiovascular disease is the leading cause of death worldwide and something that affects us all. In Britain, NHS statistics show that in England in 2007, people aged over 60 were prescribed an average of 42.4 prescription items each. Each time you receive a prescription for an individual drug from your doctor, it counts as one prescription item. That's a whole lot of drugs! Unsurprisingly, medication that treats cardiovascular disease and its risk factors is the most commonly prescribed. I often meet people who want to change their eating habits, not just because they'd like to look and feel better, but because they're shocked by the amount of medication that their own parents are on.

As fasting becomes more popular, people are becoming attracted to it as a lifestyle choice that might help their heart and circulatory system stay healthy for longer.

FASTING AND CANCER

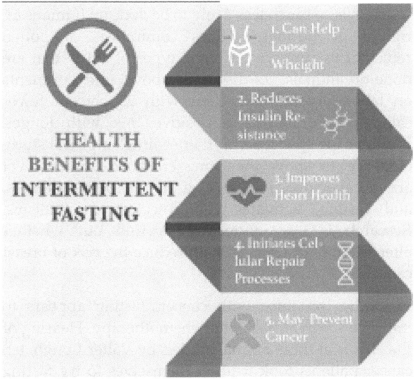

Fasting is considered to be an alternative or complementary treatment for cancer in certain sectors of complementary medicine, and has been popularized by a naturopathic doctor called Max Gerson. However, my focus is not on fasting as a stand-alone treatment but rather on exciting evidence about fasting in cancer prevention and the encouraging results from trials involving fasting during cancer treatment, particularly chemotherapy.

There's evidence that intermittent fasting, and calorie restriction more generally, fights the growth and spread of cancer cells in animals. Often when we read about research on animals, it seems so compelling that we want to see if the same thing will work for us. However, research is so much less likely to be done on humans as, rightly or wrongly, ethics committees are often reluctant to approve the same types of study that are done on animals. As discussed above, in experiments on laboratory animals, diets with 25 percent fewer calories have shown a positive link with longer, healthier life spans. So far there's little empirical study evidence to show the same effect in humans, yet anecdotal evidence is growing that restricting calories, and fasting, activates cell-protecting mechanisms. Research is also underway to find out whether alternate-day fasting can help reduce the risk of breast cancer.

In studies on mice with cancer, fasting appears to improve survival rates after chemotherapy. Hearing of the effects of these animal studies by Valter Longo, ten cancer patients took it upon themselves to try fasting before chemotherapy. The results were published in the medical journal Aging. Of these ten, the majority experienced fewer side-effects as a result of fasting than those eating normally, and the authors concluded that fasting for two to five days before chemotherapy treatment appeared to be safe. This work has yet to be taken to a truly meaningful empirical testing on humans, but it's understandable that cancer patients are excited by the potential of calorie restriction and fasting, not least by it helping the body to mitigate the effects of cancer treatment and specifically chemotherapy.

DETOXING

Personally, I no longer like the word "detox". It's been used and abused by marketeers in their quest to sell, sell, sell fancy products, when, in fact, detoxing is something that the body does naturally every hour of the day. However, until someone comes up with a better word, "detox" will have to do.

HOW WE BECOME TOXIC

A toxin is anything that has a detrimental effect on cell function or structure. Toxins are materials that our bodies cannot process efficiently. Over time they build up and, as a result, our systems function below par, leaving us drained, tired and frequently ill. People become "toxic" in many ways – through diet, lifestyle and the environment, as a natural by-product of metabolism, and through genetic lineage. Stress and harmful emotions can also create a kind of toxic environment.

Toxins include, but are not limited to:

• Food additives, flavorings and colorings.

• Household and personal cleaning chemicals, which are both inhaled and absorbed via the skin.

• Agricultural chemicals, such as pesticides, fungicides and herbicides.

•   Heavy metals, which occur naturally but are poisonous.

•   Oestrogens, which enter the environment due to human usage of the contraceptive pill and HRT.

•   Xeno-oestrogens, which are chemicals that mimic oestrogen.

…And here are the most common ways people become toxic on the inside:

•   Eating a poor diet. This includes low-fiber foods, fried foods and foods tainted with synthetic chemicals. Unlike live foods (fresh fruits and vegetables), these lack the enzymes that assist proper digestion and assimilation, and the fiber or bulk that assists proper elimination. They're also void of essential vitamins, minerals and other basic nutrients.

•   Eating too much. Over-eating puts a great amount of stress on our digestive system. The body must produce hydrochloric acid, pancreatic enzymes, bile and other digestive factors to process a meal. When we over-eat, the digestive system finds it hard to meet the demands placed upon it. The stomach bloats as the digestive system goes into turmoil. Foods aren't broken down properly and tend to lodge in the lower intestine. Vital nutrients are then not absorbed.

• Inadequate water intake. When the body isn't receiving enough water, toxins tend to stagnate, hindering all digestive and eliminative processes.

• Exposure to synthetic chemicals in food and environmental pollutants. A clean, strong system can metabolize and excrete many pollutants, but when the body is weak or constipated, they're stored as unusable substances. As more and different chemicals enter the body, they tend to interact with those already there, forming second-generation chemicals that can be far more harmful than the originals.

• Being stressed. Stress hinders proper digestion, absorption and elimination of foods.

• Overuse of antibiotics. Antibiotics have a damaging effect on the intestines, especially if they're taken for extensive periods of time. Reducing the use of unnecessary antibiotics will also help minimize the very real danger of bacterial resistance.

• Lack of exercise. This lowers metabolic efficiency, and without circulatory stimulation, the body's natural cleansing systems are weakened.

• Eating late at night. The human body uses sleep to repair, rebuild and restore itself. In essence, the body uses the sleeping hours to cleanse and build. When a person goes to sleep with a full stomach, the body isn't at rest but is busy digesting and processing food. In addition, the body requires gravity to assist the passage of food from the stomach down the digestive tract.

Q If the body detoxes itself anyway, why bother to do anything further?

A Just as your home or office can become dusty and dirty, so your body can become clogged up with toxins and waste matter from the environment. A healthy body is able to disarm toxins by breaking them down, storing them in fat tissue or excreting them. However, here's the crux – many, if not most,

people are depleted in the nutrients needed to detox optimally, and chronic health problems, sluggishness and weight gain are common results.

If you've never given your digestion much thought, don't beat yourself up about being neglectful. Unlike the head or the tips of the fingers, the gut contains very few nerve endings. What this means is, we're not so aware when things aren't working well. When you have a headache, you feel every throbbing pulse and do something about it. In contrast, gut problems go unresolved and uncared for over long periods.

The good news is, when you improve digestion, a whole range of seemingly unrelated health issues can improve. For example, it's not only the job of the white blood cells (the leukocytes) to defend your body since the digestive system forms the basis of your immune system with the action of beneficial bacteria. Improving the ecology of the gut can be achieved with a juice fast and healthy diet.

USING A JUICE FAST TO DETOX

A juice fast stands head and shoulders above other fasting techniques in its self-healing effect and is often mentioned in the context of detoxing the body.

Juice fasting is based on consuming juices and broths only, whereas intermittent fasting adds lean protein and fat for the feeling of fullness. Studies have shown that eating as little as 10g (¼oz) of essential amino acids (found in high-quality proteins) can switch off autophagy. Therefore, a juice fast is best placed to give your body a good "spring clean" because juices are typically very low in protein.

The simple act of juicing a fruit or vegetable will help you absorb more of the nutrients from it. The caveat here is that you should make the juice fresh rather than drink pasteurized fruit juice from a carton or bottle. The process of juicing eliminates a lot of the fiber that needs to be digested. Cutting out the bulk and drinking only the juice means that you can very effectively hit your antioxidant targets in one small cup. Juice provides tiny "particles" of nutrients that are readily absorbed into the bloodstream.

Fresh juices provide a highly effective fast-track and – importantly – easy delivery mechanism for the body to absorb and process key vitamins, minerals and plant chemicals (phytonutrients) that are so beneficial to our health. A fresh juice contains a concentration of nutrients that have been separated from pulp, making it easier to consume what's required to assist the healing process. In essence, a fresh juice should be considered more of a body tonic than a tasty drink.

Q   Will I get withdrawal symptoms on a juice fast?

A   The folklore of fasting is littered with stories about the dramatic side-effects of a juice fast. This is usually because the contrast between the diet and lifestyle before and after is simply too great. Or, in some cases, the enterprising individual has decided to "retox", that is go on an almighty bender before entering detox – not a good idea.

One of the most dramatic side-effects I ever witnessed was when a client was coming off a 20-year-long diet cola habit during a juice-fasting retreat. Her symptoms were akin to what you'd expect from coming off a class-A drug. The rest of the detox group watched mesmerized at her descent from bubbly, bouncy guest on arrival to a sweating, vomiting, pale-faced shadow of her former self after just 24 hours of juicing. Even I was a little worried. Luckily, her troubled time was followed by a rapid and dramatic improvement two days later, at which point she declared that she felt "reborn" and would never touch a drop of cola again.

So, learn from my diet cola story and start with a transition diet. Fasting can be a challenge physically and psychologically. I recommend having at least three days on the Countdown Plan to prepare. Juice fasting should be undertaken for between one and five days for optimum results – usually once or twice a year. Any longer requires more management and should only be considered when there are adequate reserves (body fat) or if there's a specific medical condition. Some people find that weekend-long juice fasts four times a year are helpful.

Q   What are the most common side-effects of a juice fast?

A   Let me be frank – a juice fast isn't a good idea for a romantic break or naughty weekend away. During a juice fast the capacity of the eliminative organs – lungs, liver, kidneys, and skin – is greatly increased, and masses of accumulated metabolic wastes and toxins are quickly expelled. It's like pressing the accelerator button on your body's waste disposal unit. As part of the eliminative process, your body will be cleansing itself of old, accumulated wastes and toxins. This typically throws up symptoms such as offensive breath, dark urine, increased faecal waste, skin eruptions, perspiration and increased mucus. As I said, it's not exactly romantic!

• Your digestive system is the star of a fasting program. Poor digestion can be a hidden cause of weight gain, or more accurately, water retention. For example, if your body's responding to an allergy or intolerance, it will often retain water. So, when fasting, there's often a "quick-win" water loss that equates to an extra kilo being lost.

Q   What about fiber?

A   The process of juicing extracts the pulp (fiber) of the fruits and vegetables so on a juice fast it's a good idea to restore some bulk to maintain a healthy transit of waste matter through the gastrointestinal tract. Psyllium husks, a soluble form of fiber, do just the trick as, when taken with adequate amounts of fluids, they absorb water to form a large mass. In people with constipation, this mass stimulates the bowel to move, whereas in people with diarrhea it can slow things down and reduce bowel movements.

Some recent research also shows that psyllium husks may lower cholesterol. It's thought that the fiber stimulates the conversion of cholesterol into bile acid and increases bile acid excretion. In addition, psyllium husks may even decrease the intestinal absorption of cholesterol.

Psyllium comes from the plant Plantago ovata and is native to India. It is readily available in health food shops and online stores, either as husks or in powdered form. In non-fasting, normal dietary conditions, whole grains provide dietary fiber and similar beneficial effects to psyllium, so a supplement isn't needed unless recommended by your health care practitioner.

Q   Can colon cleansing help?

A   Your bowels are not just "poo pipes". Toxins and metabolic wastes from the blood and tissues are discharged into the intestinal canal to be excreted from the body. Not surprisingly, one of the long-established techniques to support the body's elimination organs during a fast is colon hydrotherapy or enemas. This is a technique that involves taking in water into the large intestine, also known as the bowel, to assist the removal of waste.

Part 3

Results (Rejuvenate)

EAT, FAST AND PERFORM BETTER

CAN FASTING GIVE YOU A YOUNGER BRAIN?

The potential benefits of fasting go beyond weight loss and physical health. If you've ever found yourself befuddled about where you could possibly have left your keys/phone/purse/marbles, you'll know that memory loss is a very frightening thing. The threat of long-term conditions like Alzheimer's is arguably one of the most worrying aspects of ageing. But there is hope. Researchers at the National Institute on Aging in Baltimore have found evidence that fasting for one or two days each week may help protect the brain against Alzheimer's, Parkinson's and other brain diseases.

ISN'T BREAKFAST IMPORTANT "BRAIN FOOD"?

Children who eat breakfast tend to perform better in cognitive tests, but this doesn't seem to be the case for adults. Studies have shown that short-term food reduction doesn't actually impair cognitive function in adults. Prolonged dieting, on the other hand, does. This means that the perceived deterioration in brain function may, in fact, have a psychological cause – rather than being caused by a dip in blood sugar, lack of concentration may be a result of the stress of being "on a diet" (the way it tends to make you feel grumpy, miserable, and obsessive about food). Of course, it's true that the brain uses glucose for fuel, but as we've seen in previous chapters, our bodies have enough stored glucose to see us through a short fast.

In one study, published in the American Journal of Clinical Nutrition, scientists observed that fasting and non-fasting groups of adults performed similarly in cognitive tests, even after two days without food. This is thought to relate to adaptive mechanisms – as adults, when we don't have food available, it's important that we have the mental clarity to go out and find it. Our hunter- gatherer ancestors didn't have the option to pop out to the supermarket to grab a snack, and those who could think more clearly when hungry were more likely to be able to find food or outsmart predators. This was a survival advantage, and so the genetic factors that maintained cognitive function when food was scarce were passed on. As there haven't been dramatic changes in our genes since caveman times, it makes sense that the ability to think clearly when we haven't eaten for a while should still be the norm.

FASTING AND BRAIN HEALTH

Professor Mark Mattson, a renowned researcher at the National Institute on Aging, has dedicated his career to studying the effects of fasting on brain ageing. Until now, all his research has been on mice, but there's now enough evidence of the beneficial effects of fasting on the brains of mice to begin research on humans.

At the National Institute on Aging, mice have been bred to develop a susceptibility to Alzheimer's disease. If they are then put on a "fast food" diet which is high in sugar, they experience an earlier onset of learning and memory problems. But if they're made to fast every other day, they find it much easier to remember their way around a maze. Brain scans on the mice show that fasting actually encourages new brain cells (neurons) to form by placing a mild level of stress on the brain cells, which encourages them to build up a resistance to future stress, as well as building new proteins. Other researchers have found that fasting also increases the rate of autophagy in the brain, thereby getting rid of any damaged "grey matter" and making way for healthy new cells. So, while it's too early to tell whether fasting is the miracle cure for memory loss and age- related brain diseases, the research definitely sounds promising.

WHAT ELSE CAN I DO TO KEEP MY BRAIN YOUNG?

Sadly, the exact reasons why some people are susceptible to diseases such as Alzheimer's are unclear. It's generally accepted that diets rich in fruit, vegetables and healthy fats from fish, avocados and olives (typically like the Mediterranean diet) are associated with good brain health. What's good for the body is also good for the brain!

One of the most important things that you can do for your body and brain is to get active and regular fasting might just help you do that. Recent studies published in the Archives of Internal Medicine indicate that the more active we are as we get older – even if it's just gentle walking – the longer our brains will stay healthy. It sounds like the recipe for a healthy brain could be fasting combined with an active lifestyle and a real-food based diet – just what I have in mind!

CAN FASTING MAKE YOU FASTER?

I have to declare an interest here... For a few years I've loved the release that running has given me, especially after having my second baby. In fact, I've been a competitive soul from day dot. In my early youth I was good at badminton and represented Scotland in the game. In those days, not much attention was paid to sports nutrition, and since badminton is a largely anaerobic discipline it was possible to get by without thinking too much about what you were eating. Now, of course, everything has changed. Nutritionists feature large in all serious sport - not least, I imagine, because the "quick fix" route of banned substances has come under the spotlight, and, of course, we're all more aware of nutrition's role in exercise.

My running has become something of a "fix" – a means of releasing tension, either before the stress of the school run, or after the stress of a day's work. My usual preparation used to consist of an espresso and a mostly empty stomach. While that works for a quick half-hour run, it was only when I stepped up to training for the London Marathon in 2011 that I became more scientific and observant of my nutritional requirements. I also wondered whether fasting during training or pre-event could make a person run faster.

Q What's the truth about sports drinks?

A If you're a keen runner or cyclist, or harbor ambitions to run a marathon, you're probably aware of the importance of getting plenty of carbs. It's impossible to open up a running magazine or take part in a race without being bombarded with adverts for the latest energy drink or gel.

It's a fact that topping up your fuel levels with sugar – whether from fruit juice, sweets or expensive sports drinks – can make you run faster if your existing energy levels are low. Countless sports nutrition studies confirm that they do benefit performance. And the British public are buying into the dream en masse. In 2010, we drank 600 million liters of energy drinks and sports drinks.

However, topping up your blood sugar during exercise is only beneficial if you're taking part in high-intensity exercise that lasts for more than an hour, such as running a half-marathon or competing in a football match. In other cases, it won't do you any favors at all.

Q What about fasting and exercise during Ramadan?

A Interest in the effects of fasting on fitness has increased in recent years, inspired by studies on what happens to Muslim athletes during the month of Ramadan. During Ramadan, Muslims are required to observe a period of fasting from dawn until sunset. This includes avoiding not only food, but fluids too. As the dates of Ramadan change from year to year, this means that it can take place across major events in the sporting calendar, such as the 2012 Olympics. If you believe the sports nutrition adverts, you may think that not being able to eat or drink regularly would ruin an athlete's chances of winning, but that doesn't necessarily seem to be the case.

While most medal contenders at the 2012 Olympics seem to have taken the opportunity to postpone their fast until later in the year, in 1980 Tanzanian runner Suleiman Nyambui won silver in the 5,000 meters while observing the Ramadan fast. The effects of fasting on athletes' ability to compete and train during Ramadan are mixed. Several studies summarizing the research were published in the Journal of Sports Science in 2012. The overall picture was that the effects of fasting on performance are minimal, so long as overall nutritional intake and other factors, such as quality of sleep, are maintained.

Nevertheless, training while fasting – especially in the case of Ramadan, where athletes are also likely to be dehydrated through avoiding water – may make you feel more tired or reduce the amount of effort that you're able to put in. But, for mere mortals rather than Olympians, intermittent fasting has the promising ability to improve overall fitness or sports performance.

Q   Should I cut carbs?

A   As mentioned at the beginning of this chapter, the roots of how fasting may benefit performance are in our evolutionary past. Our caveman ancestors simply didn't have the opportunity to fuel up with carbohydrates before they went off to forage and hunt. Cycles of feast and famine meant that the ability to perform extended periods of physical activity on an empty stomach was an advantage when it came to survival. It's thought that our genetic make-up hasn't changed much in the 10,000 or so years since. So, it makes sense, in theory, that humans are designed to exercise without taking on extra fuel. At all times, our bodies burn both fat and carbohydrate for energy. While our storage capacity for carbohydrate is limited to around 500 calories-worth, most of us have more than enough fat stores to keep us going for a while. Say you're 70kg (11st) and your body fat is 25 percent – that means you have over 150,000 calories of fat in storage.

Aerobic training increases the proportion of fat to carbohydrate burned, making it easier to exercise for long periods of time. Just as the body adapts to any training stimulus by getting stronger or fitter, the idea is that training when fasting – when stored carbohydrate levels are low – stimulates the body to become even more efficient at using stored fat for fuel. While it might therefore seem like a no-brainer that exercising without extra carbohydrate will help your body adapt, it has long been recommended that endurance athletes consume a carbohydrate-rich diet.

Carbohydrate is stored in muscles as glycogen, where it can easily be broken down into glucose to fuel movement. Most research continues to emphasize the importance of adequate carbohydrate intake, before, during and after exercise. This is particularly important during high- intensity events, where glucose is the main fuel – stored fat is pretty good at fueling slow and steady movement, but it's glucose that your body turns to when you want to move fast. In events or training that last over an hour, it's generally recommended that 30–60g (1–2¼oz) of carbohydrate is consumed per hour, in the form of drinks, gels or food.

The mistake that many of us make is to rely on topping up our carbohydrate stores too much. This could also be the reason why many people don't lose weight when they start exercising. A typical bottle of sports drink can take half an hour of leisurely cycling to burn off, so if that's all you manage, and you add in a post-workout snack too, you could even find yourself gaining weight!

Q   What happens when you train while fasting?

A   Looking back to a study carried out by the US Army in 1988, there's no need to fear running out of glucose if you haven't eaten for a day. In fact, it seems to be possible to exercise for just as long after a three-and-a-half day- fast as it is after an overnight fast when working at a low intensity. Researchers in the same study found that blood glucose levels were maintained too.

In another small study published in the Journal of Physical Activity and Health, this time on healthy people who exercised at a relatively high intensity for an hour-and-a-half, fasting for 16–18 hours didn't impede their efforts. Interestingly, drinking a sports drink didn't make them feel or perform better either.

Meanwhile, researchers at Pennington Biomedical Research Center have discovered that consuming carbohydrates during exercise can actually decrease the expression of genes that are involved in fat metabolism. So, the more carbs you take in during exercise, the worse your body gets at tapping into its fat stores!

Sticking to plain water, or a calorie-free drink, increases the proportion of fat burned during exercise because less glucose is available. When you consume a sports drink, the glucose is rapidly delivered to your blood and provides an instant source of fuel. Without this, you need to tap into your body's fat stores.

Q   What's meant by "train low, race high"?

A   "Train low" means that some training is done without carbs to encourage the body to burn fat. As the bulk of modern sports nutrition research highlights the role of carbohydrates in enhancing performance under race conditions, the "race high" part involves taking on standard sports drinks or gels during events.

"Train low" training is different from simply training after an overnight fast, when muscle glycogen levels are still relatively high. Studies investigating the "train low" approach deplete participants' glycogen stores by putting them through an hour or more of aerobic training. After an hour's rest, participants then complete up to an hour of high-intensity exercise, all with only water to drink.

But be careful because training in a glycogen-depleted state has its risks.

These include increased levels of stress hormones, muscle breakdown, fatigue and lowered immune response. If, while fasting, you decide to add some endurance training to your schedule, especially at a high intensity, it's probably best, initially, to limit it to once a week. Allow plenty of time for recovery, and monitor your response, stopping if you feel unwell or fatigued.

FASTING FOR A STRONGER BODY

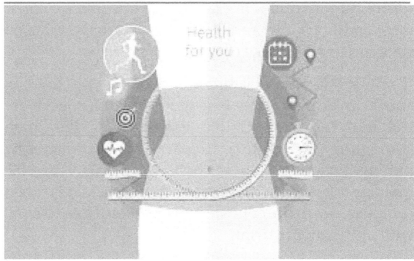

Weight-training enthusiasts use intermittent fasting as a technique to build lean mass and lose fat, with the goal of achieving a "shredded" or "ripped" physique. The explosion in popularity of intermittent fasting over the past few years is in part due to fitness experts such as Martin Berkhan, who designed the "Lean Gains" 16/8 hour fast. This method focuses the fast around the times you're scheduled to work out. The reason for this is that, in order to build muscle, you need to be in positive energy and protein balance after your workout, otherwise your muscles will be consumed for energy instead of getting bigger. Therefore, while the workout is done in the fasted state, the biggest meal of the day is right after the workout. Some people also take "branched-chain amino acid" supplements to maximize levels of growth hormone and to kick-start the muscle- building process.

FASTING AND MOTIVATION

The final motivator, when thinking about incorporating fasting with exercise, is that it could give you more energy to train. There are lots of arguments over whether diet or exercise is more important when it comes to losing weight.

You may be familiar with the saying "you can't out-train a bad diet". While it's probably true that exercise alone isn't going to get you the body you want if you pay no attention to what you eat, dieting without exercise isn't a good idea either. After all, exercise comes with an impressive array of health benefits itself from heart and lung health, to stress relief, to maintaining strong bones.

When it comes to muscle strength and the way you look, exercise is the clear winner over diet. Researchers at Ann Arbor University in Michigan looked at how women's bodies responded to diet alone versus exercise alone. They found that, as expected, diet was more effective at reducing body weight, but exercise was more effective when it came to losing fat and maintaining muscle.

The thing is, getting the motivation to exercise can be hard when you're "on a diet" because you're always eating less than you're burning off and you often feel like you just don't have the energy. The good thing about fasting is that the gaps between meals are longer so when you do eat, you get to eat more. This means that you can time your exercise around the times when you've eaten and are feeling energetic. You're more likely to work harder!

MEDITATION

For those with ambition above and beyond the physical benefits of fasting, getting into the fasting state of mind can be helped by meditation, and if you have the time and inclination at least once in your life, a week's retreat can take the fasting experience to another level.

Meditation can be viewed in scientific terms for its effects on the mind and the body. During meditation, a marked increase in blood flow slows heart rate, and high blood pressure drops to within normal ranges. Recent research indicates that meditation can also boost the immune system and reduce free radicals – in effect, a slowing down of the ageing process.

There's much talk about the power of meditation and how you can use your mind to manifest great piles of money. But, becoming more aware of your mind is not just about manipulating it or attempting only to have positive thoughts – rather, it's about the ability to direct your attention toward or away from the mind at will.

My most intensive fast was on a 10-day silent meditation retreat during my time in India. One evening, five days into the experience when I was seriously doubting my judgement about freezing my butt off in a cold cave in the Himalayas, I had what I've come to realize was a "breakthrough" moment. In spiritual terms I'd describe it as a moment of grace. With a raw, pure energy of infinite magnitude, my mind flashed through formative experiences – good and bad – that had shaped my life. As my mind was swept along on this emotional rollercoaster, my body conveniently left the room, leaving me nowhere to run or hide… or at least that was how it felt!

When I first started to meditate, I tried too hard. Furiously studying the science of the mind or contorting your face into Zen-like expressions won't work. The only way to experience meditation is actually to experience it. It can be maddening. You'll be trying to meditate for hours and then, just when you're ready to give up, you might get a flash of something akin to what you were aiming for. Yet, in that momentary shift you might see how you could choose to do a few things differently, or how some really small things have a huge impact on you, and how easy it would be to make a few minor changes. Many great thinkers have talked about breakthroughs and inspiration. The most famous of all was probably Albert Einstein, who said that no problem can be solved from the same level of consciousness that created it.

So, if you do manage to get your mind to stop its usual chatter through meditation, try asking yourself a question when all is calm. For example, if you always react to something uncomfortable by quashing the emotion with food, then meditation can create a gap to ask why. Sometimes there's a clear answer to that question, and sometimes there isn't. Usually, it takes a bit of time.

YOGA

Yoga is often lumped together with meditation since the kind of person who likes yoga is often into meditation, and vice versa. For people with a poor attention span, yoga can be a good way of getting into a calm state without the need ever to sit cross-legged.

There are many forms of yoga and it's a case of having a go and seeing which suits you best. Regardless of which tradition you choose, good yoga teachers can make you walk out of the class feeling a foot taller and ready to take on the world. My advice would be:

• If you're gentle by nature, try Hatha.

• If you're into precision and detail, go for Iyengar.

•   If you like the spiritual side of yoga, opt for Sivananda.

•   If you want yoga to help you sleep, try Yin.

•   If you're fit and physical, Ashtanga or Vinyasa "flow" yoga will be more your bag.

•   If you really want to sweat, try Bikram, or "hot yoga". It's not for the faint hearted and has some medical contra-indications, but it's considered seriously addictive by devotees.

ANTI-AGING TIPS FOR FASTING

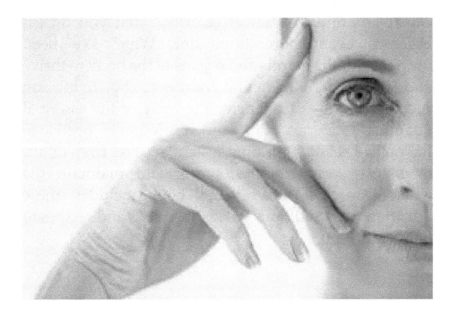

There are far too many tips which would enable you achieve that anti-aging look and feel. However, we are going to be grouping them for you to easily process and remember.

EAT WELL

The problem with most fasting information is that it only focuses on the fasting bit, not on what you need to eat. If you're eating fewer calories, what you do eat becomes even more important. Why? We need nutrients for the glands and organs of the body to thrive and burn fat. Restricting nutrients by living on processed foods can deprive the body of the essential vitamins, minerals, fats and proteins it needs to maintain a healthy immune system, recover from injury or illness, keep muscles strong and maintain the metabolism. That's why this book includes these nutrition rules and practical fasting plans and recipes to help guide you.

RULE 1: ONLY EAT "REAL" FOOD

This means no fake food and no diet-drinks. If you grew up in the UK, chances are you'll have fond memories of bright orange corn snacks and fizzy drinks that turned your tongue red or blue. It's to be hoped that now you're "all grown up 'n' stuff", you eat lots of rocket and Parmesan salads, roasted artichoke and monkfish. If only that was the case for all of us. Celebrity chefs may make out that this is the norm but it just isn't. Most people still eat a diet full of processed, refined, low-fiber, nutrient-deficient foods.

Not all processed food is bad, though. In fact, some of it's great. Canned food without added sugar or salt and freshly-frozen fruit and veg are just a couple of examples of stellar staples for your larder. It's the low-calorie, low-fat, oh-so-easy snacks and meals that you need to watch out for since they're often loaded with chemicals and hidden sugars.

Heavily processed foods can also be high in chemicals. There's a real and present danger that chemicals in the environment may have a blocking effect on hormones that control weight loss. When the brain is affected by toxins, it's possible that hormone signaling is impaired. The reason why we're unsure as to the extent of the problem is that it's impossible to test for the thousands of chemicals that are contributing to the "cocktail" effect on the body. Err on the side of caution and control what you can. Keep foods "real"!

But what makes up a real-food diet?

PROTEIN

Protein is made up of amino acids, often called the "building blocks of life", and we need all of them to stay alive and thrive. Proteins from animal sources – meat, dairy, fish and eggs – contain all the amino acids and are therefore classed as "complete" proteins. Soya beans also fall into this category. Once and for all, eggs are healthy. Eggs have had a tough time of it over the years. First the salmonella scare, then the unfair link to cholesterol. Eggs are low in saturated fat and if you eat eggs in the morning, you're less likely to feel hungry later in the day.

Vegetable sources provide incomplete proteins. If you're vegetarian or vegan, you'll get your protein from nuts, seeds, legumes and grains but you need a good variety of these to ensure that you get the full range of essential amino acids.

TOP TIP:
•   Include more beans and lentils in your meals. Examples include kidney beans, butter beans, chickpeas or red and green lentils. They're rich in protein and contain complex carbohydrates, which provide slow and sustained energy release. They also contain fiber, which may help to control your blood fats. Try adding them to stews, casseroles, soups and salads.

CARBOHYDRATES
Carbs are one of the most controversial topics in nutrition and weight loss. For years we've been told that we eat too much fat, and that saturated fat is the main cause of heart disease. But recently, some experts have challenged this view, suggesting that carbohydrate is responsible for the obesity epidemic and a whole host of diseases. Should we cut carbs, avoid fat or simply reduce our food intake and exercise more?

When the body is starved of carbohydrates it looks for energy in its glycogen stores. Water binds to every gram of glycogen so it's easy to get dramatic weight loss – the only problem is that it's mostly water weight! Along with those glycogen stores you'll begin to lose fat but not at a rate higher than a healthier (and easier) weight-loss method.

The truth is there are healthy fats and healthy carbohydrates. Avoiding carbs altogether is unnecessary and potentially dangerous. The key is in recognizing that not all carbs are created equal. Low glycemic index (GI) carbohydrates, found in fiber-rich fruits, beans, unrefined grains and vegetables, are important for good health and can actively support weight loss – for example, through reducing appetite and energy intake.

However, high-GI refined carbohydrates, such as those found in soft drinks, white bread, pastries, certain breakfast cereals and sweeteners, not only make it harder to lose weight but could damage long-term health. Studies show that eating a lot of high-GI carbohydrates can increase the risk of heart disease and Type-2 diabetes.

There's been a lot of research on low-carbohydrate diets in recent years. It was initially thought that they may damage bone and kidney health, but this doesn't seem to be the case unless you have a pre-existing kidney problem. Lowcarb diets can be effective for weight loss and also improve risk factors for heart disease and diabetes. However, they do carry risks.

First, the low intake of fruit, vegetables and whole grains on a lowcarb diet reduces the intake of certain vitamins and minerals, notably folate, which is vital for women who may become pregnant. Second, cutting out unrefined carbohydrates dramatically reduces the amount of fiber in the diet, which leads to constipation and changes the balance of gut bacteria. In the long term, this may increase the risk of colorectal cancer.

Finally, eating a lowcarb diet based on animal protein has been associated with a significantly higher risk of mortality. High levels of meat and dairy create substances called prostaglandins, which are inflammatory. Inflammation is bad news for the body. Side-effects of a very lowcarb diet can include bad breath, hair loss, mood swings, constipation and fatigue. In my opinion, this is too high a price to pay when weight loss can be achieved just as quickly without the side-effects.

For this reason, while I'd never recommend cutting out carbohydrates as a food group, my recipes focus on unrefined, low-GI carbs from whole foods rather than refined, high-GI carbs. As well as improving health, low-GI carbs release glucose into the bloodstream more slowly, which leads to a more sustained energy release, rather than the peaks and crashes you tend to experience if you eat a lot of high-GI carbs.

TOP TIP:

•   Eat bulky carbs to become slim. When you choose "big" foods like fruits, vegetables, salads and soups, which are bulked up by fiber and water, you're eating a lot of food that fills you up, but not a lot of calories.

FAT

Since fat is the greatest source of calories, eating less of it can help you to lose weight. However, fat is actually a vital nutrient and is an important part of your diet because it supplies the essential fatty acids needed for vitamin absorption, healthy skin, growth and the regulation of bodily functions. In fact, eating too little fat can actually cause a number of health problems.

The right kinds of fat, in the right amounts, can also help you to feel fuller for longer, so try not to think of fat as your mortal diet enemy, but rather a useful ally in the pursuit of your healthier lifestyle! Adding a little fat to your meals helps your body absorb nutrients and enhances the flavor of your food, so recipes have been created with this in mind. Choose monounsaturated fats or oils (e.g., olive oil and rapeseed oil) as these types of fats are better for your heart. Coconut oil can be a good choice for cooking as it's heat-stable.

TOP TIPS:
• Increase essential fats – aim for at least two portions of oily fish a week. Examples include mackerel, sardines, salmon and pilchards. Oily fish contains a type of polyunsaturated fat called omega 3, which helps protect against heart disease. If you don't eat fish, use flaxseed oil in salad dressing and snack on walnuts.

• If you use butter, stick to a thin scraping on bread and just a smidgen for flavor in cooking.

• Choose lean meat and fish as low-fat alternatives to fatty meats.

- Choose lower-fat dairy foods such as skimmed or semi-skimmed milk and reduced-fat natural yogurt.

- Grill, poach, steam or oven bake instead of frying or cooking with oil or other fats.

- Watch out for creamy sauces and dressings – swap them for tomato-based sauces. Add herbs, lemon, spices and garlic to reduced-fat meals to boost flavor.

- Use cheese as a topping, not a meal – in other words, no macaroni cheese! Choose cheese with a strong flavor, such as Parmesan or goat's cheese so that you only need to use a small amount.

RULE 2: CUT OUT SUGAR

Too much sugar makes you fat and has an ageing effect on the skin. Sugar links with collagen and elastin and reduces the elasticity of the skin, making you look older than your years. The recipes I provide use low-sugar fruits to add a little sweetness – and the occasional drizzle of a natural sweetener such as honey is fine – but, in general, sugar is bad news and best avoided.

TOP TIP:
- Stick to dark chocolate if you need a chocolate "fix" (which simply is the case sometimes!), as most people need less of it to feel satisfied.

RULE 3: WATCH THE ALCOHOL

Over the years the alcohol content of most drinks has gone up. A drink can now have more units than you think. A small glass of wine (175ml/5½fl   cup) could be as much as two units. Remember, alcohol contains empty calories so think about cutting back further if you're trying to lose weight. That's a maximum of two units of alcohol per day for a woman and three units per day for a man. For example, a single pub measure (25ml/¾fl oz) of spirit is about one unit, and a half pint of lager, ale, bitter or cider is one to one-and-a-half units.

TOP TIP:

•   If you're out for the evening, try out some healthy soft drinks such as tonic with cordial, or an alcohol-free grape juice as a tasty substitute to wine. Alcohol-free beers are also becoming increasingly popular and are available in most pubs and bars.

RULE 4: EAT FRUIT, DON'T DRINK IT

If you consume around 1 liter (35fl oz/4 cups) fruit juice, remember you'll be imbibing 500 calories. That's fine if you're juice fasting, but too much if it's simply a snack. You could tuck into a baked potato with tuna and two pieces of fruit for the same number of calories.

TOP TIPS:

•   Choose herbal teas (especially green tea, which may aid fat loss).

•   Feel free to have a cup or two of tea or coffee. A small amount of milk is allowed but keep it to a splash when you're fasting.

•   Sip water throughout the fast, aiming for a fluid intake of around 1.2–2 liters (40–70fl oz/4¾–8 cups) a day. This will not only help to keep hunger pangs at bay, it will also keep you hydrated.

RULE 5: AVOID THE PITFALLS

• Top up before you fast. When you first start fasting, you may feel hungry during the times when you'd normally have a meal and you may also feel slightly light-headed if you have sugary foods as your last meal. This isn't a sign that you're wasting away or entering starvation mode, and these feelings of hunger will usually subside once that usual meal time has passed. Try to get your carbohydrate intake from fruit, vegetables and whole grains and eat a good amount of protein, which will fill you up for longer. Following the fasting plans will make this as straightforward as possible.

• Stock up for quick meals. Make sure you always have ingredients in your fridge and cupboards for meals that can be put together quickly, such as stir-fries, soups and salads.

• Don't polish off the kids' plates. Eating the children's leftovers is a fast track to weight gain for parents. Put the plates straight into the sink or dishwasher when the children have finished their meal, so you won't be tempted!

• Downsize your dinner plate. Much of our hunger and satiation is psychological. If we see a huge plate only half full, we'll feel like we haven't eaten enough. But if the plate is small but completely filled, we'll subconsciously feel that we have eaten enough.

•   Beware of the Frappuccino effect. Black coffee only contains about 10 calories but a milky coffee can contain anything from 100 calories for a standard small cappuccino to a whopping 350+ calories for a Grande with all the trimmings. Much like the plate size, shrink your cup size and shrink your waist line. Don't be afraid to ask for half the milk – spell it out: "Don't fill up the cup." I do it all the time and the best baristas get it right first time!

•   The sandwich has become the ubiquitous carb-laden "lunch on the go". Lose the top piece of bread to cut your refined carbohydrates and instead fill up with a small bag of green salad leaves and healthy dressing.

•   Don't try to change everything at once. Bad habits are hard enough to break as it is. Focus on breaking one at a time.

•   If you're a parent, choose your meal skipping wisely. I've tried fasting with a toddler who doesn't understand why Mummy isn't eating and will, quite literally, shove a fistful of tuna pasta into my mouth.

•   Get the portions right. If you're restricting the number of meals you're having, it makes sense that the portion sizes need to be bigger than they would be if you were eating five mini-meals a day. Use the recipe section as a guide to how big your portions should be.

FASTING SAFELY

By now I hope that you have an open mind to the many benefits of fasting and that you're excited about giving it a go. If you've read this book and are still trying to decide if, when, or how to give fasting a try, remember that you'll only ever truly "get it" by trying it for yourself.

Before you launch headlong into your new fasting lifestyle, here are a few words of caution. Although fasting has been around for millennia, the science on how and when to fast is in its early stages. For example, there's very little research on how fasting affects fertility.

There are some people who should avoid fasting completely, some who should seek medical advice first, and some situations where it might not be right for you. Fasting isn't something that you should just jump into, and it doesn't suit everyone.

WHEN NOT TO FAST

You should avoid fasting if any of the following apply:

• You are pregnant, breastfeeding, or actively trying for a baby (it's okay to fast if you're getting your body ready to conceive, but please don't consider fasting if there's any chance you could already be pregnant).

• You have ever experienced an eating disorder.

• You are underweight

You should seek medical advice first if any of the following apply:

• You have a long-term medical condition such as cancer, diabetes, ulcerative colitis, epilepsy, anemia, liver, kidney or lung disease.

• You have a condition that affects your immune system.

• You are on medication, particularly medicines that control your blood sugar, blood pressure or blood lipids (cholesterol).

POSSIBLE SIDE-EFFECTS AND HOW TO MANAGE THEM

As we learnt earlier in the book, fasting may make you feel a bit "yucky" at first. Many juice fasters experience headaches through caffeine withdrawal, and feeling hungry is natural when you first try a fast. These effects don't usually last long, and most people find that they're outweighed by the positive effects of fasting.

More serious side-effects may include:

- Dehydration or over-hydration.

- Feeling dizzy or light-headed.

- Extreme fatigue.

- Constipation.

- Nausea or vomiting.

- Insomnia.

- Irregular periods.

Always err on the side of caution and stop the fast if you don't feel well. You can minimize the risk of some side-effects by approaching the fast safely.

Introduction

Given the multiple kinds of diets you have probably read about in your life, you are likely to have a few fresh ones. Perhaps one amongst them may be the Ketogenic Diet, commonly known as the Keto Diet, which is a low-carbohydrate, high-fat regimen.

The idea behind the high-fat, low-carbohydrate ratio is that instead of carbs, the body would depend on fats for nutrition, and hence the body would become leaner as a consequence of getting less fat contained throughout the body.

Ideally, the Keto Diet would encourage the body to achieve ketosis or a metabolic condition where the carbs are ketones, which are fats that are burned for energy rather than glucose. Many who embrace the Keto Diet often eat only the correct amount of protein on a regular basis that the body requires. The Keto Diet does not rely on measuring calories, compared to any of the other diets that occur. Instead, the emphasis is on the food's fat, proteins and carbohydrates make-up, as well as the weight of the servings.

But what contributed to the Keto Diet being created?

In hopes of discovering a cure for seizures, a Mayo Clinic physician by the name of Russell Wilder invented the Ketogenic Diet back in 1924. Since going on this diet, many people who have epilepsy and other disorders have reported a substantial reduction in their symptoms. This procedure goes back to Ancient Greece when physicians would change the diets of their patients and even make them rapidly push their bodies into hunger mode.

The Ketogenic Diet is a much better way for the body to reach the fasting mode without completely depriving the body of food. However, to this day, no one understands precisely why the Ketogenic Diet is so effective in treating those who have epilepsy, autism, and other identified diseases.

The high-fat, low-carbohydrate combination might be a normal meal for those on the Ketogenic Diet, which would include a balanced portion of some fruit or a protein-rich vegetable, protein such as chicken and a high-fat portion that may be butter. The high-fat portion of this diet typically comes from the food-making ingredients; this may involve heavy cream, butter, or buttermilk, and creamy dressings such as ranch could also be mixed.

Unfortunately, with its potential for instantaneous results, this natural approach to healing had to give way to the new advancement of medicinal research.

Happily, again and perhaps for really good purposes, the ketogenic diet has made its way back into the spotlight!

You see, the cornerstone of the diet is to effectively stimulate the fat-burning processes of your own body to feel what the body wants for energy during the day. This implies that all the fat you consume and the accumulated fat in your body have both been fuel reserves that can be taped over by your body! No wonder that except among some persistent, hard to lose fat regions, this plan also helps you with weight reduction. It may be one of the explanations why you selected this eBook and looked into the ketogenic process, or you might have learned stories from your social group on how the keto diet really normalizes blood glucose levels and optimizes the cholesterol measurements and you are fascinated. Only by adopting this plan alone, how about the news of type 2 diabetes getting cured as well as stories of some diseases being prevented or tumors shrinking thanks to the beneficial impact of the keto diet? Even as a result of the diet, we do overlook the risk of heart disease!

All the above-mentioned advantages derive primarily from a single major mechanism in the ketogenic diet. The name of the game is ketosis.

In this very book, all information about the keto diet and intermittent fasting is provided and lets you know how it's helpful for quick and healthy weight loss.

Chapter 1- Ketogenic Diet and Ketosis

You may be on a ketogenic diet or are contemplating it.

If you desire to kickstart with ketosis, then your ticket is for intermittent fasting.

Truth be known, it can be daunting to follow a ketogenic diet, mainly because there are too many things that you cannot consume. But be assured the truth-ketosis is spiritual.

Fortunately, whether you don't want to eat a ketogenic diet, you will easily get a route to ketosis.

When the body burns up ketones and fat for food instead of glucose, ketosis happens.

In two cases, that happens:

1. there is no food coming (fasting) or

2. little or no carbohydrates come through (ketogenic dieting).

It regularly makes ketones in the process when your system is in the fat-burning phase; hence, you are in ketosis.

For the body to be in the process of ketosis is perfectly natural, and it was definitely a popular occurrence for humans across history that had intermittent accessibility to food and fasting times in between. For those following a Western diet, though, the physiological condition of ketosis is very unusual since we are all feeding. You basically get negligible ketones in your blood while you're consuming something else than a ketogenic diet. But it's very rare for our generation of people to be in a condition of ketosis unless you seek one out purposefully.

Post 8 hours of fasting, as you wake up, ketone levels are only starting to raise. Ketone output will speed up to provide more of the energy you need if you prolong your fast until noon, and your body will finally be in the renowned fat-burning condition of ketosis. If you want to manage to burn body fat at a high pace by keeping to your fast for 16 hours or a day or a few days, and not by consuming anything ketogenic, you need to live in ketosis!

A lot of focus is given to reaching ketosis through ketogenic diets, but if you consume keto foods, where do you suppose any of the ketones come from? And not the fat on the thighs and hips. Fasting for ketosis means that only the body fat comes from the ketones that feed the brain, thereby getting rid of it.

Ketosis is a condition in which the body creates compounds that are formed by the liver, labeled ketones. Crafted to supply organs and cells with nutrition, it may substitute sugar as an additional source of food. We get much of our energy from glucose in our conventional diet, rich in carbs which are processed from the carbohydrates that we consume throughout meals. Glucose is a fast energy supply, where insulin is needed as a kind of intermediary that tells the cells to open up and enables the flow of glucose so that it can be used as a mitochondrial fuel, better known as the fuel factories in our cells. The further sugars we eat, the more glucose is found in our blood, which suggests that the pancreas has to generate more insulin to promote the extraction of energy from usable blood sugar. In an organism where the metabolism is still natural, the cells readily embrace the insulin released by the pancreas, which then contributes to the effective use of blood glucose as energy. The concern is that our cells will actually become desensitized to insulin, contributing to a condition in which the pancreas is required to inject more and more insulin into the bloodstream only to clear the blood sugar levels and normalize them.

Insulin de-sensitivity or insulin tolerance is primarily induced by the constant enhanced presence of blood glucose and is typically caused by the intake of foods high in carbon. Picture of the cells of the body like a security guard at a bar, where you need to pay a charge to enter the club. Here, you play a glucose function, and the cost paid to join the club is insulin. If the club intensity is in accordance with the standard, the security officer doesn't really notice something odd and does not increase the admission fee needed. However, if you wake up clamoring to be allowed in just about every night, the bouncer understands the dire need and jacks up the insulin charge periodically in order to let glucose in. Gradually, at such a stage that the source of insulin, which in this situation is the pancreas, no longer generates any, the admission fee grows greater and greater. This is when the situation is diagnosed with type 2 diabetes, and the normal solution will include drugs or insulin injections for a lifetime. In the existence of glucose in the body system lies the crux of the matter here. Our blood sugar levels are raised every time we take in a carb-rich meal, which is not complicated in this day and age of fast food and sugary snacks, and insulin is enabled for the conversion into energy as well as the storage of the wasted waste into fat cells. This is where the normal furor begins, with condemnations pouring in as the cause of numerous ailments and dreaded weight gain with both glucose and insulin. It wouldn't be wrong if it claimed that insulin and glucose, as certain books have made them out to be, are most certainly not the source of all bad. To refer to our present diet as the leading cause of metabolic disorders and obesity plaguing the greater part of the developing world will be much more specific.

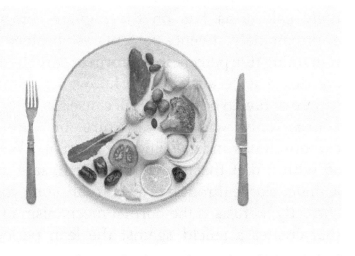

Link the ketogenic diet, which is where the shift toward the positive will be seen.

The keto diet, with a focus on being intentionally low carb, is a fat-based diet. This strategy is intended to decrease our consumption of sugar and starchy foods that are too easily affordable. Just a pleasant fact: in the old days, sugar was actually used as a preservative, and it's no accident that a number of the packaged goods we have now involve massive quantities of sugar so that it makes for longer shelf life. The hedonic appetite reaction in the brain has often been found to cause foods rich in sugar, ultimately allowing you to feed for the sake of gratification rather than actual hunger. Studies also found that sugar therapies are linked to the regions of the brain that are often responsible for opioid use and gambling. You know now that it appears like you can't resist tossing those caramelized sweets into the mouth.

So, we cut back on sugars, and this is where the fat comes in to offset the calories required to help the body. You will be looking at taking seventy-five percent of the daily calorie as fats on the regular ketogenic diet, approximately twenty percent as protein and the remaining five percent in the form of carbohydrates. We are doing it because, as we know, we want our key source of fuel to be fat. We will cause the body to induce ketosis only with the mixture of cutting down carbohydrates and growing our fat intake. We either do so with a diet that makes long-term, safe use, or we actually starve through ketosis. Yeah, sure, you heard it correctly; ketosis is the normal mechanism of the body that creates a shield against the lean periods where there is a lack of food.

Chapter 2- Intermittent fasting and the ketogenic diet

In recent years, this has also been bandied about a lot, with some seeking to shed a misleading light on the keto diet by associating it with thirst.

To make it simpler, when our bodies feel that we do not have adequate glucose in the bloodstream, the ketosis mechanism is initiated. In order to ensure the continuous availability of nutrition for our cells and tissues, it then switches to our fat reserves to transform them into ketones via the liver. It does not mean that you are necessarily killing yourself on the keto diet! Any time someone says that, he got a little worked up.

How will a person who eats 1,800 to 2,000 calories on a regular basis, which is what you're going to get on the meal plan, starve effectively?

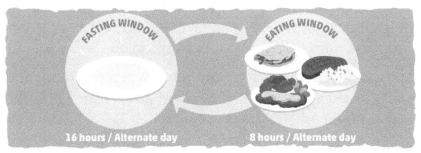

To be fair, during the hunter-gatherer days of our human past, ketosis comes in very handy. This was a time where agriculture wasn't that common, and what you searched or found relied on the food you consumed. This produced a scenario where there could be no calories for days at a time, so our bodies sent insulin to ferry it through our organs as glucose made its way through the environment, as well as hoarding the leftover glucose into fat cells for potential usage.

The body then reached the condition of ketosis by using the accumulated fats to provide nutrition during the lean periods when there was really little food to be found.

Our hunger hormones, like ghrelin, decrease their development during this stage, and the hormones that regulate satiety, like leptin, see their levels increased. All this is how our bodies want to make the most of it to make it easier for us to feel as comfortable as possible if nutritional supplies are scarce.

Today, quick forward to modern days, where food is practically only one or two streets away, or maybe just a car ride away, and we're not going to experience food scarcity like our predecessors in the Paleolithic. However, our bodies also retain the processes and pathways that have enabled them to function. That is the main explanation why we reduce carbohydrates and raise our regular fat consumption on the keto diet.

The condition of ketosis is triggered when we do so, and we get to reap all the biochemical advantages that the diet confers.

The fat we consume often goes into replenishing the body's fat reserves, which is why it won't be wrong to claim again when on the ketogenic diet, one should not starve!

How the Intermitting Fasting Works

From the context of weight reduction, intermittent fasting operates by finding it more challenging to overeat during the day. A basic guideline such as "skip breakfast" or "eat only between 5 pm and 8 pm" will help keep you from reaching for sweets or consuming calorie-dense drinks that lead to weight gain during the day.

You'll also find it impossible to overeat, even though you work up a ferocious appetite when fasting. In fact, intermittent fasting appears to decrease the intake of daily energy and encourage fat loss.

This ensures that as long as you adhere to a shorter feeding time or a fixed number of meals, you can be willing to consume as much as you like and meet your objectives.

Your body may need to adapt itself to this new eating pattern when you first attempt intermittent fasting. Hunger pangs and strong cravings may strike you hard at first, but they will soon recede when your cells feast on accumulated fat and ketones.

Insulin removal, ketone synthesis and autophagy are the main pathways behind your ability to quickly lose weight and boost your health in the process. Our insulin levels drop incrementally as we accumulate time in a fasting condition. This facilitates the liberation of fat from our fat cells and activates the mechanism known as ketogenesis that generates ketones.

You'll reach a deeper state of ketosis as you continue your easy, become more successful at burning fat, and speed up the self-cleaning mechanism known as autophagy.

Benefits of Intermitting Fasting

1. **Enhanced regulation of blood sugar and resistance to insulin**

This will also help boost blood sugar levels and improve one's cells' insulin response by allowing the body an occasional break from calorie intake. One research study showed that for six meals a day, intermittent fasting could also be a healthier option than having the same calorie deficit.

The two dietary strategies can function synergistically to boost blood sugar regulation when paired with the keto diet, which has also been shown to assist with insulin tolerance and type 2 diabetes. More study on the results of using them in tandem, however, is needed.

2. Psychic Clarity

Your brain will essentially operate on ketones, which are extracted through fat dissolution in the liver until the body is keto-adapted.

Fat is thought to be one of the body's most energy-efficient resources to work on, and your mind is a major energy user.

When you do not regularly refill on grains and fruits, most high-carb supporters fight for the malnutrition your body endures. They expect you to take a granola bar and an apple around you everywhere you go, but the advantage of Keto is that you don't.

And if the body is full of glycogen (which is more definitely if you are in ketosis), the excess of fat from the meals you consume and shop you have will depend on it. That ensures that your brain powerhouse will operate at maximum capacity all the time. Less emotional fogginess and more attention.

You can begin to lose fat automatically when you get used to dieting. In other terms, feed only when you are starving. Don't arrange the fasting; let it arise spontaneously.

3. Fitness

People still claim that if you don't use the benefit of pre- and post-exercise meals while you work out, you're going to lose muscle.

This is not inherently real, and when you're adapted to ketosis, it is much less so.

In the long run, fasting while practicing can contribute to a variety of advantages, including:

1. **Greater mutation adaptations** - Studies indicate that when you work out in a fasting condition, your training efficiency will improve in the long run.
2. **Enhanced muscle synthesis**- Experiments indicate that when you exercise in a fasting condition and use sufficient nutrient consumption, muscle gains are improved.
3. **Increased reaction to post-workout meals**- Studies suggests that the accelerated ingestion of nutrients after a short exercise will contribute to better outcomes.

Mechanism Behind the Benefits

Intermittent fasting is so effective that it can be used to reduce calories, trigger ketosis, and enable the mechanisms of autophagy induced by protein restriction and hunger.

This is what happens to our cells as we consume three or more meals a day, which meets our normal calorie requirements fully. Your cells will also be backed up with non-essential proteins and poisonous chemicals, sometimes after consuming the healthiest diets, but what can you do?

You soon, not from cooking, but from being consumed by other commitments, to ensure you clean your real bedroom. You need to fast with food to ensure sure the cells will clean themselves.

Not only can this fasting phase trigger this cleanup for your cells, but it will increase the output of your ketones and facilitate fat burning as well. Simply stated, by incorporating intermittent fasting into the keto diet, coupled with the consequences of autophagy, you can enjoy the advantages of Keto more easily.

In addition, you will raise ketone amounts, lose more fat, and improve autophagy more than you can with intermittent fasting alone if you begin to implement intermittent fasting and exercise together.

Overall, the evidence for intermittent fasting shows that it will be a perfect complement to the keto lifestyle for certain persons, whether you include activity or not. Before you start, though, it is important to be acquainted with the unpleasant signs that can occur.

Chapter 3- How autophagy and ketosis are synergic?

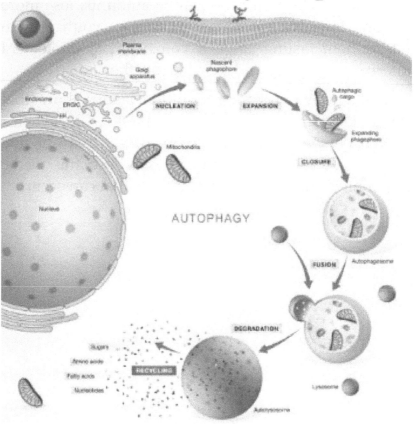

In order to reconstruct healthy, healthier cells, autophagy is the body's method of wiping out dead cells.

Auto" implies self, and "phagy" implies eating." So, 'self-eating' is the literal sense of autophagy.

That is often referred to as "self-devouring." Although it might seem like something you would wish to occur

---

to your body, your ultimate wellbeing is actually advantageous.

It is since autophagy is an evolved method of self-preservation by which the organism can extract and regenerate sections of dysfunctional cells for cellular repair and hygiene.

The aim of autophagy is to eliminate debris and return to optimum smooth operation through self-regulation.

Around the same moment, it's recycling and washing, almost like touching the body on a reset button. Plus, as a reaction to different stressors and contaminants accumulated in our bodies, it encourages resilience and adaptation.

Note that autophagy simply means "self-eating." Therefore, it makes sense that it is understood that intermittent fasting and ketogenic diets induce autophagy.

The most successful method to cause autophagy is by fasting.

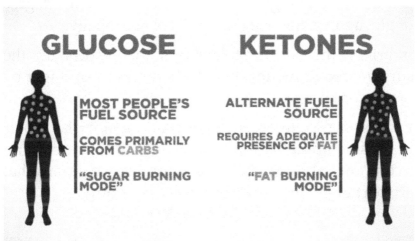

Ketosis, a high-fat and low-carb diet, offers the same advantages to eating without fasting, such as a shortcut that causes the same advantageous biochemical adjustments. It allows the body a break to concentrate on its own wellbeing and repair by not stressing the body with an external load.

You receive about 75 percent of the recommended daily calories from fat in the keto diet and 5 to 10 percent of your calories from carbohydrates.

This alteration in calorie sources allows the biochemical processes in the body to change. Instead of the glucose that is extracted from carbohydrates, it would start using fat for food.

In reaction to this ban, the body will begin to start creating ketone bodies that have several protective effects. Khorana says studies show that ketosis, which has neuroprotective functions, may also cause starvation-induced autophagy.

In all diets, low glucose levels exist and are related to low insulin and high levels of glucagon. And the degree of glucagon is the one that initiates autophagy.

It brings the constructive stress that wakes up the survival repair mode when the body is low on sugar by fasting or ketosis.

Exercise is one non-diet region that can also play a part in causing autophagy. Physical activity can, according to one animal research, cause autophagy in organs that are part of the processes of metabolic control.

Chapter 4- Keto Diet and weight loss

When we start on a ketogenic diet, one of the first items we still lose is most certainly water weight. As adipose fats, the body stores glucose, although there is a limited supply of glucose that is processed as glycogen, composed mainly of water. Glycogen is intended to provide rapid bursting capacity, the kind we use when we run or raise weights. The body switches to glycogen as the first source of energy supply as we cut carbohydrates, which is why water weight is lost in the initial phases. This initial blast of weight reduction may be a morale booster for everyone, and for people who conform to the keto diet, it is a positive signpost for what is to come. Water weight is readily lost and gained, as a side note. This suggests that even those who first see certain outcomes in the keto diet and then wish to get off the track for some reason, as carbohydrates become the daily calorie mainstay, the odds are their weight would swell back up.

For the rest that conforms to the ketogenic diet, what comes next will be the fat burning process of the body that is responsible for the impressive effects of weight loss shown by many. The underlying principle is also the same in that adipose fats are still activated by the organs and cells of the body as energy sources, contributing to a normal state of depletion of fat and thus accompanying reducing weight.

The burning of fat is not the sole explanation that the keto diet demonstrates weight reduction.

Hunger reduction and improvement of pleasure during meals are also explanations that people are better able to lose weight whilst on a diet. One of the long-standing ideals of weight management has always been the adage of drinking less and doing more. The entire premise is to establish a calorie shortage in such a way that the body is forced to depend on its stored energy reserves to make up for the requisite expenditure. That seems quick and straightforward on paper, but it may be as challenging as scaling Mount Everest for someone who has been through scenarios where you have had to deliberately curtail your food on a hungry stomach!

Through the ketogenic diet, thanks to the modification of the hormones that regulate sensations of appetite and fullness, you realize that you will have normal hunger suppression. In addition, the food we usually eat while on a diet often assists with weight reduction. It is understood that fats and protein are more relaxing and rewarding than sugary carbs. We do two items almost concurrently as we turn to a high-fat diet when cutting back on the carbohydrates. Only because we feel like it, not because we are very hungry, easing back on carbohydrates, particularly the sugar stuff, reduces the urge to consume. Charging high the consumption of fat often causes the satiety impact even easier and helps you to feel complete. This is part of so many keto dieters claim that without having the smallest pinch of hunger, they will go for two and a half or even two meals a day.

We account for a regular caloric consumption that varies from 1,800 to 2,000 calories on our keto meal schedule, but we do not even use calorie limits to minimize weight. The truth is that those tiny and harmless-looking snacks that fill the period between dinners will not appear much in your life when you feel fullness and enjoyment from your meals! Think about it: the usual go-to sweets, donuts, candy, and cookies, are left out purely, so you are less inclined to give in to hedonistic appetite induced mainly by the same sugar treats in reducing extra calories which would have otherwise been converted to adipose fat tissue, that goes a very long way.

To sum up, without the usual calorie limit in most weight reduction diets, the ketogenic diet provides for meals. It also offers a supporting hand in the production of symptoms of hunger suppression such that you do not have to struggle with those treacherous hunger pangs! The lack of carb munchies is also present, which may theoretically disrupt any diet. With as minimal disturbance to our everyday life as possible, this helps one to experience normal weight loss. There is no need to deploy calorie counters, no need for a problematic six to eight meals a day, and certainly no strange or amusing workout exercises required. If you pair it with the satisfying high-fat keto meals, you enter a scenario where hunger could indeed become an outsider.

As another good spin-off, having to re-learn what real hunger feels like still arrives. We get incidents of hunger on a carb-rich diet, and our blood sugar levels appear to fluctuate dramatically as our cells become increasingly desensitized by insulin. The propensity to feed on impulse is often enhanced by sugar, which can really ruin any diet! We will also have to wake up and take care anytime we feel those hunger pangs when we cut back on carbohydrates and ratchet up on the fats, so that will be proper signs that the body needs extra energy.

Chapter 5- Benefits of Ketogenic Diet

All in all, the straightforward method to the keto diet has inspired individuals to engage with it, resulting in many variants of the keto diet that are available. The keto diet method has been one of the most attempted regimes, and in the last few years, it has grown tremendously in prominence.

Although the key advantage of Keto is successful weight loss, metabolic boosting and hunger control, such advantages include the following-

1. Acne may be decreased by the keto diet since glucose restriction can tip the dynamics of bacteria in the intestine that influences the face.
2. It is known to deter and cure some cancers and, in addition to radiation and chemotherapy, is seen as a supportive medication since it allows cancer cells to undergo additional oxidative stress, allowing them to die.
3. This diet provides your body with a better and healthy source of energy and thus will make you feel more energetic throughout the day.
4. A reduction in cholesterol is caused by keto diets, and the presence of healthy cholesterol is improved.
5. The brain and nerve cells are reinforced and preserved. In addition, it is understood to manage diseases such as Alzheimer's, Parkinson's etc.
6. Many types of research have shown that the keto diet helps to lower down the low-density lipoproteins or the bad cholesterol over time and have been shown to eliminate diseases such as type 2 diabetes.
7. It aids in losing weight as the body burns down the fat as the prior energy source, and one will primarily be using the fat stored in the body as an energy source while in a fasting mode.

8. A Keto diet has been shown to improve cholesterol levels and triglyceride levels most associated with arterial buildup.
9. Known for managing epilepsy-like disorders, Ovarian polycystic disease, etc.
10. The ketogenic diet promises many keto advantages, but a true effort is to initiate the keto diet. It is a restrictive diet that seeks to reduce one's carb consumption to about 50 grams a day, so visiting a dietician to work out and modify the diet according to one's needs is advantageous.

Chapter 6- The 15-day Meal Plan with Low-Carb Recipes that fit the Intermittent Fasting Diet

Eating Keto involves limiting the net carb consumption such that energy and ketones are generated by your body metabolizing fat. For many, this means reducing net carbs to 20 grams a day.

The keto diet could be perfect for you if you are trying to optimize advantages such as curing type 2 diabetes or if you want to lose the extra kilos

A more balanced low-carb diet could be a safer option for you if you want more carbohydrates in your diet and if you don't have type 2 diabetes or have a lot of weight to lose. It may be better to adopt mild low carb, but it may also be less successful than Keto, suggesting you may get more modest outcomes.

Day 1

Breakfast- Scrambled eggs

Lunch-Bacon and Zucchini Noodles Salad

Dinner- Spinach Soup

Day 2

Breakfast- Keto Frittata

Lunch-Keto Roasted Pepper and Cauliflower

Dinner-Buffalo Blue Cheese Chicken Wedges

Day 3

Breakfast- Breakfast Bowl

Lunch-Lunch Tacos

Dinner-Lemon Dill Trout

Day 4

Breakfast- Poached Eggs

Lunch-Simple Pizza Rolls

Dinner-Special Fish Pie

Day 5

Breakfast- Bright Morning Smoothie

Lunch-Lunch Stuffed Peppers

Dinner-Cauliflower Bread Garlic Sticks

Day 6

Breakfast-Pumpkin Muffins

Lunch-Lunch Stuffed Peppers

Dinner- Buffalo Blue Cheese Chicken Wedges

Day 7

Breakfast- Keto Breakfast Mix

Lunch-Lunch Caesar Salad

Dinner-Sage N Orange Breast of Duck

Day 8

Breakfast-Pumpkin Pie Spiced Latte

Lunch-Keto Roasted Pepper and Cauliflower

Dinner- Salmon with Caper Sauce

Day 9

Breakfast- Strawberry Protein Smoothie

Lunch-Keto Slow Cooker Buffalo Chicken Soup

Dinner-Cauliflower Bread Garlic Sticks

Day 10

Breakfast-Delicious Eggs and Sausages

Lunch-Special Lunch Burgers

Dinner-Tossed Brussel Sprout Salad

Day 11

Breakfast-Bright Morning Smoothie

Lunch-Keto Lunch Jambalaya

Dinner- Spinach Soup

Day 12

Breakfast-Keto Frittata

Lunch-Lunch Tacos

Dinner-Special Fish Pie

Day 13

Breakfast-Feta and Asparagus Delight

Lunch-Keta Chicken Enchilada Soup

Dinner-Bok Choy Stir Fry

Day 14

Breakfast-Scrambled Eggs

Lunch- Simple Pizza Rolls

Dinner- Lemon Dill Trout

Day 15

Breakfast-Strawberry Protein Smoothie

Lunch-Bacon and Zucchini Noodles Salad

Dinner-Spinach Soup

The list of food items in this meal plan is not exhaustive. You can change the menu as per the availability of the products.

If you wish to avoid your breakfast or any other meal in order to practice fasting, then you are supposed to keep drinking water in that period of time and also make sure that you take multi-vitamins prescribed by a physician.

Following provided is a list of foods that you can take while on intermittent fasting inspired keto diet-

1. Vegetables
2. Proteins
3. Oil and good fats
4. Beverages
5. Seeds and nuts

6. Diary

The list of foods provided under are to be completely avoided or should be taken in a minimal amount-

1. Processed Foods
2. Artificial Sweeteners
3. Alcohol
4. Milk
5. Refined fats
6. Legumes
7. Soy Products
8. Grains

Chapter 7- Breakfast Recipes

7.1 Delicious Poached Eggs

Ready in about 45 minutes|Servings-4| Difficulty-Easy

Ingredients

- Three minced garlic cloves
- One tablespoon of ghee
- One chopped white onion
- One chopped Serrano pepper
- Salt and black pepper to the taste
- One chopped red bell pepper
- Three chopped tomatoes
- One teaspoon of paprika
- One teaspoon of cumin

- A quarter teaspoon of chili powder
- One tablespoon of chopped cilantro
- Six eggs

Instructions

1. Heat the pan over medium heat with the ghee, add the onion, stir and cook and stir for ten minutes.
2. Add the garlic and Serrano pepper, stir and cook over medium heat for a minute.
3. Add red bell pepper and cook for 10 minutes, stirring and cooking.
4. Add the tomatoes, pepper, salt, chili powder, paprika and cumin, stir and cook for 10 minutes.
5. In the pan, crack the eggs, season them with pepper and salt, cover the pan and cook for another 6 minutes.
6. In the end, sprinkle with cilantro and serve.

7.2 Delicious Eggs and Sausages

Ready in about 45 minutes | Servings-6 | Difficulty-Easy

Ingredient

- Five tablespoons of ghee
- Twelve eggs
- Salt and black pepper as per taste
- One of torn spinach
- Twelve slices of ham
- Two chopped sausages
- One chopped yellow onion
- One chopped red bell pepper

Instructions

1. Heat a saucepan over medium heat with one tablespoon of ghee, add the onion and sausages, stir and cook for five minutes.
2. Add the bell pepper, pepper and salt, stir and cook for an additional three minutes and place in a bowl.
3. Melt and divide the rest of the ghee into 1two cups of cake molds.
4. In each cupcake mold, add a slice of ham, divide each spinach and then the sausage mix.
5. Break an egg on top, place everything in the oven and bake for 20 minutes at 425 ° Fahrenheit
6. Before serving, leave your cupcakes to cool down a bit.

7.3 Delicious Breakfast Bowl

Ready in about 30 minutes|Servings-1| Difficulty-Easy

Ingredients

- Four ounces of ground beef
- One chopped yellow onion
- Eight sliced mushrooms
- Salt and black pepper as per taste
- Two whisked eggs
- One tablespoon of coconut oil
- Half a teaspoon of teaspoon smoked paprika
- One avocado, pitted, peeled and chopped
- Twelve pitted and sliced black olives

Instructions

1. Heat a saucepan over medium heat with the coconut oil, add the onions, mushrooms, pepper and salt, stir and cook for five minutes.
2. Add the beef and paprika, stir, cook and transfer to a bowl for 10 minutes.
3. Over medium heat, heat the pan again, add the eggs, some pepper and salt and scramble.
4. Put the beef mix back in the pan and stir.
5. Add the olives and avocado, stir, and cook over medium heat for a minute
6. Transfer and serve in a bowl.

7.4 Keto Breakfast Mix

Ready in about 20 minutes | Servings-2 | Difficulty-Easy

Ingredients

- Five tablespoons of unsweetened coconut flakes
- Seven tablespoons of Hemp seeds
- Five tablespoons of Ground Flaxseed
- Two tablespoons of ground Sesame
- Two tablespoons of unsweetened cocoa, dark
- Two tablespoons of Psyllium husk

Instructions:

1. Grind the sesame and the flaxseed. Ensure that you only grind the sesame seeds for a short time.
2. In a jar, mix all the ingredients and shake them well.
3. Keep refrigerated until ready for consumption.
4. Serve softened with black coffee or still water and, if you want to increase your fat intake, add

coconut oil. It also combines well with cream or with cheese from mascarpone.

7.5 Pumpkin Pie Keto Spiced Latte

Ready in about 20 minutes|Servings-2| Difficulty-Easy

Ingredients

- Two cups of strong and freshly brewed coffee
- One cup of Coconut Milk
- A quarter cup of Pumpkin Puree
- Half teaspoon of Cinnamon
- One teaspoon of Vanilla Extract
- Two teaspoons of Pumpkin Pie Spice Blend
- 15 drops of Liquid Stevia
- Two tablespoons of Butter
- Two tablespoons of Heavy Whipping Cream

Instructions

1. Cook the pumpkin, butter, milk and spices over medium-low flame,
2. Add two cups of solid coffee and blend together until bubbling.
3. Remove from the stove, apply cream and stevia, and then whisk together with an electric mixer.
4. Top with whipped cream and enjoy.

7.6 Keto Frittata

Ready in about one hour 10 minutes|Servings-4| Difficulty- Moderate

Ingredients

- Nine ounces of spinach
- Twelve eggs

- One ounce of pepperoni
- One teaspoon of minced garlic
- Salt and black pepper to the taste
- Five ounces of shredded mozzarella
- Half cup of grated parmesan
- Half cup of ricotta cheese
- Four tablespoons of olive oil
- A pinch of nutmeg

Instructions

1. Squeeze out the spinach liquid and put it in a bowl.
2. Mix the eggs with the salt, nutmeg, pepper, and garlic in another bowl and whisk well.
3. Add the spinach, ricotta and parmesan and whisk well.
4. Pour this into a saucepan, sprinkle on top with mozzarella and pepperoni, place in the oven and bake for 45 minutes at 375 ° Fahrenheit.
5. Leave the frittata for a few minutes to cool down before serving.

7.7 Keto Fall Pumpkin Spiced French Toast

Ready in about 20 minutes | Servings-2 | Difficulty-Easy

Ingredients

- Four slices of Pumpkin Bread
- One large Egg
- Two tablespoons of cream
- Half teaspoon of Vanilla Extract
- 1/8 teaspoon of Orange Extract
- A quarter teaspoon of Pumpkin Pie Spice

- Two tablespoons of butter

Instructions

Cook the pumpkin, butter, milk and spices over a medium-low flame.

Add two cups of solid coffee and blend together until bubbling.

Remove from the stove, apply cream and stevia, and then whisk together with an electric mixer.

Top with whipped cream and serve.

7.8 Scrambled Eggs

Ready in about 20 minutes | Servings-1 | Difficulty-Easy

Ingredients

- Four chopped bell mushrooms
- Three whisked eggs
- Salt and black pepper to the taste
- Two chopped ham slices
- A quarter cup of chopped red bell pepper
- Half cup of chopped spinach
- One tablespoon of coconut oil

Instructions

Heat a saucepan over medium heat with half the oil, add the mushrooms, spinach, bell pepper and ham, stir and simmer for four minutes.

Heat up another pan over medium heat with the rest of the oil, add the eggs and scramble them.

Stir in the vegetables and ham, pepper and salt, stir, simmer and cook for one minute and then serve.

7.9 Feta and Asparagus Delight

Ready in about 35 minutes | Servings-2 | Difficulty-Easy

Ingredients

- Twelve asparagus spears
- One tablespoon of olive oil
- Two chopped green onions
- One minced garlic clove
- Six eggs
- Salt and black pepper to the taste
- Half cup of feta cheese

Instructions

1. Heat a pan over medium heat with some water, add asparagus, stir for eight minutes, drain well, chop two spears and reserve the remainder.
2. Over medium heat, heat a pan with the oil, add the garlic, onions and chopped asparagus, stir and cook for five minutes.
3. Add salt, pepper and eggs, stir, cover and cook for five minutes.
4. On top of your frittata, arrange the whole asparagus, sprinkle with cheese, place in the oven at 350 ° F and bake for nine minutes.
5. Divide and serve between plates.

7.10 Eggs Baked in Avocados

Ready in about 30 minutes | Servings-4 | Difficulty-Easy

Ingredients

- Two avocados, cut in halves and pitted
- Four eggs
- Salt and black pepper to the taste
- One tablespoon of chopped chives

Instructions

1. Scoop some of the avocado halves with some flesh and assemble them in a baking dish.
2. In each avocado, crack an egg, season with pepper and salt, place them at 425 degrees F in the oven and bake for 20 minutes.
3. In the end, sprinkle the chives and serve them for breakfast.

Chapter 8- Lunch Recipes

8.1   Lunch Caesar Salad

Ready in about 10 minutes|Servings-2| Difficulty-Easy

Ingredients

- One pitted, peeled and sliced avocado
- Salt and black pepper to the taste
- Three tablespoons of creamy Caesar dressing
- One cup of cooked and crumbled bacon
- One grilled and shredded chicken breast

Instructions

1. Mix the avocado with the chicken breast and bacon in a salad bowl and stir.
2. Add salt and pepper, Caesar dressing, toss to coat, split into two bowls and serve.

8.2 Keto Lunch Jambalaya

Ready in about 40 minutes|Servings-2| Difficulty-Moderate

Ingredients

- One medium cauliflower
- One coarsely chopped green pepper
- Two stalks of coarsely chopped celery
- One diced small onion
- Two minced cloves of garlic
- Three cubed boneless chicken breasts
- Eight ounces of sliced smoked sausage
- Eight ounces of ham, cubed
- Fourteen and a half ounce can of diced tomatoes, undrained
- Eight ounce can of tomato sauce
- Three teaspoons of Cajun Seasoning
- Salt and pepper according to taste
- Cooking oil

Instructions

1. Heat two tablespoons of oil in an 8-quart Dutch oven or skillet.
2. On a medium-high flame, sauté the peppers, garlic, chicken, celery, onion and Cajun seasoning until the chicken is almost cooked.
3. Add the cauliflower, ham and sausage. Mix thoroughly.
4. Add the tomato sauce and tomatoes to the mix. Bring it to a simmer, and then turn it back to low.
5. Cover until the cauliflower is moist but not mushy, and cook for around twenty minutes.
6. Season with salt and pepper and then serve after removing from heat.

8.3 Lunch Tacos

Ready in about 40 minutes|Servings-3| Difficulty-Moderate

Ingredients

- Two cups of grated cheddar cheese
- One small pitted, peeled and chopped avocado
- One cup of cooked favorite taco meat
- Two teaspoons of sriracha sauce
- A quarter cup of chopped tomatoes
- Cooking spray
- Salt and black pepper as per taste

Instructions

1. Spray on a lined baking dish with some cooking oil.
2. Cover on the baking sheet with cheddar cheese, put in the oven at 400 degrees F, and bake for 15 minutes.
3. Spread the taco meat over the cheese and cook for a further 10 minutes.
4. Meanwhile, combine the avocado with tomatoes, sriracha, salt and pepper in a bowl and swirl.
5. Spread this over the layers of taco and cheddar, let the tacos cool down a little, use a pizza slicer to slice and serve for lunch.

8.4 Keto Chicken Enchilada Soup

Ready in about 40 minutes|Servings-3| Difficulty-Moderate

Ingredients

- Six oz. Shredded chicken

- Two teaspoons of Cumin
- One teaspoon of Oregano
- One teaspoon of Chili Powder
- Half teaspoon of Cayenne Pepper
- Half cup of chopped cilantro
- Half medium Lime, juiced
- three tablespoons of Olive Oil
- Three stalks of diced Celery
- One medium diced Red Bell Pepper, diced
- Two teaspoons of garlic, minced
- Four cups of Chicken Broth
- One cup of Diced Tomatoes
- Eight oz. of Cream Cheese

Instructions

1. Heat the oil in a pan and add the celery and pepper. Add the tomatoes and cook for 2-3 minutes once the celery is soft.
2. Add the spices to the pan and mix well.
3. Add the chicken broth and the cilantro to the mixture, boil, and then reduce to low for 20 minutes to simmer.
4. Then add the cream cheese and bring it back to the boil. Once it has cooked, reduce the heat to low and cover and cook for 25 minutes.
5. Scrap the chicken and add it to the pot, then top it with half the lime juice.
6. Mix together everything.
7. Serve with coriander, sour cream or shredded cheese.

8.5 Simple Pizza Rolls

Ready in about 40 minutes|Servings-6| Difficulty-Moderate

Ingredients

- A quarter cups of chopped mixed red and green bell peppers
- Two cups of shredded mozzarella cheese
- One teaspoon of pizza seasoning
- Two tablespoons of chopped onion
- One chopped tomato
- Salt and black pepper to the taste
- A quarter cups of pizza sauce
- Half cup of crumbled and cooked sausage

Instructions

1. On a lined and lightly oiled baking dish, spread mozzarella cheese, sprinkle pizza seasoning on top, put at 400 °F in the oven and bake for 20 minutes.
2. Spread the sausage, onion, tomatoes and bell pepper all over and drizzle the tomato sauce at the top. Taking the pizza crust out of the oven.
3. Place them back in the oven and bake for ten more minutes.
4. Take the pizza from the oven, leave it aside for a few minutes, break it into six pieces, roll each slice and eat it for lunch.

8.6 Lunch Stuffed Peppers

Ready in about 50 minutes|Servings-4| Difficulty-Moderate

Ingredients

- Four big banana peppers cut into halves lengthwise
- One tablespoon of ghee
- Salt and black pepper to the taste
- Half teaspoon of herbs de Provence
- One pound of chopped sweet sausage
- Three tablespoons of chopped yellow onions
- Some marinara sauce
- A drizzle of olive oil

Instructions

1. Season the banana peppers with pepper and salt, drizzle with the oil, rub well and bake for 20 minutes in the oven at 325 ° F.
2. Meanwhile, over medium, prepare, heat a skillet, add the pieces of sausage, mix and cook for 5 minutes.
3. Combine the onion, herbs, salt, pepper and ghee, mix well and simmer for 5 minutes.
4. Take the peppers out of the oven, load them with the sausage mix, place them in a dish that is oven-proof, drizzle them with the marinara sauce, placed them back in the oven and bake for another 10 minutes.
5. Serve and enjoy.

8.7 Special Lunch Burgers

Ready in about 35 minutes | Servings-8 | Difficulty-Moderate

Ingredients

- One pound ground brisket
- One pound ground beef

- Salt and black pepper as per taste
- Eight butter slices
- One tablespoon of minced garlic
- One tablespoon of Italian seasoning
- Two tablespoons of mayonnaise
- One tablespoon of ghee
- Two tablespoons of olive oil
- One chopped yellow onion
- One tablespoon of water

Instructions

1. Mix the beef, pepper, salt, Italian herbs, mayo and garlic with the brisket in a bowl and stir well.
2. Form 8 patties into each one to create a pocket.
3. With butter-slices, stuff each burger and seal it.
4. Over medium pressure, heat the pan with the oil, add the onions, stir and simmer for 2 minutes.
5. Apply the water, swirl and pick them up in the pan corner.
6. Put the burgers with the onions in the pan and cook them for ten minutes over moderate flame.
7. Flip them over, apply the ghee, and simmer for ten more minutes.
8. Break the burgers into buns and place them on top of caramelized onions.

8.8 Keto Roasted Pepper and Cauliflower

Ready in about 50 minutes | Servings-4 | Difficulty-Moderate

Ingredients

- Two halved and de-seeded Red Bell Peppers
- Half head of cauliflower cut into florets
- Two tablespoons of Duck Fat
- Three medium diced green Onions
- Three cups of Chicken Broth
- Half cup Heavy Cream
- Four tablespoons of Duck Fat
- Salt and pepper as per taste
- One teaspoon of Garlic Powder
- One teaspoon of Dried Thyme
- One teaspoon of Smoked Paprika
- A quarter teaspoon of Red Pepper Flakes
- Four oz. Goat Cheese

Instructions

1. Preheat the oven to 400 °F

Clean, de-seed, and half-slice the peppers

Broil until the flesh is burnt and blackened for about 10-15 minutes.

Place in a container with a cover to steam when finished cooking cauliflower.

Sprinkle two tablespoons of melted duck fat, pepper and salt into sliced cauliflower florets.

Cook for 30-35 minutes in the oven.

Pick off the skins of the peppers by gently peeling them off.

Heat Four tablespoons of duck fat in a pot and add the diced green onion.

To toast, apply seasonings to the plate, then add red pepper, chicken broth, and cauliflower to the skillet.

For 10-20 minutes, let this boil.

Bring the mixture to an immersion blender. Make sure that it emulsifies both fats.

Then apply the cream and combine.

Serve with some bacon and goats' cheese. Add thyme and green onion to garnish.

8.9 Bacon and Zucchini Noodles Salad

Ready in about 10 minutes|Servings-2| Difficulty-Easy

Ingredients

- One cup of baby spinach
- Four cups of zucchini noodles
- 1/3 cups of crumbled bleu cheese
- 1/3 cups of thick cheese dressing
- Half cup of cooked and crumbled bacon
- Black pepper as per taste

Instructions

1. Mix the spinach with the bacon, zucchini noodles and the bleu cheese in a salad dish, and toss.
2. Apply the black pepper and cheese dressing as per taste, toss well to cover, distribute into two bowls and eat.

8.10 Keto Slow Cooker Buffalo Chicken Soup

Ready in about 6 hours and 20 minutes | Servings-2 | Difficulty- Hard

Ingredients

- Three Chicken Thighs, de-boned and sliced
- One teaspoon of Onion Powder
- One teaspoon of Garlic Powder
- Half teaspoon Celery Seed
- A quarter cup of butter
- Half cup of Frank's Hot Sauce
- Three cups of Beef Broth
- One cup of Heavy Cream
- Two oz. Cream Cheese
- A quarter teaspoon of Xanthan Gum
- Salt and pepper as per taste

Instructions

1. Begin by de-boning the chicken thighs, break the chicken into chunks and place the remainder of the ingredients in a slow cooker in the crockpot with the exception of cream, cheese, and xanthan gum.
2. Set a low, slow cooker for 6 hours (or a high one for 3 hours) and cook fully.
3. Remove the chicken from the slow cooker until it is done, and shred it with a fork.
4. Using the slow cooker to combine cream, cheese, and xanthan gum. Combine it all together
5. Transfer the chicken to the slow cooker and blend.
6. Season it with salt, pepper, and hot sauce. Serve.

Chapter 9- Dinner Recipes

9.1 Buffalo Blue Cheese Chicken Wedges

Ready in about 40 minutes|Servings-2| Difficulty-Moderate

Ingredients

- One head of lettuce
- Bleu cheese dressing
- Two tablespoons of crumbled blue cheese
- Four strips of bacon
- Two boneless chicken breasts
- 3/4 cup of any buffalo sauce

Instructions

1. Boil a big pot of salted water.
2. Add two chicken breasts to the water and simmer for 30 minutes, or until the internal temperature of the chicken reaches 180 °C.
3. Let the chicken rest for 10 minutes to cool.
4. Take apart the chicken into strips using a fork.

5. Cook and cool bacon strips, crumble reserve,
6. Merge the scrapped chicken and buffalo sauce over medium heat, then mix until warm.
7. Break the lettuce into wedges and apply the appropriate amount of blue cheese dressing to it.
8. Add crumbles of blue cheese.
9. Add the chicken-pulled buffalo.
10. Cover with more crumbles of blue cheese and fried crumbled bacon.
11. Serve.

9.2 Cauliflower Bread Garlic sticks

Ready in about 55 minutes | Servings-2 | Difficulty-Moderate

Ingredients

- Two cups of cauliflower rice
- One tablespoon of organic butter
- Three teaspoons of minced garlic
- A quarter teaspoon of red pepper flakes
- Half teaspoon of Italian seasoning
- 1/8 teaspoon of kosher salt
- One cup of shredded mozzarella cheese
- One egg
- One cup of grated parmesan cheese

Instructions

1. Preheat the oven to 350° F.
2. Sauté the red pepper flakes and garlic for nearly three minutes and transfer to a bowl of cooked cauliflower. Melt the butter in a small skillet over low heat.

3. Mix the Italian seasoning and salt together.
4. Afterward, refrigerate for 10 minutes.
5. Add the mozzarella cheese and egg to the cauliflower mixture until slightly cooled.
6. A creamy paste in a thin layer lined with parchment paper on a thinly oiled 9-9 baking dish.
7. Bake for thirty minutes.
8. Remove from the oven and finish with a little more parmesan and mozzarella cheese.
9. Put them back in the oven and cook for an extra 8 minutes.
10. Remove from the oven and slice into sticks of the appropriate duration.

9.3 Tasty Baked Fish

Ready in about 40 minutes | Servings-4 | Difficulty-Moderate

Ingredients

- One pound of haddock
- Three teaspoons of water
- Two tablespoons of lemon juice
- Salt and black pepper as per taste
- Two tablespoons of mayonnaise
- One teaspoon of dill weed
- Cooking spray
- A pinch of old bay seasoning

Instructions

1. With some cooking oil, spray a baking dish.
2. Apply the lemon juice, fish and water and toss to cover a little bit.

3. Apply salt, pepper, seasoning with old bay and dill weed and mix again.
4. Add mayonnaise and spread evenly.
5. Place it at 350 ° F in the oven and bake for thirty minutes.
6. Split and serve on a plate.

9.4 Spinach Soup

Ready in about 25 minutes | Servings-8 | Difficulty-Easy

Ingredients

- Two tablespoons of ghee
- Twenty ounces of chopped spinach
- One teaspoon of minced garlic
- Salt and black pepper as per taste
- Forty-five ounces of chicken stock
- Half teaspoons of nutmeg, ground
- Two cups of heavy cream
- One chopped yellow onion

Instructions

1. Heat a pot over medium heat with the ghee, add the onion, stir and simmer for 4 minutes.
2. Stir in the garlic, stir and simmer for a minute.
3. Add spinach and stock and simmer for 5 minutes.
4. Blend the broth with an immersion mixer and reheat the soup.
5. Stir in pepper, nutmeg, salt, and cream, stir and simmer for a further 5 minutes.
6. Ladle it into cups and serve.

9.5 Tossed Brussel Sprout Salad

Ready in about 30 minutes | Servings-2 | Difficulty-Easy

Ingredients

- Six Brussels sprouts
- Half teaspoon of apple cider vinegar
- One teaspoon of olive/grapeseed oil
- A quarter teaspoon of salt
- A quarter teaspoon of pepper
- One tablespoon of freshly grated parmesan

Instructions

1. Break and clean Brussels sprouts in half lengthwise, root on, then cut thin slices through them in the opposite direction.
2. Cut the roots and remove them until chopped.
3. Toss the apple cider, oil, pepper and salt together.
4. Sprinkle, blend and eat with your parmesan cheese.

9.6 Special Fish Pie

Ready in about One hour 20 minutes | Servings-6 | Difficulty-Moderate

Ingredients

- One chopped red onion
- Two skinless and medium sliced salmon fillets
- Two skinless and medium sliced mackerel fillets
- Three medium sliced haddock fillets
- Two bay leaves
  - A quarter cup and two tablespoons of ghee
  - One cauliflower head, florets separated
  - Four eggs
  - Four cloves
  - One cup of whipping cream
  - Half cup of water

- A pinch of nutmeg
- One teaspoon of Dijon mustard
- One and a half cup of shredded cheddar cheese
- A handful of chopped parsley
- Salt and black pepper as per taste
- Four tablespoons of chopped chives

Instructions

1. In a saucepan, place some water, add some salt, bring to a boil over medium heat, add the eggs, simmer for ten minutes, heat off, drain, cool, peel and break into quarters.
2. Place the water in another kettle, bring it to a boil, add the florets of cauliflower, simmer for 10 minutes, rinse, add a quarter of a cup of ghee, add it to the mixer, blend properly, and place it in a bowl.
3. Add the cream and half a cup of water to a saucepan, add the fish, toss and cover over medium heat.
4. Put to a boil, reduce heat to a minimum, and steam for 10 minutes. Put the cloves, onion, and bay leave.
5. Take the heat off, put the fish and set it aside in a baking dish.
6. Heat the saucepan with the fish, add the nutmeg, combine and simmer for 5 minutes.
7. Remove from the oven, discard the bay leaves and cloves and blend well with one cup of cheddar cheese and two tablespoons of ghee.
8. On top of the fish, set the egg quarters in the baking dish.

9. Sprinkle with cream and cheese sauce on top of the remaining cheddar cheese, chives and parsley, cover with cauliflower mash, sprinkle with the remaining cheddar cheese, and place in the oven for 30 minutes at 400 ° F.
10. Leave the pie until it is about to slice and serve, to cool down a little.

9.7 Lemon Dill Trout

Ready in about 20 minutes | Servings-4 | Difficulty-Easy

Ingredients

- Two pounds of pan-dressed trout (or other small fish), fresh or frozen
- One and a half teaspoons of salt
- A quarter teaspoon of pepper
- Half cup of butter or margarine
- Two tablespoons of dill weed
- Three tablespoons of lemon juice

Instructions

1. Cut fish lengthwise and season its inside with pepper and salt.
2. With melted butter and dill weed, prepare a frying pan.
3. For about two to three minutes per side, fry the fish flesh side down.
4. Remove the fish.
5. Add lemon juice to butter and dill to create a sauce.
6. Serve the fish and sauce together.

9.8 Sage N Orange Breast of Duck

Ready in about 20 minutes | Servings-4 | Difficulty-Easy

Ingredients

- Six oz. Duck Breast (~6 oz.)
- Two tablespoons of Butter
- One tablespoon of Heavy Cream
- One tablespoon of Swerve
- Half teaspoon of Orange Extract
- A quarter teaspoon of Sage
- One cup of spinach

Instructions

1. Score the duck skin on top of the breast and season with pepper and salt.
2. Brown butter in a saucepan over medium-low heat, and swerve.
3. Add the extract of sage and orange and cook until it is deep orangey in color.
4. Sear duck breasts for few minutes until nicely crunchy.
5. Flip the Breast of the Duck.
6. Add the orange and sage butter to the heavy cream and pour it over the duck.
7. Cook until finished.
8. In the pan that you used to make the sauce, add the spinach and serve with the duck.

9.9 Salmon with Caper Sauce

Ready in about 30 minutes | Servings-3 | Difficulty-Easy

Ingredients

- Three salmon fillets

- Salt and black pepper as per taste
- One tablespoon of olive oil
- One tablespoon of Italian seasoning
- Two tablespoons of capers
- Three tablespoons of lemon juice
- Four minced garlic cloves
- Two tablespoons of ghee

Instructions

1. Heat the olive oil pan over medium heat, add the skin of the fish fillets side by side, season with pepper salt and Italian seasoning, cook for two minutes, toss and cook for another two minutes, remove from heat, cover and leave aside for 15 minutes.
2. Put the fish on a plate and leave it aside.
3. Over medium heat, heat the same pan, add the capers, garlic and lemon juice, stir and cook for two minutes.
4. Remove the heat from the pan, add ghee and stir very well.
5. Put the fish back in the pan and toss with the sauce to coat.
6. Divide and serve on plates.

9.10 Bok Choy Stir Fry

Ready in about 20 minutes | Servings-2 | Difficulty-Easy

Ingredients

- Two minced garlic cloves
- Two cups of chopped bok choy
- Two chopped bacon slices
- Salt and black pepper to the taste

- A drizzle of avocado oil

Instructions

1. Heat a pan over medium heat with the oil, add the bacon, stir and brown until crunchy, move to paper towels and drain the oil.
2. Return the saucepan to medium heat, stir in the garlic and bok choy, and cook for 4 minutes.
3. Stir in salt, pepper and bacon, stir, cook for another 1 minute, divide among plates and serve.

Chapter 10- Appetizer and Snacks Recipes

10.1 Cheeseburger Muffins

Ready in about 40 minutes | Servings-9 | Difficulty-Easy

Ingredients

- Half cups of flaxseed meal
- Half cups of almond flour
- Salt and black pepper to the taste
- Two eggs
- One teaspoon of baking powder
- A quarter cups of sour cream

For the filling

- Half teaspoons of onion powder
- Sixteen ounces of ground beef

- Salt and black pepper to the taste
- Two tablespoons of tomato paste
- Half teaspoons of garlic powder
- Half cups of grated cheddar cheese
- Two tablespoons of mustard

Instructions

1. Mix the almond flour with the flaxseed meal, pepper, salt and baking powder in a bowl and whisk together.
2. Add the sour cream and eggs and stir very well.
3. Divide it into a greased muffin pan and use your fingers to press well.
4. Over medium-high heat, heat a pan, add beef, stir and brown for a couple of minutes.
5. Stir well and add pepper, salt, garlic powder, onion powder and tomato paste.
6. Cook for an additional 5 minutes and take the heat off.
7. Fill the crusts with this mixture, place them in the oven at 350 degrees F and bake for fifteen minutes
8. Spread the cheese on top, put it in the oven again and cook the muffins for another 5 minutes.
9. Serve with mustard and your preferred toppings.

10.2 Pesto Crackers

Ready in about 30 minutes | Servings-6 | Difficulty-Easy

Ingredients

- Half teaspoons of baking powder
- Salt and black pepper to the taste
- One and a quarter cups of almond flour
- A quarter teaspoon of basil, dried

- One minced garlic clove
- Two tablespoons of basil pesto
- A pinch of cayenne pepper
- Three tablespoons of ghee

Instructions

1. Mix the pepper, salt, almond flour and baking powder together in a bowl.
2. Stir in the garlic, basil and cayenne.
3. Add whisk the pesto.
4. Also, add ghee and with your finger, mix your dough.
5. Spread this dough on a baking sheet and bake it at 325 degrees F in the oven for 17 minutes.
6. Leave your crackers aside to cool down, cut them and serve.

10.3 Tomato Tarts

Ready in about One hour and 20 minutes | Servings-4 | Difficulty-Easy

Ingredients

- A quarter cups of olive oil
- Two sliced tomatoes
- Salt and black pepper to the taste

For the base

- Five tablespoons of ghee
- One tablespoon psyllium husk
- Half cups of almond flour
- Two tablespoons of coconut flour
- A pinch of salt

For the filling

- Two teaspoons of minced garlic
- Three teaspoons of chopped thyme
- Two tablespoons of olive oil
- Three ounces of crumbled goat cheese
- One small thinly sliced onion

Instructions

1. On a lined baking sheet, spread the tomato slices, season with pepper and salt, drizzle with a quarter of a cup of olive oil, place in the oven at 425 degrees F and bake for 40 minutes.
2. Meanwhile, mix psyllium husk with almond flour, coconut flour, pepper, salt and cold butter in your food processor and stir until you've got your dough.
3. Divide this dough into cupcake molds of silicone, press well, place it in the oven at 350 degrees F and bake for 20 minutes.
4. Remove the cupcakes from the oven and leave them aside.
5. Also, take slices of tomatoes from the oven and cool them down a bit.
6. On top of the cupcakes, divide the tomato slices.
7. Heat a saucepan over medium-high heat with two tablespoons of olive oil, add the onion, stir and cook for 4 minutes.
8. Add the thyme and garlic, stir, cook for another 1 minute and remove from the heat.
9. Spread the mix over the tomato slices.
10. Sprinkle with the goat cheese, put it back in the oven and cook for five more minutes at 350 degrees F.
11. Arrange and serve on a platter.

10.4 Pepper Nachos

Ready in about 30 minutes | Servings-6 | Difficulty-Easy

Ingredients

- One pound of halved mini bell peppers
- Salt and black pepper as per the taste
- One teaspoon of garlic powder
- One teaspoon of sweet paprika
- Half teaspoons of dried oregano
- A quarter teaspoon of red pepper flakes
- One pound of ground beef meat
- One and a half cups of shredded cheddar cheese
- One tablespoon of chili powder
- One teaspoon of ground cumin
- Half cups of chopped tomato
- Sour cream for serving

Instructions

1. Mix the chili powder, pepper, salt, paprika, oregano, cumin, flakes of pepper and garlic powder in a bowl and stir.
2. Over medium heat, heat a pan, add beef, mix and brown for 10 minutes.
3. Add the mixture of chili powder, stir and take the heat off.
4. On a lined baking sheet, arrange the pepper halves, stuff them with the beef mix, sprinkle the cheese, place in the oven at 400 degrees F and cook for 10 minutes.
5. Remove the peppers from the oven, sprinkle with the tomatoes and divide among the plates and serve with sour cream.

10.5 Pumpkin Muffins

Ready in about One hour 25 minutes|Servings-18|Difficulty-Easy

Ingredients

- A quarter cups of sunflower seed butter
- 3/4 cups of pumpkin puree
- Two tablespoons of flaxseed meal
- A quarter cups of coconut flour
- Half cup of erythritol
- Half teaspoons of ground nutmeg
- one teaspoon of ground cinnamon
- Half teaspoons of baking soda
- One egg
- Half teaspoons of baking powder
- A pinch of salt

Instructions

1. Mix the butter with the pumpkin puree and egg in a bowl and mix well.
2. Stir well and add coconut flour, flaxseed meal, erythritol, baking powder, baking soda, nutmeg, cinnamon and a pinch of salt.
3. Spoon this into an oiled muffin pan, add in the oven at 350 degrees F and cook for 15 minutes.
4. Let the muffins cool and serve them as a snack.

10.6 Fried Queso

Ready in about One hour 20 minutes|Servings-6|Difficulty-Easy

Ingredients

- Two ounces of pitted and chopped olives,

- Five ounces of cubed and freeze queso Blanco
- A pinch of red pepper flakes
- One and a half tablespoons of olive oil

Instructions

1. Over medium-high heat, heat a pan with the oil, add cheese cubes and fry until the lower part melts a bit.
2. Flip the spatula cubes and sprinkle on top with black olives.
3. Let the cubes cook a little more, flip and sprinkle with the red flakes of pepper and cook until crispy.
4. Flip, cook until crispy on the other side, then move to a chopping board, cut into tiny blocks, and then serve.

10.7 Tortilla Chips

Ready in about 25 minutes | Servings-6 | Difficulty-Easy

Ingredients

For the tortillas

- Two teaspoons of olive oil
- One cup of flaxseed meal
- Two tablespoons of psyllium husk powder
- A quarter teaspoon of xanthan gum
- One cup of water
- Half teaspoons of curry powder
- Three teaspoons of coconut flour

For the chips

- Six flaxseed tortillas
- Salt and black pepper to the taste
- Three tablespoons of vegetable oil

- Fresh salsa for serving
- Sour cream for serving

Instructions

1. Combine psyllium powder, flaxseed meal, xanthan gum, olive oil curry powder and water in a bowl and mix until an elastic dough is obtained.
2. On a working surface, spread coconut flour.
3. Divide the dough into six pieces, place each portion on the work surface, roll it into a circle and cut it into six pieces each.
4. Over medium-high heat, heat a pan with vegetable oil, add tortilla chips, cook on each side for 2 minutes and transfer to paper towels.
5. Put in a bowl of tortilla chips, season with pepper and salt and serve on the side with sour cream and fresh salsa.

10.8 Jalapeno Balls

Ready in about One hour 20 minutes | Servings-3 | Difficulty-Easy

Ingredients

- Three slices of bacon
- Three ounces of cream cheese
- A quarter teaspoon of onion powder
- Salt and black pepper as per taste
- One chopped jalapeno pepper
- Half teaspoons of dried parsley
- A quarter teaspoon of garlic powder

Instructions

1. Over medium-high heat, heat a skillet, add bacon, cook until crispy, switch to paper towels, remove the fat and crumble.
2. Reserve the pan's bacon fat.
3. Combine the jalapeno pepper, cream cheese, garlic powder and onion, parsley, pepper and salt in a bowl and stir thoroughly.
4. Use this blend to mix bacon crumbles and bacon fat, stir softly, form balls, and serve.

10.9 Maple and Pecan Bars

Ready in about 40 minutes|Servings-12| Difficulty-Easy

Ingredients

- Half cups of flaxseed meal
- two cups of pecans, toasted and crushed
- one cup of almond flour
- Half cups of coconut oil
- A quarter teaspoon of stevia
- Half cups of coconut, shredded
- A quarter cups of maple syrup
- **For the maple syrup**
- A quarter cups of erythritol
- Two and a quarter teaspoons of coconut oil
- One tablespoon of ghee
- A quarter teaspoon of xanthan gum
- 3/4 cups of water
- Two teaspoons of maple extract
- Half teaspoons of vanilla extract

Instructions

1. Combine ghee with two and a quarter teaspoons of xanthan gum and coconut oil in a heat-proof bowl, stir, put in your oven and heat up for 1 minute.
2. Add the extract of erythritol, water, maple and vanilla, mix well and fire for 1 minute more in the microwave.
3. Mix the flaxseed meal and the coconut and almond flour in a bowl and stir.
4. Add the pecans, and stir them again.
5. Apply a quarter of a cup of maple syrup, stevia, and half a cup of coconut oil, and mix well.
6. Spread this in a baking dish, push well, position it at 350 degrees F in the oven and cook for 25 minutes.
7. To cool off, leave it aside, break into 12 bars and act as a keto snack.

10.10 Broccoli and Cheddar Biscuits

Ready in about One hour 35 minutes | Servings-12 | Difficulty-Easy

Ingredients

- Four cups of broccoli florets
- One and a half cups of almond flour
- One teaspoon of paprika
- Salt and black pepper to the taste
- Two eggs
- A quarter cup of coconut oil
- Two cups of grated cheddar cheese
- One teaspoon of garlic powder
- Half teaspoons of apple cider vinegar
- Half teaspoons of baking soda

Instructions

1. In your food processor, place the broccoli florets, add some pepper and salt and combine well.
2. Mix pepper, salt, paprika, baking soda and garlic powder with almond flour in a bowl and stir.
3. Apply the coconut oil, cheddar cheese, vinegar and eggs and stir.
4. Attach the broccoli and stir some more.
5. Shape Twelve patties, arrange them on a baking sheet, put them at 375 degrees F in the oven and bake for 20 minutes.
6. Switch the broiler in the oven and broil the biscuits for another 5 minutes.
7. Arrange and serve on a platter.

Chapter 11- Dessert Recipes

11.1 Chocolate Truffles

Ready in about 20 minutes|Servings-22| Difficulty-Easy

Ingredients

- One cup of sugar-free chocolate chips
- Two tablespoons of butter
- 2/3 cups of heavy cream
- Two teaspoons of brandy
- Two tablespoons of swerve
- A quarter teaspoon of vanilla extract
- Cocoa powder

Instructions

1. In a fire-proof mug, add heavy cream, swerve, chocolate chips and butter, stir, put in the microwave and heat for 1 minute.
2. Leave for 5 minutes, blend well, and combine with the vanilla and the brandy.
3. Stir again. Set aside for a few hours in the fridge.
4. Shape the truffles using a melon baller, cover them in cocoa powder and then serve them.

11.2 Keto Doughnuts

Ready in about 25 minutes | Servings-24 | Difficulty-Easy

Ingredients

- A quarter cups of erythritol
- A quarter cups of flaxseed meal
- 3/4 cups of almond flour
- One teaspoon of baking powder
- One teaspoon of vanilla extract
- Two eggs
- Three tablespoons of coconut oil
- A quarter cups of coconut milk
- Twenty drops of red food coloring
- A pinch of salt
- One tablespoon of cocoa powder

Instructions

1. Mix together the almond flour, cocoa powder, baking powder, erythritol and salt in a bowl and stir.
2. Mix the coconut oil with vanilla, coconut milk, food coloring and eggs in another bowl and stir.

3. Mix mixtures, use a hand mixer to stir, move to a bag, cut a hole in the bag and shape a baking sheet with 12 doughnuts.
4. Place it in the oven at 350 degrees F and cook for 15 minutes.
5. On a tray, place them and eat them.

11.3 Chocolate Bombs

Ready in about 20 minutes│Servings-12│ Difficulty-Easy

Ingredients

- Ten tablespoons of coconut oil
- Three tablespoons of chopped macadamia nuts
- Two packets of stevia
- Five tablespoons of unsweetened coconut powder
- A pinch of salt

Instructions

1. Place coconut oil in a casserole dish and melt over medium heat.
2. Apply stevia, salt and cocoa powder, mix well and remove from the heat.
3. Spoon this into a tray of candy and store it for a while in the freezer.
4. Sprinkle the macadamia nuts on top and hold them in the refrigerator until served.

11.4 Simple and Delicious Mousse

Ready in about 10 minutes│Servings-12│ Difficulty-Easy

Ingredients

- Eight ounces of mascarpone cheese

- 3/4 teaspoons of vanilla stevia
- One cup of whipping cream
- Half-pint of blueberries
- Half-pint of strawberries

Instructions

1. Combine the whipped cream with mascarpone and stevia in a cup and blend well with your mixer.
2. Assemble twelve glasses with a coating of strawberries and blueberries, then a layer of milk, and so on.
3. Serve cool.

11.5 Strawberry Pie

Ready in about 2 hours and 20 minutes | Servings-12 | Difficulty-Hard

Ingredients

For the filling

- One teaspoon of gelatin
- Eight ounces of cream cheese
- Four ounces of strawberries
- Two tablespoons of water
- Half tablespoon of lemon juice
- A quarter teaspoon of stevia
- Half cups of heavy cream
- Eight ounces of chopped strawberries for serving
- Sixteen ounces of heavy cream for serving

For the crust

- One cup of shredded coconut

- One cup of sunflower seeds
- A quarter cup of butter
- A pinch of salt

Instructions

1. Mix the sunflower seeds with coconut, butter and a pinch of salt in your food processor and stir well.
2. Place this in a greased springform pan and push the bottom well.
3. Heat a skillet over medium heat with the water, add gelatin, mix until it dissolves, remove the heat and leave to cool off.
4. Add it to your food processor, mix and blend well with 4 ounces of cream cheese, lemon juice, strawberries and stevia.
5. Stir well, pour half a cup of heavy cream and scatter over the crust.
6. Before slicing and serving, top with 8 ounces of strawberries and 16 ounces of heavy cream and keep in the refrigerator for 2 hours.

11.6 Keto Cheesecakes

Ready in about 25 minutes | Servings-9 | Difficulty-Easy

Ingredients

For the cheesecakes

- Two tablespoons of butter
- Eight ounces of cream cheese
- Three tablespoons of coffee
- Three eggs
- 1/3 cups of swerve
- One tablespoon of sugar-free caramel syrup

For the frosting

- Three tablespoons of sugar-free caramel syrup
- Three tablespoons of butter
- Eight ounces of soft mascarpone cheese
- Two tablespoons of swerve

Instructions

1. Combine eggs with cream cheese, two tablespoons butter, one tablespoon caramel syrup, coffee, and 1/3 cup swerve in your blender and pulse very well.
2. Spoon this into a pan of cupcakes, place it at 350 degrees F in the oven and cook for 15 minutes.
3. To cool down, leave aside and then keep in the freezer for three hours.
4. Meanwhile, mix three tablespoons butter with three tablespoons caramel syrup, two tablespoons swerve and mascarpone cheese in a bowl and mix well.
5. Spoon the cheesecakes over and serve them.

11.7 Peanut Butter Fudge

Ready in about 2 hours and 15 minutes | Servings-12 | Difficulty-Hard

Ingredients

- One cup of unsweetened peanut butter
- A quarter cups of almond milk
- Two teaspoons of vanilla stevia
- One cup of coconut oil
- A pinch of salt

For the topping

- Two tablespoons of swerve
- Two tablespoons of melted coconut oil
- A quarter cups of cocoa powder

Instructions

1. Combine peanut butter with one cup of coconut oil in a heat-proof bowl, stir and heat in your microwave until it melts.
2. Add stevia, a pinch of salt and almond milk, mix it well and pour into a lined loaf pan.
3. Keep it for 2 hours in the refrigerator and then slice it.
4. Mix two tablespoons of cocoa powder and melted coconut in a bowl and swirl and stir well.
5. Drizzle over your peanut butter fudge with the sauce and serve.

11.8 Chocolate Pie

Ready in about 3 hours and 30 minutes | Servings-10 | Difficulty-Hard

Ingredients

For the filling

- One tablespoon vanilla extract
- Four tablespoons of sour cream
- One teaspoon of vanilla extract
- Four tablespoons of butter
- Sixteen ounces of cream cheese
- Half cup of cut stevia
- Two teaspoons of granulated stevia
- Half cup of cocoa powder
- One cup of whipping cream

For crust

- Half teaspoons of baking powder
- One and a half cups of the almond crust
- A quarter cup of stevia
- A pinch of salt
- One egg
- One and a half teaspoons of vanilla extract
- Three tablespoons of butter
- One teaspoon of butter for the pan

Instructions

1. With one teaspoon of butter, oil a springform pan and leave aside for now.
2. Mix the baking powder with a quarter cup of stevia, almond flour and a pinch of salt in a bowl and stir.
3. Add three tablespoons of butter, one teaspoon of egg, and one and a half teaspoons of vanilla extract, then mix till the time the dough is ready.
4. Press it well into the springform pan, place it at 375 degrees F in the oven and cook it for 11 minutes.
5. Take the pie crust out of the oven, cover it with tin foil and cook for another 8 minutes.
6. Take it out of the oven again and set it aside to cool down.
7. Meanwhile, add sour cream, four tablespoons of butter, one tablespoon of vanilla extract, half a cup of cocoa powder and stevia to the cream cheese in a bowl and mix it well.

8. Mix two teaspoons of stevia and one teaspoon of vanilla extract with the whipping cream in another bowl and stir using your mixer.
9. Combine two mixtures, pour into the pie crust, spread well, place for 3 hours in the refrigerator and serve.

11.9 Raspberry and Coconut Dessert

Ready in about 20 minutes|Servings-12| Difficulty-Easy

Ingredients

- Half cup of coconut butter
- Half cup of coconut oil
- Half cup of dried raspberries
- A quarter cups of swerve
- Half cup of shredded coconut

Instructions

1. Mix the dried berries in your food processor very well.
2. Heat a pan over medium heat with the butter.
3. Stir in the coconut, oil and swerve, stir and cook for 5 minutes.
4. Pour half of this and spread well into a lined baking pan.
5. Add raspberry powder and also spread.
6. Spread the rest of the butter mix on top and keep it in the fridge for a while.
7. Cut and serve into pieces.

11.10 Vanilla Ice Cream

Ready in about 3 hours 20 minutes | Servings-6 | Difficulty-Hard

Ingredients

- Four eggs, yolks and whites separated
- A quarter teaspoon of cream of tartar
- Half cups of swerve
- One tablespoon of vanilla extract
- One and a quarter cups of heavy whipping cream

Instructions

1. Mix the egg whites with the tartar cream in a bowl and swerve and swirl using your mixer.
2. Whisk the cream with the vanilla extract in another bowl and mix thoroughly.
3. Combine and gently whisk the two mixtures.
4. Whisk the egg yolks very well in another bowl and then apply the combination of two egg whites.
5. Gently stir, put it into a container and leave it in the refrigerator for 3 hours until the ice cream is eaten.

Chapter 12- Smoothie Recipes

12.1 Minted Iced Berry Sparkler

Ready in about 30 minutes | Servings-2 | Difficulty-Easy

Ingredients

- One cup of mixed frozen berries
- One lime or lemon
- One cup of fresh mint
- Twenty drops liquid Stevia extract (Clear / Berry)
- One large bottle of water
- Ice

Instructions

1. Wash the mint.
2. Cut the lime into wedges that are thin.

3. Using your option of sparkling or still water to put mint, frozen berries, lemon wedges or lime and leftover ingredients into all in a jar.
4. Let yourself relax for 15 minutes or more. The longer you keep it, the taste gets bolder.
5. Serve.

12.2 Body Pumping Smoothie

Ready in about 10 minutes | Servings-2 | Difficulty-Easy

Ingredients

- One beetroot
- One Apple
- Three tablespoons of yogurt
- Handful of mint
- One thumb of a two-inch ginger
- Half teaspoon of black salt or rock salt
- One teaspoon of honey or sugar
- A quarter cup of water

Instructions

1. Clean and remove the beet peel.
2. Slice the medium-sized apple and remove the nuts.
3. Add all the ingredients into the blender.
4. Add ice, then proceed to mix into a paste that is smooth.
5. Add juice from the lemon.
6. Enjoy and serve.

12.3 Kiwi Dream Blender

Ready in about 10 minutes | Servings-2 | Difficulty-Easy

Ingredients

- A quarter average avocado

- One small wedge of Galia melon (or Honeydew, Cantaloupe)
- One scoop of vanilla whey protein powder (vanilla or plain)
- powdered gelatin
- Six drops liquid Stevia extract
- Ice as per the need
- A quarter cups of coconut milk (or coconut cream or full-fat cream)
- A quarter cup of kiwi berries or kiwi fruit
- One tablespoon of chia seeds (or psyllium)
- Half cups of water

Instructions

1. Strip and peel the avocado and put it in a blender.
2. Add the kiwi, melon and the remaining ingredients to the flesh.
3. Blend until completely smooth.
4. Serve.

12.4 Keto Smart Banana Blender

Ready in about 10 minutes | Servings-2 | Difficulty-Easy

Ingredients

- One cup of Spinach
- One cup of Banana
- Half cup of water and yogurt
- Two tablespoons of Pomegranate
- Two tablespoons of Almond meal/Almonds
- One teaspoon of Cinnamon powder
- One teaspoon of Vanilla sugar or Honey or Sugar and vanilla extract
- Ice

Instructions

1. Clean the spinach and chop it coarsely.
2. Cut the Banana into medium-sized portions.
3. To make a half-cup of milk, blend two to three tablespoons of yogurt with water.
4. In a blender, mix all ingredients and process until smooth.
5. If the ideal thickness is met, add ice when blending.
6. Then serve.

12.5 Bright Morning Smoothie

Ready in about 15 minutes | Servings-2 | Difficulty-Easy

Ingredients

- Two cups of Washed Spinach
- Two Large Strawberries
- A quarter cup of Lemon Juice or Fresh Squeezed Orange Juice
- Two tablespoons of Chia Seeds or Powder
- One cup of Green Tea
- One cup of Ice
- Four tablespoons of sweetener of choice

Instructions

1. Place all of the ingredients in a mixer.
2. Blend it all until smooth.
3. Let it rest for about 5-10 minutes, then serve.

12.6 Keto Iced Strawberry and Greens

Ready in about 10 minutes | Servings-2 | Difficulty-Easy

Ingredients

- Half cup coconut water
- One cup of ice
- One cup of washed spinach
- Three large strawberries
- Sweetener to taste

Instructions

1. Blend all the ingredients together in a blender until smooth.
2. Let it rest for 5 minutes and then serve chilled.

12.7 Strawberry Lime Ginger Punch

Ready in about 10 minutes | Servings-2 | Difficulty-Easy

Ingredients

- Two cups of water
- Two tablespoons of raw apple cider vinegar
- Three packets of NuStevia or any other sweetener
- Juice of one lime
- Half teaspoon of ginger powder
- Five frozen strawberries

Instructions

1. Blend all the ingredients together in a blender until smooth.
2. Let it rest for 5 minutes and then serve chilled.

12.8 Mexican Comfort Cream

Ready in about 20 minutes | Servings-2 | Difficulty-Easy

Ingredients

- Two handfuls of almonds blanched
- One cup of almond milk (unsweetened)
- One large egg

- Two tablespoons of whole or ground chia seeds
- One tablespoon of lime zest
- One teaspoon of cinnamon powder or one whole cinnamon stick
- Three tablespoons of erythritol or another healthy low-carb sweetener
- Twenty drops of liquid Stevia extract (Clear / Cinnamon)
- Two cups of warm water

Instructions

1. Put in a bowl lime zest, the blanched almonds and cinnamon stick and cover with two teaspoons of hot water.
2. Let it rest for about eight hours or overnight.
3. Remove the lime zest and cinnamon stick after the almonds have been softened and put them in a shallow saucepan.
4. Mix almond milk. Purée until it's really smooth.
5. Steam the mixture and mix cinnamon and sweeteners before it begins to sizzle.
6. Whisk the egg when stirring constantly and pour it gently into the mixture.
7. Stir for a minute or two over the sun.
8. Remove from the heat and add in the seeds of chia.
9. To thicken the remainder.
10. Serve cold and pour in a bottle.

12.9 Strawberry Protein Smoothie

Ready in about 10 minutes | Servings-2 | Difficulty-Easy

Ingredients

- Half cup water

- One cup of ice
- One scoop of strawberry protein powder
- One egg
- Two tablespoons of cream
- Two strawberries

Instructions

1. Blend ice cubes and water together.
2. Apply the egg, powder and strawberries and start blending.
3. Pour in the cream.
4. Blend it again until smooth in a blender.
5. Serve and enjoy.

12.10 Low-Carb Caribbean Cream

Ready in about 2 hours and 10 minutes | Servings-1 | Difficulty-Moderate

Ingredients

- Half cup of unsweetened coconut milk
- A quarter cups of coconut water or water (iced)
- One shot of dark or white rum
- One slice of fresh pineapple
- Five drops of liquid Stevia extract

Instructions

1. In an ice cube tray, freeze the coconut water for 1-2 hours.
2. Blend coconut milk and pineapple until creamy.
3. Add the coconut water ice cubes and rum to the serving bottle.
4. Add the combined solution.

5. Use the pineapple to garnish.
6. Serve and enjoy.

Introduction

Congratulations on downloading Intermittent Fasting for women: *The Ultimate Beginners Guide for Permanent Weight Loss, Slow the Aging Process, and Heal Your Body with the Self-cleansing Process of Metabolic Autophagy.*

This book is your ultimate guide to intermittent fasting. In this book, you'll explore everything about intermittent fasting; what it is, how it works, and how best you can adapt it to suit your needs as a woman. The intermittent fasting diet is one of the best ways to lose weight since it's not restrictive but instead advocates for a change in lifestyle.

You'll notice that this book covers many facets of intermittent fasting, thus offering as much guidance you need to help you get started. This book also discredits the common belief that breakfast is the most important meal of the days hence can't be skipped. Moreover, nutritionists will tell you to eat multiple small meals during the day to stay healthy, but the intermittent fasting diet overrides this principle. The science behind the intermittent fasting is backed by various research studies that have proved that you can actually skip breakfast.

We all have a tendency to naturally fast that makes it easy to integrate intermittent fasting into our lifestyles. In fact, once you adjust to your new lifestyle of intermittent fasting, you'll be surprised that you actually don't eat as much as you think you do or you need to. Intermittent fasting will help you to not only fulfill your weight loss goals but also meet your dietary needs, fight off diseases, and maintain a healthy lifestyle.

Even then, as you read this book keep in mind that everyone's experience with intermittent fasting is different. This is the key to implementing it in your life because you'll find it easy to stick to the intermittent fasting plan that is convenient for you. It's never too late to make significant changes to your lifestyle with intermittent fasting. You can begin today.

Chapter 1: Obesity and Its Impact on Women

Obesity has a negative impact on the health of women, yet 2 in 3 women in the United States are obese. What is obesity, and how do you know you are obese? Obesity is a disorder that is characterized by having an excessive amount of body fat. It is diagnosed when your body mass index is (BMI) 30 or higher. This is calculated by dividing your weight in kilograms by your height in meters squared. Wondering what your BMI is? Can you use online BMI calculators to find out your BMI? Even then, BMI is considered less accurate in some people, especially if you're very muscular since muscles weigh more than fat. The other ways to find out if your weight is healthy is by measuring your waist circumference. If your waist circumference is more than 35 inches, then you have a higher risk of experiencing the problems associated with obesity.

Your body needs calories to work properly. However, when your body is storing more calories than its burning over time, you become obese because it means you're gaining weight. However, environmental factors can also influence obesity. When you are extremely obese, you are likely to have a myriad of health problems in addition to having low self-esteem. As a woman, you are also at risk of suffering from diseases like diabetes, heart disease, and even certain types of cancers.

Obesity Risk Factors

Although women of all ages, ethnicities, and races can be obese, obesity tends to be more common among African American Women and Latina or Hispanic women. Other risk factors for obesity among women include the following:

Genetics and family background. For some people, obesity runs in the family. This is not to say that there's a single fat gene. Rather, many genes work together resulting in your likelihood of gaining excess weight. Additionally, the kind of food you're given as a child by your caregivers and parents can influence your weight gain as an adult.

Metabolism. The rate at which your body breaks down calories will often vary from one person to the other due to various reasons affecting your weight loss and gain. When you have more muscle and less fat, your body burns fat quickly. On the contrary, when you have more fat and less muscle, you're more likely to gain weight. Moreover, your metabolism may also be affected by hormonal changes at puberty, during pregnancy, and when you get into menopause.

Trauma. You may sometimes go through life issues that you don't have control over or are not your fault that affects how fast you gain weight. Women who experience negative events in their childhood like alcoholic parents or abuse are more likely to be obese as adults.

Sleep: Lack of high-quality sleep could also lead to weight gain. This is because not getting quality sleep can affect your hormone levels, which eventually has an effect on your food choices and appetite. Not getting enough sleep may also affect your level or exercise and physical activity throughout the day.

Medicines. Some of the medicines that you may be taking such as those used in treating mental health conditions, high blood pressure, and sleep can lead to weight gain. Medicines may also make it difficult to lose weight. If you're taking prescription medicine and you notice you're gaining extra weight, don't hesitate to talk to your doctor to give you alternative medicine or ways of losing weight.

With so many factors contributing to unhealthy weight gain, you always have to be alert to know what is making you gain weight to make sure you keep your weight under control. When you're overweight or obese, it increases your risk of having serious health conditions such as:

Cancer. Women who are obese have a high risk of suffering from various types of cancer such as cancer of the thyroid, ovarian, pancreatic, multiple myeloma (blood plasma cells), meningioma (cancer of tissue covering spinal cord and brain, kidney, liver, stomach, esophagus, endometrial, colon, rectal, breast and gall bladder.

Breathing problems. When you're overweight, you'll most likely experience sleep apnea. This causes you to stop breathing or take in slow breaths during sleep. Consequently, you'll not get enough oxygen in your body or brain during sleep. This can lead to more serious health issues like heart disease.

Heart disease. Your risk of having heart disease increases with excess weight. Therefore, you must strive to keep your weight in check in order to stay healthy and avoid heart disease that is a leading cause of death among women.

Diabetes. Having extra weight predisposes you to diabetes. On the contrary, you can prevent diabetes when you lose weight or keep your weight within the recommended range. Weight loss is also important in controlling your blood glucose, especially if you already suffer from diabetes. In fact, you'll less likely need medicine to keep your blood sugar in control.

Pregnancy problems. You might find it difficult getting pregnant when you are obese. If you're already pregnant, you're likely to experience complications like preeclampsia (dangerously high blood pressure) and gestational diabetes. Thus, you'll need close monitoring and regular prenatal care to ensure early detection and prevention of such problems.

High blood pressure. If you've obesity, you're more likely to have high blood pressure and may be advised by your doctor to lose some weight to reduce your blood pressure. When you have high blood pressure, it can damage your arteries resulting in related health conditions like heart disease and stroke.

Stroke. Being obese increases your chances of suffering from a stroke. This is particularly serious when most of your weight is around your waist than thighs and hips.

High cholesterol. When your weight is more excess, your body will change the way it processes food. Thus, your bad cholesterol increases while your good cholesterol is reduced. Consequently, the buildup of fatty plaque increases within your arteries. An increase in bad cholesterol can lead to heart disease.

You need to know when to start working towards losing weight. A 3 to 5 % loss is capable of helping lower your risk of health problems while making you healthier. Therefore, take time to discuss with your doctor the amount of weight you must lose.

Chapter 2: The Skinny on Intermittent Fasting

Losing excessive body weight/fat can be a challenge. In most cases, you'll have to give up something you love and embrace a change of lifestyle by hitting the gym. But did you know that you can lose fat, improve your metabolism, and enjoy all the other health benefits without giving up the foods you love? Intermittent fasting is an incredible solution to shedding off excess fat that comes with other benefits you'll enjoy. So, what is intermittent fasting? Although most people think of it as a diet, it is not. Intermittent fasting is a pattern of eating that cycles between periods of eating and fasting and has been proven to be effective in weight loss while sustaining the results.

Interestingly, intermittent fasting is a practice that has been in existence for a long time. What makes intermittent fasting unique is the way in which you schedule your meals. You don't change what you eat, instead what changes are when you eat. That is, instead of dictating the foods you should eat, it dictates when you should eat. Thus, with intermittent fasting, you get lean and building your muscle mass without cutting down your calories. Even then, most people opt for intermittent fasting for the sole reason of losing fat.

Who Invented the Intermittent Fasting Diet

Fasting is not a new thing. It has been practiced since human evolution. In fact, the human body is wired to fast. The hunter and gatherer population did have much food to store, and they would sometimes have nothing to eat due to scarcity. As such, they adopted the ability to function without food for long periods that are essentially fasting. There's also a religious angle to fasting for Christians and Muslims alike.

However, the current wave of intermitted fasting diet was popularized by Dr. Michael Mosley. Intermittent fasting has generated a steady positive buzz with more and more people embracing it. Dr. Mosley explains the science behind intermittent fasting. He, however, attributes the success and popularity of intermittent fasting to the fact that it's mostly psychological and teaches you better ways of eating. That is, when you get used to eating vegetables and good protein, you'll eventually crave healthy food whenever you're hungry.

Why Do You Fast

Intermittent fasting is a simple yet effective strategy for taking shedding off all the bad weight so that you only keep the good weight. This approach requires very little change in behavior. Thus, it's simple yet meaningful enough to make a difference. When you fast, a couple of changes take place in your body both at the molecular and cellular level. To understand why you need to fast to lose weight, you first must understand what happens to your body when it is in the fed and absorptive state. In the fed state, your body is absorbing and digesting food. It actually begins when you start eating and would typically last for five hours as digestion and absorption of the food you ate takes place. When your body is in this state, it can hardly burn fat due to high insulin levels. From the fed state, your body enters the postabsorptive state during which no meal processing is taking place. This stage lasts between 8 and 12 hours after the last meal before you enter the fasted state. It is during the fasted state that your body burns fat because your insulin levels are low. In the fasted state, your body burns fat that is usually inaccessible in the fed state. Fasting helps to put your body in the fat burning state that is rare to achieve when you're on a normal eating schedule.

Intermittent fasting changes the hormones in your body to utilize your fat stores effectively. Your human growth hormone levels go up dramatically, thus speeding up protein synthesis, thereby influencing your body's fat loss and muscle gain by making the fat available for use as a source of energy. What this means is that your body will be burning fat and packing muscle faster. When your insulin levels drop due to heightened insulin sensitivity making the fat stored in your body more accessible to be converted to energy, some changes in gene functions relating to protection and longevity will be amplified, and your cells will initiate repair processes efficiently and quickly. Moreover, fasting promotes autophagy that removes all the damaged cells while contributing to the renewal of cells in addition to supporting the body's regenerative processes.

What You Should Eat During Intermittent Fasting

One of the reasons why intermittent fasting is appealing is because there are no food rules. The only restrictions are on when you can eat and not what you can eat. However, this is not to say that you should be downing bags of chips and pints upon pints of ice cream. Remember, the idea is to adopt a healthy eating lifestyle. So what should you eat anyway? Well, a well-balanced diet is key to maintaining your energy levels. If your goal is to lose weight, you must focus on including nutrient-dense foods on your menu like veggies, fruits, nuts, whole grains, seeds, beans, lean proteins, and dairy. Think about unprocessed, high fiber, whole foods that offer flavor and variety. Here are some foods you should eat in plenty during intermittent fasting:

Water. Although you're not eating, it's important to make sure your stay hydrated to maintain the health of major organs in the body. To tell if you have adequate water, make sure your urine is pale yellow. Dark urine is a sign of dehydration that can cause fatigue, headaches, or even lightheadedness. If you can't stand plain water, you can add mint leaves, a squeeze of lemon juice or cucumber slices.

Fish. Dietary guidelines advocate for the consumption of at least eight ounces of fish weekly. Fish is a rich source of protein, ample quantities of Vitamin D and healthy fats. Moreover, limiting your calorie consumption can alter your cognitive ability; hence, fish will come in handy as brain food.

Avocado. It's obviously strange to eat high-calorie food when you're actually trying to lose weight. Well, the thing about avocadoes is that they're packed with monounsaturated fat that is satiating. Thus, you can be sure to stay full for longer hours than you would when you eat other foods.

Cruciferous vegetables. Foods like Brussels sprouts, broccoli, and cauliflower, are laden with fiber. Eating these foods will keep you regular while preventing constipation. Furthermore, you'll also fee full, which is great when you're fasting for hours.

Beans and legumes. Carbs are a great source of energy; hence, you can consider including low-calorie carbs like legumes and beans in your eating plan. Besides, foods like black beans, lentils, and chickpeas have been found to decrease body weight.

Potatoes. Potatoes are not necessarily bad. If anything, they offer a satiating effect that could lead to weight loss. However, this doesn't include potato chips and French fries.

Eggs. It's important to get as much protein as possible to build muscle and stay full. A large egg will give you six grams of proteins. When you eat hard boiled eggs, you're less likely to feel hungry.

Berries. You need immune boosting nutrients like vitamin c, and there's no better way to achieve this than including berries in your meal plan.

Probiotics. The bacteria in your gut aren't happy when you go for hours without food. As such, you could experience side effects like constipation. You can counter this unpleasant feeling taking probiotic-rich foods like kefir, kraut, or kombucha.

Whole grains. It's ridiculous to be on a diet and eat carbs. Well, with intermittent fasting, you can include whole grains that are rich in protein and fiber to stay full. Moreover, eating whole grains will speed up your metabolism. Think about millet, amaranth, sorghum, kamut, spelled, faro, bulgur, and freekeh, among others.

Nuts. Although nuts may contain high calories, they're most certainly important because of the good fat.

According to research, polyunsaturated fat found in walnuts has the ability to alter physiological markers for satiety and hunger.

What to Consider Before Starting Intermittent Fasting

Before you begin intermittent fasting for weight loss, you need to know that this eating pattern is not for everyone. First off, you should not attempt intermittent fasting before consulting a health professional if you're underweight or you have a history of battling eating disorders. Intermittent fasting is also not recommended if you have a medical condition. Some women have also reported various effects like a cessation of a menstrual period. Ultimately, you need to be careful when you go into intermittent fasting because it has been previously found that this eating pattern is not beneficial for women compared to men. If you have fertility issues or are trying to conceive, then consider holding off intermittent fasting. Expectant and lactating mothers are also advised against intermittent fasting.

The main side effect that you'll experience when you go into intermittent fasting is hunger. Additionally, you may experience general body weakness. Your brain may also perform well. However, these are temporary, and your body will adapt to your new eating pattern over time. It's advisable that you consult your doctor before starting intermittent fasting for women if you have any of the following conditions;

- Diabetes/Problems with blood sugar regulations
- Low blood pressure
- You are underweight
- Eating disorders
- Amenorrhea
- Breastfeeding
- Trying to conceive
- Taking medications

Always look at the potential benefits of intermittent fasting before you go for it. If the risks far outweigh the benefits, this could be dangerous hence not worth trying. For instance, if you're pregnant, you definitely have more energy needs; therefore, taking on intermittent fasting would definitely be a bad idea. This also applies when you're having problems sleeping or are under chronic stress. Intermittent fasting is also discouraged if you have a history of eating disorders because it could actually cause further problems that can mess your health. While intermittent fasting has produced results for thousands of people across the globe, you must keep in mind that this is not a gateway to eating a diet comprising of highly processed food or even skipping meals randomly. Generally, intermittent fasting has an outstanding safety profile since it's not dangerous to go without food for a while when you're well-nourished and healthy.

When Do You Fast

If you're looking to get on the intermittent fasting train, you need to know when you will be fasting in order to achieve the desired outcome. There are three common ways of approaching the fast as follows:

Eat stop eat. This involves fasting for 24 hours once or twice in seven days. However, you can take calorie-free beverages during this fasting period. This is one of the best ways to start intermittent fasting because the occasional fasting will equally help you realize the many benefits of fasting.

Up day, down day. With this method of fasting, you will keep on reducing your calorie intake daily. That is, when you eat very little one day (down day), you revert to your normal caloric intake the next day (up day). The advantage of this eating pattern is that it allows you to eat every day while you still reap the benefits of fasting.

Alternate day fasting. With this schedule, you get to fast for longer periods on alternate days weekly. You fast for 24 hours and only eat one meal every day.

Lean gains. With this approach, you'll fast for 16 hours within every 24 hours and only eat during the eight-hour window. Keep in mind that sleep is included so this is not as tough as it may seem. The good thing about this fast is that you can start your 8-hour eating period at a time that works best for you. This means that you could actually skip breakfast and instead have lunch and dinner. Since this is something you'll do every day, it eventually becomes a habit making it remarkably easy to stick to it.

Chapter 3: Why Intermittent Fasting Is the Best Way for Weight Loss

Most of the weight loss diet fads will often demand that you give up certain things in order for you to see the results. Well, this is not the case with intermittent fasting that almost blends into your normal eating and sleeping pattern. Even then, the truth is that fasting in itself can be intimidating. Not eating for a couple of hours is something many people find difficult. Yet this method comes close to your lifestyle than a diet. So make sure that you identify an intermittent fasting plan that fits into your schedule, and you're able to keep up with comfortably. This will minimize the chance of having to quit because you're not putting any strain on your body.

Think about this; you fast while sleeping and break the fast when you wake up in the morning! Even more interesting, most people often fast for 12 hours and have another 12 hours of eating. As such, you can easily extend the fasting window to 16 hours and eat for eight hours to realize the benefits of intermittent fasting. Here are reasons why you should consider intermittent fasting as your weight loss regime:

Intermittent fasting is convenient. One of the reasons many people give up on other kinds of weight loss diets is because they're unable to follow through. When you have a busy lifestyle juggling between a number of things that are vying for your attention and are on a diet, the latter will definitely suffer.

On the contrary, intermittent fasting comes with convenience. For instance, when doing the 16:8 intermittent fast, you don't have to think about preparing breakfast in the morning or even lunch. Yes, you can skip breakfast.

What's more? When it's time to feed, you don't have to worry about what kind of food you should eat. Intermittent fasting is quite flexible with the foods you can include in your diet. In fact, in most instances, nothing will really change. You could even eat at a restaurant yet still enjoy the benefits of fasting.

Moreover, intermittent fasting lets you enjoy special occasions with family and friends without worrying about excess calories. However, this does not mean that you eat highly processed foods. The idea here is to develop a healthy yet convenient to implement eating pattern that can eventually be part of your lifestyle.

Intermittent fasting makes life simple. Intermittent fasting is not just convenient but also simple to follow. Whether you're always on the go or are into skipping a meal or two, this eating pattern is convenient and perfect for you. College students will particularly find intermittent fasting appealing because they can hardly find a balance between school work and maintaining a healthy social life. When you take on intermittent fasting, you'll realize there'll be fewer decisions you have to make daily. Instead, you'll have more energy to handle the most important tasks of the day. This is contrary to the effect that most diets will have on your body like feeling overwhelmed and tired in addition to being expensive and complex.

Intermittent fasting saves you time and money. If you were to go on a regular diet, no doubt you'll have to go out of your way to spend time and money to conform to a certain menu. Not to mention the amount of time that would go into shopping for the food supplies, prepping and eventually cooking at least six meals in a day. The truth is that this can be draining. However, with intermittent fasting, there's no need to get out of your normal lifestyle. If anything, it will save you money and time since you'll be having fewer meals in a day. Consequently, you don't have to spend time thinking about what you should eat or even spending a lot of time preparing the food.

Intermittent fasting strengthens your will power while improving your concentration and focus. Intermittent fasting is all about self-discipline. That is, you must learn to say no. In fact, there'll be numerous times during your fast when you'll crave food, but you must resist this urge to eat. Every time you resist this urge helps you develop your willpower as well as strengthen your ability to steer clear of distractions and temptations even in other areas of life. In addition, it'll also go a long way in improving your ability to focus and concentrate on achieving specific goals that you have yet to accomplish. Generally, you tend to be sharper and alert when you're hungry than when you've got a full tummy. This is attributed to the fact that fasting will free up all the valuable energy hence avoiding distractions while staying focused on an important goal.

Intermittent fasting lets you eat what you want and still lose weight. With intermittent fasting, weight loss is more about when you eat as opposed to what you eat. As such, it gives you more freedom to eat what you want to eat. Since you're fasting, you'll typically settle down for a larger meal and consequently more calories than you would normally eat per meal for three to six meals. Therefore, intermittent fasting is more about timing than the composition of your diet. Even then, you should avoid eating processed junk food, particularly those with empty calories since they will undo the benefits of your fast. Since intermittent fasting is more of a lifestyle, you'll do well to cut down on sweeteners and processed sugars and replace processed foods with whole foods. Ultimately, you should focus on having a balanced diet that includes whole grains, vegetables, fruits, and protein. If you're aiming at losing weight, you also must not take in too many calories during your feeding window.

Intermittent fasting helps you embrace a healthy lifestyle and avoid dangerous eating diets. Since intermittent fasting is not a diet, it's a lifestyle that can be sustained through the years. Intermittent fasting is more of a wellness revolution because it helps you to adapt to a lifestyle of eating healthy foods and avoiding dangerous diets. If you're on intermittent fasting, you should not overeat junk food; otherwise, you'll end up gaining weight. Remember, intermittent fasting isn't an excuse for indulging in your favorite chocolate cookie or ice cream without giving a care. Rather, intermittent fasting reprograms your brain so that you're accustomed to taking reduced calories than you would normally consume. This helps you to avoid the trap of overeating. In fact, you'll be surprised that over time you'll be able to say no to your favorite cookies not because you deny yourself a treat, but you simply don't want. When you're consuming fewer calories than you're taking, you'll definitely begin to burn fat and lose weight over time.

Intermittent fasting lets you have bigger meals that are more satisfying. When you have to eat every 2-3 hours, you tend to think about food for the better part of the day. Consequently, you'll hardly have big meals, particularly if you are physically inactive. Having infrequent meals in a large volume will often provide you with more calories and is much more satisfying hence a great way to feel fuller for longer periods. When you eat large meals infrequently, you'll have increased adherence to the diet over time.

Intermitted fasting helps to establish a more structured way of eating. When you are on the regular eating plan, you will, in most instances, find yourself snacking in between meals mindlessly. From a couple of cookies to a slice of cake and ice cream, there's always something you can chew on. This will definitely contribute to you gaining excess weight. Intermittent fasting helps you to structure your eating pattern without necessarily getting rid of your favorites. Instead, you eliminate the habit of eating every so often by taking better control of your diet.

Intermittent fasting improves your hunger awareness. Hunger and thirst are processed in the same part of the brain. Thus, it is common to find that you're eating throughout the day not because you're hungry but for other reasons. This can be anything from stress, boredom, happiness, or even sadness, among others. Sometimes, the mere smell of food can make you assume you're actually hungry. Thus, when you're on a fast, you'll have a heightened sense of hunger awareness that will make you realize that real hunger feels like and how to differentiate it from the hunger that is triggered by other factors.

You can still eat out and enjoy social gatherings during intermittent fasting. Unlike many weight loss diets, intermittent fasting is not restrictive in terms of the foods you need to include on your menu. So you don't have to worry about missing out on social gatherings or even eating out! In fact, this pattern of eating accommodates the social nature of human beings as we tend to build social events around food. Since most of the occasions take place in the evening, you can always stick to your fasting routine and join the rest of the gathering at the table. Intermittent fasting gives you the freedom to eat food that is served at social gatherings as well as restaurants while staying within your calorie range for the day. This makes it simple and easy to maintain. So you don't have to write off the idea of eating out.

You can still travel the world while fasting. If you love traveling, you might be hesitant about attempting intermittent fasting. However, the interesting thing is that you can still travel the world and not worry about missing new experiences because of breaking your fast outside your feeding window. You can easily integrate intermittent fasting into your diet so that you are enjoying new experiences while losing weight. This way, you don't have to eat unhealthy food or even abandon your intermittent fasting plan for weight loss. Intermittent fasting can work for you whenever and wherever you are.

Intermittent fasting helps to improve the quality of your sleep. Although most people embrace intermittent fasting solely to lose weight, it comes with other added benefits among them quality sleep. This is attributed to the fact that when you're fasting, your body digests food before you sleep. This eventually helps you to sleep better because your insulin and fat levels are better controlled. Getting quality sleep can also contribute to weight loss.

Intermittent fasting makes you feel happy. This is another added advantage of fasting for weight loss. When you lose excess weight, you will not only feel lighter but also happier because you'll be more confident in your body. Moreover, you'll also have more energy because generally, digestion often takes much of your body's energy. This is in addition to feeling more healthier and in control.

Intermittent fasting is easy to follow. In most cases, starting a diet is easy. However, many people tend to give up after several weeks of watching what you're eating and counting calories. On the contrary, intermittent fasting gives you much freedom making it a lot easier to stick with it in the long term.

Intermittent fasting helps in muscle growth. Although many people have reported that intermittent fasting resulted in the loss of muscle when done properly, intermittent fasting can contribute to muscle building. However, this will require you to tailor your intermittent fasting approach in a manner that limits your fasting period to between 10 and 12 hours so that you're not inhibiting the body's ability to build muscle. You may also have to extend your feeding window to 10 hours so that you get all the nutrients you need.

Well, intermittent fasting does more than just helping you achieve your goal of losing weight. It actually presents many other benefits that will generally improve your lifestyle. This means that you must stay committed to the intermittent fasting plan that works for you to make sure that you get the results you desire. Eventually, intermittent fasting will become part of your lifestyle.

Chapter 4: Impact of Intermittent Fasting on Your Body

A number of studies have backed up the fact that intermittent fasting presents powerful benefits to your brain and body. Some of the top benefits you'll experience when you embark on intermittent fasting for weight loss include the following:

Speeds up fat burning and weight loss. Intermittent fasting is one of the top strategies for burning fat effortlessly. Fat burning during intermittent fasting is actually a result of being in a calorie deficient state that promotes loss of fat. A study done on animals found that intermittent fasting for a period of up to 16 weeks helps in the preventions of obesity with the results being seen in just six weeks. According to researchers, intermittent fasting activates metabolism while also helping to burn more fat through the generation of body heat. When you're fasting, your insulin levels will be low. The body will break down carbohydrates into glucose that the cells will draw energy from or convert it into fat hence store it for later use. Insulin levels are low when you're not consuming food. Thus, during fasting, your insulin levels are likely to be low, prompting the cells to get their glucose from fat stores as energy. When this process is done repeatedly, it results in weight loss. Most research suggests that intermittent fasting may be an effective weight management strategy. The fact that you'll most likely be eating fewer calories than you're burning means that your body will mostly be relying on the fat stores for energy which will translate to significant weight loss.

Boosts growth hormone production. The physiology of fasting is interesting. As such, the power of fasting is not in the reduction of calories, but hormonal changes that take place. Fasting triggers increased the production of the human growth hormone (HGH) that is produced in the pituitary gland. This hormone is instrumental in the normal development in adolescents, children, and adults. In adults, a deficiency of the growth hormone results in an increase in body fat, a decrease in bone mass, and lower lean body mass. Upon release by the pituitary gland, the growth hormone lasts for just a few minutes in the bloodstream. This hormone goes to the liver for metabolism before conversion into various growth factors with the most important one being the Insulin-Like Growth Factor 1 (IGF1).

This Insulin-Like Growth Factor 1 is linked to high insulin levels as well as most poor health outcomes. Even then, the brief pulse of IGF1 from the human growth hormone only lasts for a few minutes. All hormones are secreted in brief bursts naturally ostensibly preventing the development of resistance that requires high levels as well as the persistence of those levels. This explains how insulin resistance develops. The human growth hormone is usually secreted during sleep as a counter-regulatory hormone. Together with adrenaline and cortisol, this the growth hormone increases your blood glucose by breaking down glycogen to counter insulin. These hormones are secreted in a pulse just before you wake up during a counter-regulatory surge. This is normal as it helps the ready prepare for the upcoming day.

It's, therefore, wrong to say that you derive the energy for the day from breakfast because usually, your body has already given a big shot for great stuff and fuel for the day. Therefore, you absolutely don't need to rely on all your sugary cereals for energy. This is also the reason why you least feel hungry in the morning even when you haven't eaten for 12 hours. The growth hormone tends to go down with age while abnormally low levels can result in low bone and muscle mass. Fasting stimulates the secretion of the human growth hormone. That is, when you fast, there's a spike in the morning and regular secretion throughout the day. This is critical to the maintenance of lean bone and muscle mass while the stored fats burn. When the growth hormone is elevated by fasting, your muscle mass increases.

Prevents insulin resistance. When you eat, the body breaks down the food into glucose that goes in the bloodstream for transportation to the cells. Your cells rely on this glucose as fuel to function properly. Insulin is a hormone that allows the cells to absorb glucose. Thus, whenever you eat insulin is produced, signaling the cells to absorb glucose. When the cells receive this glucose, they effectively receive energy. Even then, this is not always the case. In some instances, the communication between insulin and the cells can go off so that the glucose is not received in the cells but is instead stored as fat. This is referred to as insulin resistance. That is, as more and more insulin is produced, the cells do not respond by receiving glucose. Insulin resistance can be caused by various reasons, yet your pancreas can only produce so much insulin before it is fatigued, leading to insulin deficiency and subsequently, diabetes. When this happens, you'll constantly feel tired, cold, and lousy. This resistance is dependent on not only the levels of insulin but also the persistence level. Intermittent fasting is a great and easiest way of increasing your insulin sensitivity. When you burn the available glucose and glycogen that is the stored glucose, your body goes into ketosis where you draw energy from ketones.

Reduces the risk of heart disease. Heart disease is a leading killer across the world. CDC puts the number of people who die from heart disease in the United States at 610,000 annually. According to research, intermittent fasting can improve certain aspects of cardiovascular health. You can reduce the risk of heart disease by making changes to your lifestyle. This includes exercising, eating right, limiting your intake of alcohol, and not smoking. Intermittent fasting restricts the calories you consume on a given day it will improve your glycemic control, cardiovascular risk as well as insulin resistance. In one study, individuals who followed an alternate day fasting plan for successfully lost weight had a notable reduction in their blood sugar levels, inflammatory markers, blood pressure, triglycerides, LDL cholesterol, and the total cholesterol. Triglycerides are a type of fat that is found in the blood and is linked to heart disease.

Increases metabolic rate. Intermittent fasting helps in improving insulin sensitivity that is key in the prevention of diabetes, increasing metabolic rate, and weight management. It's a common belief that skipping meals will result in the body adapting to the calorie deficit by lowering the metabolic rate to save energy. It has been established that extended periods of fasting can lead to a drop in metabolism. However, some studies have also shown that when you fast for short periods, you can increase your metabolism. In fact, one study conducted among 11 healthy men found that after a three day fast, their metabolism actually increased by 14%. This increase is attributed to the rise in norepinephrine hormone that, together with insulin, promotes fat burning. Based on these findings, intermittent fasting is far much significant with great weight loss advantages when compared to the other diets that are aimed to focus on calorie restriction for losing weight. Even then, the effects of intermittent fasting on metabolism are still under study because several other studies have found that your muscle mass doesn't decrease much during intermittent fasting.

Intermittent fasting changes how cells, genes, and hormones function. There's a raft of activities that go on in your body when you fast for extended periods. One of the things that happens is that your body will initiate important cellular repair processes as well as a change in the levels of hormones to make stored fat more accessible. More specifically, there'll be a significant drop in the insulin levels resulting in fat burning as the stored fats become a primary source of energy. The growth hormone in the blood may increase up to five times that also facilitates fat burning and muscle gain. Fasting also results in beneficial changes, molecules, and genes that are related to protection against disease and longevity. Cellular repair processes are also initiated when you're fasting promoting the removal of waste material from the cells.

Reduces inflammation and oxidative stress in the body. Oxidative stress is a step in most of the chronic diseases and aging. It involves unstable molecules known as free radicals that react with other molecules like DNA and protein and damage them. A number of studies show that intermittent fasting enhances your body's resistance to oxidative stress. In addition, intermittent fasting also helps in fighting inflammation that is a common cause of diseases, especially when your body is able to go into autophagy.

Induces a number of cellular repair processes. When you fast for extended periods, the cells in your body begin to initiate a waste removal process that is known as autophagy. This process not only involves breaking down but also metabolizing dysfunctional and broken proteins that accumulate in within the cells over time. Increased autophagy is able to offer protection against a number of diseases such as Alzheimer's disease.

Helps in the prevention of cancer. Cancer is a disease that is characterized by the growth of cells that is uncontrolled. Studies have found that fasting has a number of benefits on metabolism that could actually lead to a reduced risk of cancer. There's also evidence on cancer patients showing that fasting reduced some of the side effects of chemotherapy. It's important to note that these studies have mostly been done in animals; hence, there's a need for further studies in humans.

Fasting has anti-aging effects. Various forms of fasting have been found to improve healthspan and lifespan significantly. This has been demonstrated with caloric restriction in animals that reduces the number of calories by between 20 and 30%. Intermittent fasting also slows down the aging process and increases your lifespan by manipulating mitochondrial networks. Mitochondria are power generators found in the cells.

They produce most of the energy the cells need for survival. Studies have shown that intermittent fasting helps to keep the mitochondrial networks fused hence keeping the mitochondria strong with the ability to process energy. This is crucial for vibrant aging and longevity. Fasting also delays the aging process and prevent diseases by triggering adaptive cellular stress responses that result in a better ability to cope with more stress while counteracting the disease. Thus, when your mitochondria work better, so will your body.

Intermittent fasting is therapeutic. When practiced well, intermittent fasting offers therapeutic benefits that are psychological, spiritual, and physical. For physical benefits, intermittent fasting can help cure diabetes. In addition, it has been proven to be extremely useful in the reduction of seizure-related brain damage as well as seizures themselves as well as improve symptoms of arthritis. Fasting also offers spiritual benefits, as is widely practiced by different religions around the world. It contributes towards purifying your soul and body when practiced within the religious context. The psychological angle of fasting is in the fact that it takes your will and self-control, which is a powerful psychological benefit. You learn how to ignore hunger and practice restraint from eating for a certain duration. This is a great practice because it's about training your mind. A successful intermittent fasting plan will have powerful effects on your psychological perspective. In fact, intermittent fasting has been proven to have positive results in women, especially in relation to improving the sense of control, pride, achievement, and reward. Moreover, it is handy for improving your self-esteem.

You need to understand how intermittent fasting will affect you before you get into it because this signals a change of lifestyle. While it may seem difficult to execute because your body is used to a certain way of eating, it's doable, and the results are incredible. The only thing you should never do is wake up one morning and jump into it. Rather, take time to prepare psychologically and begin slowly to increase your success rate, especially if you're looking to embrace healthy living by making a lifestyle change.

Chapter 5: Benefits of Intermittent Fasting

You've probably been told to make sure that you eat a balanced diet. Thus, it's odd to think that depriving yourself a meal or more can actually be a necessity. Interestingly, evidence points to the benefits of intermittent fasting on your wellbeing. Different forms of intermittent fasting will yield different benefits that go beyond weight loss. Some of the benefits of intermittent fasting include:

Weight and body fat loss. The majority of people who try intermittent fasting do it because they want to lose weight. Unlike other weight loss plan, intermittent fasting makes you adapt to an eating pattern that defines when you should eat and when you should fast. The whole idea behind intermittent fasting it offers you flexibility while making you eat fewer meals. This is not equivalent to counting calories as is usually the norm with most of the weight loss regimens. When you alter your eating pattern, then you're likely to eat much less hence taking fewer calories. In addition, intermittent fasting will enhance the hormonal function that facilitates weight loss. That is, a dip in the levels of insulin, along with a higher presence of the growth hormone and an increase in the amount of norepinephrine increases the rate at which fat is broken down into energy. As such, fasting on a short-term basis will increase your metabolic rate, thus helping you to burn more fats. Thus, intermittent fasting works to lose weight by reducing the amount of food you eat as well as boost your metabolic rate. It's estimated that you can experience up to 8% weight loss over a period of 3-24 weeks with intermittent fasting. When you have significant weight loss, your waist circumference will also reduce indicating loss of belly fat that is actually harmful.

Stable glucose level. Studies conducted in both people and mice show that various kinds of intermittent fasting can improve the way your body responds to sugar. In mice, researchers were able to reboot the pancreas that produces insulin, thereby reversing diabetes. Various forms of fasting that involve extended hours of unrestricted eating, followed by five days of eating a restricted fasting diet has been found to cause big improvements in individuals with high blood sugar. Losing weight, eating healthy, and moving more can help in fighting off the development of type 2 diabetes. Losing weight makes you more insulin sensitive hence driving your blood sugar down. When you eat, your body releases insulin in your bloodstream to supply cells energy. However, if you're pre-diabetic, your insulin resistant meaning your blood sugar levels are constantly elevated. Thus intermittent fasting can help to stabilize your glucose levels since it requires your body to produce insulin less often hence restoring your insulin secretion and promoting the generation of new insulin-producing pancreatic beta cells according to research.

Improves digestive health. The cells with the gastrointestinal tract are constantly working. In some instances, these cells work to the extent of being passed out a part of excreta. You can repair these digestive cells with intermittent fasting by making sure your body gets to autophagy. This gets rid of the old cells and activates your immune system accordingly. This also applies to a chronic gut immune response that is capable of inflaming bowels. Getting them to rest allows them a chance to restore and repair. An extended night fast and autophagy will give your gut a chance not only to relax but also recharge.

Improved brain health. Studies conducted in mice show that intermittent fasting could actually improve brain health by boosting your brainpower. As you grow older, the amount of blood flowing to your brain decreases while the neurons shrink, and the brain volume declines. Intermittent fasting halts the aging process keeping you mentally healthy and sharp. By boosting your brain health, intermittent fasting can lower your risk of neurodegenerative diseases like Parkinson's and Alzheimer's.

Furthermore, fasting reduces obesity and is able to protect you from diabetes, both of which can increase your risk of developing Alzheimer's disease. Intermittent fasting also helps in improving your brain by hindering the degeneration of nerve cells. According to one study, intermittent fasting plays an important role in guarding neurons in the brain from excitotoxic stress. In addition, it also speeds up autophagy in the neurons helping your body to eliminate all the damaged cells while generating new ones. This is important in helping the body defend itself from diseases. Your memory and learning ability also improve with intermittent fasting. Studies have shown that memory and mood are boosted after periods of caloric restriction.

Decreased risk of cancer. Cancer has become prevalent over the past few years, affecting people of all ages and race. The good news is that autophagy promises to reduce the likelihood of having cancer. Autophagy has received attention from medical professionals for its role in the prevention of cancer. This is because cancer occurs when there's a cellular disorder thus by promoting cell inflammation as well as regulation of damage response to the DNA by foreign bodies and regulating genome instability it helps to keep cancer at bay.

Promotes longevity. Intermittent fasting can help promote the overall length of life. This concept dates back to the 1950s when scientists discovered autophagy as well as the great potential it holds in determining the quality of life. That is, you don't necessarily need to take in too many nutrients to ensure your wellbeing rather, work toward promoting the internal process that recycles the damaged cell parts and eliminates the toxic body cells.

Improve immune system. Autophagy is powerful and highly effective when it comes to keeping your immune system in top shape. It achieves this by promoting inflammation in cells as well as actively fighting diseases through non-selective autophagy. When cellular inflammation happens, it boosts the cells of the immune system whenever it is attacked by diseases. Autophagy induces inflammation by depriving cell proteins of nutrition, thereby causing them to work more actively. This initiates the required immune response that keeps diseases and infections away. It also eliminates harmful elements that include tuberculosis, micro bacterium, as well as other viral elements from the cell.

Regulates inflammation. You can either reduce or boost the immune response with autophagy depending on what is required. This, in turn, prevents and promotes inflammation. When there's a dangerous invasion, autophagy will boost inflammation by signaling the immune system to attack. On the other hand, it can also decrease the inflammation within the immune system by getting rid of the signals that cause it.

Improved quality of life. The internet is awash with tons of methods and techniques that guarantee quality health and quality life in general. The truth is that none of these methods that include diets, anti-aging creams, and other products can lead closer to autophagy during intermittent fasting. The cellular degeneration and regeneration processes during autophagy are guaranteed to make you appear youthful in contrast to your actual age. This is especially important to your skin that is exposed to harsh elements of pollution as well as other substance that cause wrinkles leading to a decline in your skin quality with layers of toxic substances forming over your skin cells.

Decreased risk of neurodegenerative diseases. When your body achieves autophagy, you'll have a decreased risk of developing neurodegenerative diseases like Alzheimer's and Parkinson's. Here's how. Neurodegenerative diseases will work well on the basis of the accumulated toxic and old neurons that pile up in certain areas of the brain spreading to the surrounding areas. Therefore, autophagy replaces the neuron parts that are useless and, in their place, regenerate new ones effectively keeping these diseases in check.

Enhanced mental performance. Intermittent fasting enhances the cognitive function in addition to being useful in boosting brain power. Intermittent fasting will boost the brain-derived neurotrophic factor (BDNF) levels. This is a protein within the brain that is able to interact with the other parts of your brain that are responsible for controlling the learning, memory, and cognitive functions. The brain-derived neurotrophic factor is also capable of protecting and stimulating the growth of new brain cells. When you are on intermittent fasting, your body will go into the ketogenic state, thereby using ketones to burn body fat to energy. Ketones are also capable of feeding your brain, thus improving your mental productivity, energy, and acuity.

Prevention of diseases. Intermittent fasting has been associated with the prevention of diseases. According to research, intermittent fasting plays an important role in improving the number of risk markers for chronic disease that include lowered cholesterol, lowered blood pressure, and reduced insulin resistance. A study in the World Journal of Diabetes reveals that patients who have type 2 diabetes and are on short term daily intermittent fasting are likely to experience a drop in their lower body weight and have better variability of post-meal glucose. Intermittent fasting will also enhance stress markers resistance, reduce inflammation and blood pressure and promote better glucose circulation and lipid levels hence reducing the risk of cardiovascular diseases such as cancer, Alzheimer's, and Parkinson's. Intermittent fasting can also slow down the progression of certain cancers like skin and breast cancer by increasing the levels of tumor-infiltrating lymphocytes. These are the cells that are sent by the immune system to attack the tumor.

Improved physical fitness. Intermittent fasting influences your digestive system; hence, your level of physical fitness. Having a small feasting window and an extended fasting window encourages proper digestion of food. As a result, you have a healthy and proportional daily intake of food as well as calories. As you get used to this process, it is unlikely that you will experience hunger. You don't have to worry about slowing down your metabolism because, in reality, intermittent fasting will enhance your metabolism making it more flexible as your body has the capability to run on fats and glucose along for energy effectively.

The use of oxygen is important in the success of your training. In fact, in order to perform well, you must adjust your breathing habits during workouts. Generally, the maximum amount of oxygen that your body uses per kilogram of your body weight or per minute is referred to as VO2. This is also known as wind. The amount of wind you have influences your performance. More wind means better performance.

Consequently, top athletes will have twice as much VO2 level compared to those without training. A study carried out on a fasted group that skipped breakfast and a non-fasted group that had breakfast an hour before found that the VO2 levels of both groups were 3.5L/min at the beginning. There was a notable increase in the wind in the fasting group at 9.7% compared to an increase of 2.5% in those who took breakfast.

Enhances bodybuilding. When you have a short feasting window, it automatically translates to fewer meals meaning you can concentrate your daily intake of calories in 1-2 meals. Bodybuilders find this approach to be great compared to splitting your calories in 5-6 meals spread throughout the day. You need a certain amount of protein in maintaining your muscle mass. You can still maintain your muscle mass with intermittent fasting even though this eating pattern doesn't focus on your protein intake. Since your growth hormone reaches unbelievable levels after 48 hours of fasting, you're able to maintain muscles even without having to eat proteins or even having protein shakes and bars.

Increased insulin sensitivity. Insulin sensitivity refers to your body cell's level of sensitivity in response to insulin. High levels of insulin sensitivity are good as it allows the cells to use blood glucose effectively, thereby reducing the amount of blood sugar in your system. When your insulin levels are low, you will experience insulin resistance. When this happens, you will experience abnormal levels of blood sugar, which, when not managed, will result in type 2 diabetes. Insulin sensitivity will vary between different people and will change according to various dietary factors and lifestyle. Therefore, improving it could be beneficial to those people who are living with or are at risk of developing type 2 diabetes. According to a 2014 review investigating the effect of intermittent fasting in obese and overweight adults, intermittent fasting has the ability to reduce insulin resistance. Even then, there was no significant effect on glucose levels.

Intermittent fasting will provide amazing results when done right. From the loss of excessive weight to a reversal of type 2 diabetes, many benefits are linked to intermittent fasting. Even then, you need to stay committed and be consistent with your intermittent fasting protocol in order to achieve results. Most importantly, make sure you have a goal you'd like to achieve at the beginning of your fasting period. While at it remember that unlike many weight loss diets, fasting doesn't have a standard duration because it's just about depriving your body food for a given time.

Intermittent fasting is nothing curious or queer rather; it's part of normal everyday life. It's the most powerful and oldest intervention you can think of, yet so many people are not aware of its power to rejuvenate the body as well as its therapeutic potential. You don't have to put pressure on yourself to produce results in the beginning, especially if your goal is to lose weight. Take time to transition, allowing your body to adjust accordingly. This may mean starting with a plan that is close to your current eating plan, slowly advancing to intermittent eating plans that require you to fast for longer durations.

Chapter 6: Intermittent Fasting: The Best Anti-Aging Diet

Countless celebrities and entrepreneurs use intermittent fasting to reverses the effects of aging. However, not everyone understands the scientific aspect of intermittent fasting and its link with anti-aging. This chapter looks into the scientific aspect of intermittent fasting while introducing concepts related to aging healthily. To understand the relationship between fasting and anti-aging, you first need to understand the difference between the various fasting methods. For starters, the short-term fasting plans with a fasting window of between 16 and 20 hours offer multiple independent benefits. These fasts that are also known as micro-fasts support metabolic healthy by controlling body weight, lowering your insulin levels, and improving glycemic control. As such, short term fasting is an incredible choice to embrace when your goal is solely weight loss. During short fasts, your fat mass may reduce while physical strength remains the same.

The other benefits of fasting include an increase in brain-derived neurotrophic factor (BDNF) signaling within your brain, cardiovascular support, and reduced risk of cancer recurrence. On the other hand, fasting for extended periods will stimulate physiological changes that offer unique benefits of fasting that fall within functional areas like longevity, immune strength, and healthy aging.

The physiological effects of extended fasting are more pronounced than the effects of short-term fasts lasting less than 24 hours because of the body's ability to switch to fat and ketone catabolism upon the depletion of glycogen reserves during extended fasting. Extended fasting also increased the white blood cells that are a biomarker for immune health and is useful for adjunct therapy alongside chemotherapy for killing cancer cells. The rationale behind this is that cancer cells grow and thrive on glucose; thus, when you go on extended fasts; you starve the cancer cells and support the anti-cancer immune efforts.

Anti-Aging Benefits of Intermitted Fasting

Out of all interventions that are aimed at countering aging, calorie restriction is that most efficient. Generally, fasting for extended periods results in calorie restriction that reduces calories by between 20 and 40%. This is not recommended for performance and is unpopular among biohackers owing to mental distraction. Calorie restriction promotes five mechanisms that are essential for healthy aging. The following are mechanisms of extended fasting that promote healthy aging.

These processes are:

Cell proliferation (IGF-1 and TOR; specifically mTOR): Cell proliferation promotes balanced cell growth. It is the ability of the human system to be in the anabolic state with the presence of calories. That is, whenever calories are abundant, cells are in an anabolic state. When you're intermittent fasting results in caloric restriction that tends to shift the balance in the system through stimulation of catabolic pathways. The two pathways that are important in this process are the mammalian target of rapamycin (mTOR) and insulin-like growth factor-1 (IGF-1). Both IGF-1 and mTOR are nutrient sensors that regulate the cellular resources depending on the availability of calories. When you fast, fewer calories are leading to the down-regulation of mTOR and IGF-1, thus signaling repurposing and recycling of organelles and cells. A decline in mTOR signaling has been found to lead to lifespan extension.

Moreover, its inhibition is known to be a longevity assurance mechanism with the availability of rapamycin as well as other mTOR inhibitors making this pathway a valuable target for interventions that extend lifespan. Dr. Jason Fung, a proponent of intermittent fasting, agrees that mTOR is a protein sensor. He further says that eating fats alone and no protein can theoretically modulate MTOR positively. Thus, you can include fat-based drinks in your micro-fast.

Decreased Inflammation (NF-kB): The human body is bound to experience cumulative damage as you age. The damage is often identified by the immune receptors, thereby stimulating the production of multiple proinflammatory molecules. In the worst-case scenario, the accumulated damage is so extensive that the inflammation becomes continuous that either accompanies numerous age-related diseases or contributes to them. Inflammation on its own is not necessarily bad since its part of healing. However, evidence suggests that chronic inflammation and specifically age-associated inflammation, also referred to inflaming, heavily correlates with poor health biomarkers. Calorie restriction during intermittent fasting will inhibit nuclear factor kB (NF-kB) that exerts the anti-inflammatory effect. NF-kB is believed to the master regulator of inflammation, thus minimizing its activity will downregulate various parts of the proinflammatory signaling. Animal models suggest that this anti-inflammatory effect may have cognitive enhancing properties. One study focused on fasting as eustress; a form of stress that is beneficial versus distress; the negative stressors of life that speed up aging. The conclusion was that intermittent fasting led to a reduction of the plasma inflammatory factors. Thus, intermittent fasting can improve cognitive function and preserve the brain from distress through regulation of inflammatory response pathway. By engaging in intermittent fasting, you're able to attain the beneficial levels of stress that is necessary for your physiology and psychology.

Improved mitochondrial physiology (AMPK/SIRT): Mitochondria are the organelles that make up a cell. They're crucial in the production of cellular energy that enables the cells to do more work. This work is equivalent to physical labor, as is the case with the muscle cells or cognitive tasks in the case of brain cells. Aging tends to weaken the general quality of your body's mitochondrial network, thereby decreasing the destruction of already damaged or dysfunctional mitochondria as well as the generation of new mitochondria. However, when you fast and experience calorie restriction, these processes will be supported, giving rise to a high quality of your mitochondrial network. The two pathways that are mostly associated with mitochondrial support are sirtuins (SIRT genes) and AMP-dependent kinase (AMPK). Both pathways are sensitive to the shifts in the NADH/NAD+ ratio. Calorie restriction triggers an increase in NAD+ accumulation that activates sirtuins and AMPK. Studies have concluded that the fact that sirtuins need NAD for their enzymatic activity links metabolism to diseases associated with aging and aging. Both sirtuins and AMPK are central to mitochondrial biogenesis as well as processes of mitophagy (mitochondrial removing and recycling of the organelles that are dysfunctional that are associated with age) are important in maintaining a younger mitochondrial network. When cells are deprived of glucose during an extended fast, the production of ATP initially drops. When AMPK senses the decrease in ATP, it limits the utilization of energy as it upregulates numerous other processes that replenish ATP. As a result, mitochondria and cells are able to better make ATP in the future. Calorie restriction activates the AMPK pathway in a number of tissues in animal models. However, this has not been studied in humans. Sirtuins also play an important role in aging as a biological stress sensor. Increasing and manipulating the expression of sirtuins in yeast promotes longevity.

Enhanced autophagy (FoxO): Autophagy can loosely be translated to self-eating. That is a cleaning mechanism that involves removal of organelles, old cell membranes as well as other cellular junk that has accumulated with time and is an impediment to optimal cellular performance. When the old and broken parts of your cells are removed, the growth hormone that is usually amplified during fasting will signal the body to start the production of new replacements. The result of autophagy is the renovation and recycling process of cells. mTOR will induce the activation of the forkhead box proteins. Both mitophagy and autophagy are FoxO-dependent suggesting that the transcriptional molecule is an integral component of the processes.

Increased antioxidant defenses (Nrf2): As humans age, there's an increase in the reactive oxygen species (ROS) while the natural antioxidant defenses decrease. Over time, this imbalance becomes greater even as the damage accumulates while the mitochondrial dysfunction becomes more prevalent. The normal production of oxidants in specific types of cells is important in the regulation of pathways (ROS are involved in some of the signaling processes). Therefore, it is valuable to strike the right balance as we age. This balance is may be critical for the optimization of mitochondrial performance and is referred to as mitohormesis with the idea being the need for the right amount of ROS with too little resulting in subpar performance while high amounts of ROS cause damage. This is important for those tissues that rely on the production of large amounts of ATP for metabolism such as heart, brain, and muscle. Among the understandings from mitorhormesis is that a certain amount of ROS is required to trigger adaptive responses that upregulate the antioxidant defenses as well as make mitochondria and cells better in dealing with toxins and stress. Thus, intermittent fasting can help in promoting anti-oxidant defenses. Calorie restriction will activate the nuclear factor (erythroid-derived 2) like 2 (Nfr2) that is a regulator of the cellular resistance to the oxidants. This protein plays a role in supporting antioxidant defenses through:

- Catabolism of peroxides and superoxide; eliminating all the bad stuff.
- Regeneration of oxidized proteins and cofactors (regrowing more of the good old stuff)
- Increase of redox transport (increasing efficiency of existing machinery)
- Synthesis of reducing factors (Creation of new good stuff)

Overall, Nrf2 is not the only mechanisms that promote antioxidant support and defenses. All the five mechanisms that are interrelated owing to the complex nature of human systems contribute to healthspan longevity. Like it is with all these other mechanisms, they support each other. For instance, mTOR is not only categorized under cell proliferation and autophagy.

Intermittent Fasting for Lifespan and Healthspan

Lifespan refers to the duration of time that you've lived. On the other hand, the duration within which you've been functional and healthy, and not just being alive is referred to as the healthspan. Calorie restriction that is initiated by any form of intermittent fasting is important in affecting both your lifespan and healthspan. It's not unusual to focus on the lifespan within the longevity and aging space at the expense of the quality of life you're living.

On the contrary, the duration of time you're functional and healthy is correlated with a higher quality of life. Your healthspan can be mediated by many things among them; dietary interventions, social interactions, exercise, family, and community. Social interaction is positively related to life satisfaction and longevity. Thus, healthspan it may be more valuable to emphasize lifespan alone.

Damage Accumulation vs. Programmed Aging

The debate between the importance of damage accumulation and programmed aging is unending. Humans are complex systems that involve a combination of both. Damage accumulation is characterized by mitochondrial and cellular damage, both of which happen at the cellular level with each amplifying the effects of the other. That is the changes in gene expression speed up damage accumulation, which in turn affects the ability of the cell to have healthy gene expression. On the other hand, programmed aging refers to changes in the manner in which our genes are expressed as we age. Some of the genes are underexpressed, while others are overexpressed.

Aging Benefits of Intermittent Fasting

The scientific aspect of the mechanisms that are involved in promoting longevity and aging go beyond the context of fasting. These mechanisms determine nootropics as well as the other techniques that we can use in supporting healthy aging. Although there are many benefits that arise when a certain degree of temporary starvation is induced, it's important to note that there are more ways to trigger these responses. Most importantly, you need to keep in mind that while some of the benefits will occur while you're in the fasted state, others will happen when you start eating normally. Thus, starvation primes the systems for rejuvenation even though it is refeeding that is credited for rebuilding new organelles and cells, thus increasing health.

Intermittent Fasting and Anti-aging Compounds

Excessive levels of pyrimidine and purine are signs that your body might be experiencing an increase in the levels of certain antioxidants. Specifically, researchers have found significant increases in carnosine and ergothioneine. A study on the individual variability in human blood metabolites found that the number of metabolites decreases as you age. These metabolites include ophthalmic acid, isoleucine, and leucine. This study also found that fasting significantly boosted the three metabolites and concluded that this explains how fasting extends the lifespan in rats. It is believed that the hike in antioxidants may be a survival response because when in the fasted state, the body experiences extreme levels of oxidative stress. Thus, the production of antioxidants can help in avoiding the potential damage that is a result of free radicals.

Intermittent Fasting and the Anti-Aging Molecule

Research has found that being in the fasted state is instrumental in triggering a molecule that can cause a delay in the aging of arteries. This is important in the prevention of chronic diseases that are age-related like cardiovascular disease, cancer, and Alzheimer's and is evidence that aging can be reversed. Vascular aging is the most important aspect of aging. Thus, when people grow older, they vessels supplying blood to various organs become more sensitive and more likely to experience aging damage; thus studying is vascular aging is important. According to the research done on starving mice generated a molecule known as beta-hydroxybutyrate that prevented vascular aging. This molecule is also a ketone that is produced by the liver and is handy as an energy source; then the glucose level is low. Ketones are mostly produced during starvation or fasting or when you're on a diet comprising low carbs and after a prolonged exercise. This molecule also promotes the multiplication and division of cells lining the blood vessels. This is a market of cellular youth.

Additionally, this compound is also able to delay vascular aging through endothelial cells that line lymphatic vessels and blood vessels. This can prevent the kind of cell aging that is referred to as cellular aging or senescence. Cellular senescence is defined as the irreversible cell cycle while at the same time preserving the cellular viability. Cellular senescence is suggested to work as a tumor suppressor mechanism as well as tissue remodeling promoter after wounding. These cells show marked changes in morphology that includes irregular shape size, enlarged size, multiple and prominent nuclei, increased granularity, accumulation of lysosomal, and mitochondrial mass.

Chapter 7: The Golden Key: Autophagy

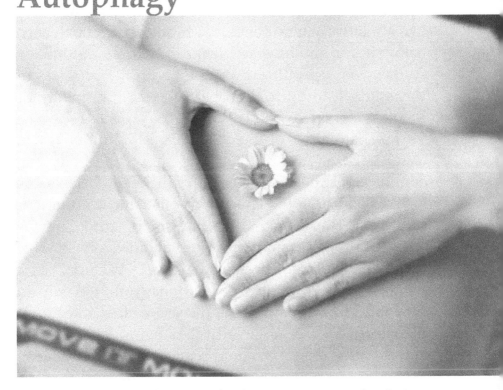

The cells in the human body are constantly being damaged as metabolic processes take place hence the need for autophagy to clear these damaged cells. The word autophagy comes from two Greek words; 'auto' which means self and 'phagy' meaning eating. Thus, autophagy is the process where the body consumes its own tissue in the wake of metabolic processes that occur due to certain diseases and starvation. Researchers consider autophagy to be a survival mechanism or the body's clever way of responding to stress to protect itself.

When you think of it as a form of self-eating, it's definitely scary. So is autophagy good for your health? Definitely! This is the body's normal way of initiating the process of cellular renewal. Autophagy may seem like a relatively new concept, yet our bodies have been using it for millions of years. The first autophagy studies were conducted on yeast with the progress of this study leading to a Nobel Prize in Physiology or Medicine for Dr. Yoshinori Ohsumi, a Japanese scientist for his discoveries of the mechanisms of autophagy in October 2016. According to the study, the body can eliminate all the clutter within whenever it feels the need to conserve the energy for other most important purposes. The cleaning mechanism of autophagy is critical in the elimination of just about every kind of toxins, misfolded proteins, germs, bacteria, and pathogens. So beneficial is autophagy that is key in preventing diseases like liver disease, cancer, infections, diabetes, cardiomyopathy, neurodegeneration, autoimmune diseases. Autophagy offers multiple anti-aging benefits by helping in destroying and reusing damaged components that occur within cells. Thus, this process uses the waste generated within cells to create new building materials that facilitate regeneration and repair. Although the process of autophagy doesn't require any outside help, you'll definitely begin feeling more relaxed and energetic once it takes place.

While recent studies have revealed the role of autophagy in cleaning and defending the body from the negative effects of stress, the exact way autophagy processes work is just beginning to be understood. Several processes are involved. For instance, lysosomes form part of the cells that are capable of destroying large damages cells such as mitochondria as well as help in transporting the damaged parts, so they are used to generate fuel. To sum it up, the damaged material must be transported by a lysosome, before it's deconstructed and spit back out for repurposing.

Essential Autophagy Steps

The process of autophagy involves the following steps as follows:

1. Creation of phagophore by a protein kinase complex as well as a lipid kinase complex. These two work together in sourcing a membrane that will eventually become the phagophore.
2. Once the phagophore is formed, the next step is its expansion. In this stage, a protein that is known as LC3 is bonded with the just formed phogophore through multiple autophagy-related proteins that are referred to as the ATG. When the bonding of the two is complete, the LC3 protein then becomes LC3-II. This formation occurs around cytoplasm material, which is then due to be degraded. This material may be random or selected specifically if it includes misfolded proteins and damaged organelles. When the process of replacement begins, ATG-9, a transmembrane protein acting as a protector of the site of phagophore formation is formed. This protein is assumed to help in expansion by increasing the number of phagophore membrane by supplying them from adjacent membrane locations.
3. The phagophore undergoes changes in its shape becoming elongated and closing, thereby becoming an autophagosome. The autophagosome serves as a holder of materials that are then degraded.
4. Both lysosome and autophagosome membranes fuse together. The lysosomal lumen (space within a lysosome) have hydrolases. Hydrolases break down molecules into smaller pieces using water to demolish the chemical bonds. When the lysosome

and autophagosome fuse together, an exposure of the material that is inside the autophagosome to chemical wrecking balls occurs. The fusion converts the lysosome into an autolysosome.

5. The hydrolases degrade all material found within the autophagosome together with the inner membrane. The macromolecules that are the result of this process are waddled around by permeases that are on the autolysosome membrane until they get back to their original cytoplasm. At this point, the cell may reuse the macromolecules.

Well, this is how autophagy works. It's a complex yet important process that is still being studied to ensure further understanding.

There are different kinds of autophagy that include micro and macroautophagy as well as chaperone-mediated autophagy. Macroautophagy is the most popular of the three. It is an evolutionarily conserved anabolic process that involves the formation of autophagosomes (vesicles) that surround cellular organelles and macromolecules. Apart from humans' mold, yeast, flies, worms, and mammals also benefit from autophagy.

Macroautophagy is the process where catalyzation of non-functional cellular constituents to lysosome of cells takes place. What this process does is a separation of the cytoplasm of cells that includes different cell organs, degrading them to amino acids.

Inducing Autophagy With Intermittent Fasting

One of the common questions about autophagy is when does it occur? Generally, autophagy is usually active in all the cells. However, there's increased response to acute energy shortage, nutrient deprivation, and stress. This means that you can cause your body to go into autophagy using good stressors such as temporary calorie restriction and exercise. These have been linked with longevity, weight control as well as inhibiting a number of age-related diseases.

You can induce autophagy through intermittent fasting. When you restrain yourself from eating food for a while, it will eventually trigger autophagy. When you fast for long, your body will start feeling deprived of supply hence can begin catabolic processes at the macromolecular level. This means identifying those processes that are misusing the available energy like parasites, pathogens, mold, fungi, and bacteria within that don't give back anything for elimination. Once your body goes into autophagy, it begins the elimination by identifying all misfolded proteins and recycling them to produce energy and new cells. Not only does this process clean your body but also promote restrengthening. The body also identifies chronic inflammations, disorders, and diseases that make us ill and use the energy of the body and eliminates them. When the elimination begins, even chronic inflammations that have troubled you for years will go away, making autophagy a powerful mechanism of treatment. This also has a powerful anti-aging effect because it stops those processes that hasten the signs of aging. Autophagy also has a great impact on the cognitive function in addition to stopping neurodegenerative disorders and reversing their effects. This means that disorders like Parkinson's and Alzheimer's can be brought under control. Autophagy also promotes cardiovascular health, lowers immunity problems, hypertension, and chronic inflammation. This process is guaranteed to give you a boon for a rejuvenated life.

Studies suggest that the autophagy process starts anywhere between 24 and 48 hours after your last meal. This is perhaps one of the best ways of inducing autophagy. Therefore, if you would like to trigger autophagy, then you must fast for longer. Alternate day fasting and water fasting are the most ideal. If you opt for alternate day fasting, make sure that you don't eat anything during the 36-hour fasting window. Don't consume any calories from soft drinks or juices either. On the other hand, if you go for the water fast, you must do it for 2 to 3 days as your recommended fasting window of between 24 to 48 hours.

Ultimately, the best intermittent fasting you can employ to induce autophagy is alternate day fast without consuming any calories in the fasting window. If you feel you're up to it, you can take it a notch higher with a 2- t0 3-day water fast once in three months. Looking at the benefits, it's definitely worth restraining yourself from eating to get your body into autophagy.

Exercise is another source of good stress that has been found to induce autophagy. According to recent research, exercise induces autophagy in a number of organs that take part in metabolic regulation like liver, muscle, adipose tissue, and pancreas. Although exercise has many benefits to the body, it's a form of stress since it breaks down tissues and causes them to be repaired so that they grow back stronger. Although the extent of exercise required to boost autophagy is not clear, research suggests that going into intense exercise is most beneficial. If you want to combine fasting and exercise, then you must approach it with caution. You just might be surprised that you actually feel energetic once you get the hang of fasting.

Apart from fasting and exercise, there are certain foods which, when eaten, will contribute towards inducing autophagy. Generally speaking, you need to focus on low carb foods, some of which include the following:

Herbs and spices such as cayenne pepper, black pepper, ginseng, ginger, cinnamon, turmeric, cumin, cardamom, parsley, thyme, cilantro, coriander, rosemary, and basil.

Berries and other fruits; strawberries, raspberries, blueberries, elderberries, cherries and cranberries.

Drinks; tea and coffee. Your coffee and tea should have no cream, milk, or sugar. As such, it's better to go for herbal, green, or black tea. Avoid fruit tea since it's too sweet. You may also have distilled vinegar or apple cider.

Alcoholic drinks; vodka, vermouth, gin, whiter, and red wine.

You could also try foods that are healthy for your body that include the following:

Fruits such as; olive, avocado, coconut, watermelon, cantaloupe, and honeydew.

Veggies; squash, tomato, peas, spinach, bell pepper, pickles, beetroot, green beans, carrots, and turnip.

Seeds and nuts; brazil nuts, almonds, cashews, chia seeds, chestnuts, flax seeds, macadamia, hazelnuts, pecans, peanuts, pistachios, pine nuts, pumpkin seeds, sunflower, sesame seeds, walnuts, peanut butter, almond butter, cashew butter, and macadamia nut butter.

Dairy and milk; blue cheese, buttermilk, brie cheese, Colby cheese, cheddar cheese, cottage cheese, cream cheese, Monterey jack cheese, mozzarella, feta cheese, swiss cheese, parmesan, mascarpone, sour cream, heavy cream, skimmed milk, and whole milk.

Fats; coconut milk, coconut cream, red palm oil, olive oil, MCT oil, macadamia oil, flaxseed oil, coconut oil, cocoa butter, avocado oil, beef tallow, lard, lard, ghee and butter.

Protein shakes with water; whey protein shake, hemp protein shake, rice protein shake, pea protein shake, and microgreens blend.

Drinks; almond water, almond milk, coconut water, kombucha, and coconut milk.

Alcoholic drinks; cognac, tequila, champagne, beer, mint liquor and chocolate liquor.

There's more to learn about autophagy and the best way of inducing it. Combing fasting and regular exercise as part of your daily routine is a great place to start. If you're taking certain medications for any health condition, you must consult your doctor before you go into fasting.

Uses of Autophagy

The main function of autophagy is degrading and breaking down organelles in cells. This process contributes to the repair of cells. Autophagy also acts as part of the body's repair mechanism. Autophagy also plays an important role in a number of cellular functions like yeast the high levels of autophagy are activated by nutrient starvation. In addition to degrading unnecessary proteins, autophagy is also helpful in recycling amino acids that in turn, are important in synthesizing proteins that are crucial for survival. In the case of animals, they experience nutrient depletion after birth due to severing transplacental food supply. It is at this point that autophagy is activates helping to mediate the nutrient depletion. Another function of autophagy is xenophagy, which is the breaking down of the infectious particles.

Benefits of Autophagy

Although autophagy presents multiple benefits, there are two major benefits of this process:

Autophagy eliminates waste cells, misfolded proteins, and pathogens from your body. Autophagy is instrumental in ridding the body of all waste that is making you sick and contributing to inefficient functioning. It removes the pathogens that live inside your body, thriving on your energy and making you experience good health. The presence of wasted cells and misfolded proteins often clutter your body. Autophagy comes in to recycle and clean them up, giving your body new cells while also releasing energy that your body can use when there's an extreme shortage.

Autophagy helps to improve muscle performance. When you exercise, the stress on your cells causes energy to go up, making parts get worn out faster. Autophagy, therefore, helps in removing the damage and keeping the energy needs in check.

Autophagy helps in the prevention of neurodegenerative disorders. Most of the neurodegenerative disorders are a result of damaged proteins forming around neurons. Thus, autophagy offers protection by eliminating these proteins. In particular, autophagy will help clear proteins associated with Alzheimer's, Parkinson's, and Huntington's diseases.

Autophagy enhances metabolic efficiency. Autophagy can be activated to help in improving the work of mitochondria the smallest part of the cell. This makes the cells work efficiently hence becoming more efficient.

Autophagy slows down the progression of certain diseases. Diseases too need energy for them to spread in the body. Thus, by starving them of energy, they're unable to function. For instance, cancer cells usually function like the normal body cells thriving on glucose obtained through food. When you go on a fast and deprive the body of this energy, the progression of cancer stops dramatically since they can't rely on fat energy to spread. In the same way, when you live on a fat diet, your body will begin burning fat hence literally starving cancer. This also applies to other chronic inflammations that flourish in your body silently because of the availability of energy that will begin to go when you're on extended fasts.

Autophagy helps fight against infectious diseases. Autophagy removes toxins that cause infections in addition to helping your body improve the way your body responds to infections. Most importantly, viruses and intracellular bacteria can be removed by autophagy.

Common Misconceptions About Autophagy

Intermittent fasting has become popular over the years, effectively shifting the spotlight on autophagy. As a result, many people have come up with speculations and assumptions about autophagy that are untrue. Here are some of the false beliefs about people hold autophagy:

You can trigger autophagy with a 24-hour fast. Neither will a 16-hour or 24-hour fast trigger autophagy. This is because this is such a short time frame. Instead, if you want to trigger autophagy within a short time, then high-intensity exercise is recommended. The reason autophagy can't happen after a 24-hour fast is simple. Fasting doesn't happen soon after your last meal because then your body has to digest the food and draw energy from it. Thus, after your last fast, the body will be in a postabsorptive state of metabolism for a couple of hours. Remember, it takes more time to digest certain foods. Foods like fibers, vegetables, fat, and protein don't digest that easy. Because of this, the body will not be getting into the fasted state until after a period of 5 to 6 hours of going without food. The reason is simple. Before that, you're still in a fed state as your body thrives on the calories you've consumed. For example, if you had your last meal at 7pm, it will not be until midnight when you actually begin the actual physiological fast. Therefore, while you'll claim to be going on a 16- to 20-hour fast, in reality, you've spent about 12 hours fasting. This is such a short time to trigger autophagy. Even then, your fast is not in vain because you'll still experience the other benefits of intermittent fasting that include; low inflammation levels, reduced insulin levels, and fat burning.

More is better. You need a minimum of three days fasting to experience autophagy. That is by the time you're getting to your third day of fasting; you'll enjoy benefits of autophagy and fasting as this will energize your body to fight off tumors, cancer cells as well as boost the production of stem cells. Even then, prolonged autophagy is not the best. If anything, it can have side effects that include providing ample ground for the production of bacteria and Brucella. Extended autophagy may also see the resilience of tumor cells because they're strengthened, thus becoming more resistant to treatment. The essential autophagy gene ATG6/BECN1 that encodes Beclin 1 protein and is vital in reducing cancer cells may instead feed the cancer cells, thus giving them the strength they need to survive. Finally, there's a risk of muscle wasting and sarcopenia that affects longevity. Although you can't dispute the fact that autophagy is incredible, you need to be aware that it's not good to always be in this state. Otherwise, you'll end up with unwanted repercussions as well as health hazards. Thus, it's best to induce autophagy intermittently; don't make it a constant process.

Autophagy means starvation. Some people believe that autophagy will make you starve. This is untrue. Although you have to avoid eating for an extended period to achieve autophagy, this is totally different from starvation. Staying away from food for a couple of days will not make you starve because people who are starving don't even have the energy to go about their lives and daily activities like someone who is practicing intermittent fasting will. Intermittent fasting doesn't deprive your body of energy since the body stores unused energy as fats that it resorts to whenever there's scarcity. This is not only in overweight and obese people but also those with a lean mass.

Additionally, autophagy breaks down misfolded proteins and old cells that serve as additional sources of energy when you are not feasting. Thus, your body turns to other body components for energy. After a couple of days of fasting, you get to experience ketosis where your normal metabolism is suspended due to the absence of new food consumption. Thus, the body begins to use ketones and stored fats to draw energy for the muscle and brain. You eventually get to improve your lifespan through basal autophagy.

Autophagy makes you build muscle. This is an outright lie because you need calories to build muscles. Therefore, building muscles during autophagy will be close to impossible since there's no additional source of energy when you're staying away from food. Moreover, proteins are essential to muscle building are it requires a vital process that is referred to as protein synthesis. Intermittent fasting limits your protein intake is limited; thus, your body easily switches to a catabolic state where it breaks down as opposed to an anabolic state where it grows. Remember, autophagy can still breakdown old protein floating around your body cells that are central to muscle protein synthesis. However, experts point to the fact that with proper meal choice, you can maintain your muscle mass during intermittent fasting.

Coffee hinders autophagy. Taking coffee doesn't have any impact on your body's ability to achieve autophagy. In fact, taking coffee is good for inducing autophagy and ketosis because coffee contains polyphenols, that is a compound that promotes autophagy. Thus, coffee supports the process of autophagy. Caffeine also contributes to the body enjoying lipolysis that burns fat while reducing insulin, thus improving ketones and boosting AMPK. Although it doesn't hinder autophagy, you shouldn't take your coffee with sugar, sweeteners or even cream as these can increase the insulin level, thus stopping any benefit, you'd get from fasting.

When you exercise, you stop autophagy. Exercising is among the proven ways of inducing autophagy. Simply put, activity triggers autophagy. Resistance training is an excellent way of increasing mTOR signaling. While exercising will not activate mTOR in the same manner that eating does, exercise will translocate mTOR complex near the cellular membrane, preparing it for action as soon as you begin eating. By working out, you become more sensitive to activating mTOR; this will trigger more growth after working out. In addition, you also get to activate autophagy with in-depth resistance training that can help in reducing the breakdown and destruction of muscles by regulating the IGF-1 as well as its receptors. Apart from fasting, the other best approach to increasing autophagy is working out. Ultimately, you can combine both in order to attain the best results.

Eating fruits will not stop autophagy. Most of the fruits are laden with fructose that is digested by the liver before being stored as liver glycogen. When you have excess levels of fructose, it's converted to triglycerides. Thus, eating fruits will definitely work against ketosis and autophagy as it promotes liver glycogen storage. The content of glycogen in the liver makes sure that there's a balance between the mTOR and AMPK. When you consume fruits with a regulated amount of fats and protein may help in remaining in a catabolic state of breaking down molecules. Even then, the chance of experiencing autophagy is quite slim.

Most of the autophagy research has been done on yeast and rats. Genetic screening studies have found at least 32 different autophagy-related genes. Research continues to show the importance of autophagic processes as a response to stress and starvation. As you may know, insulin is the hormone that is responsible for letting glucose in the blood to enter the cells, thus energizing them for proper functioning. Thus, the more glucose you ingest, the more likely it will be stored in the blood effectively raising your insulin levels and blood sugar. Even then, the insulin will only get active and begins working if magic when its level decreases, thereby regulating your blood level. It's important to understand that fasting for extended periods is not easy; hence, you'll do well to start with intermittent fasting, which, when done on a regular basis produces the benefits of autophagy.

Chapter 8: The Seven Types of Intermittent Fasting Diets

Intermittent fasting is about changing your pattern of eating. You can choose to abstain from eating partially or entirely for a specified period before you can begin eating again. As such, there are many different methods of fasting. These methods vary in terms of the number of days, hours, and calorie allowances. With intermittent fasting, every person's lifestyle and experience is unique; hence, different styles will suit different people. Here are 7 common types of intermittent fasting diets:

The 12:12 Diet

With this diet, you need to adhere to a 12-hour fasting window and a subsequent 12-hour feeding window every day. This means that if you eat dinner at 9 p.m., you won't have breakfast until 9 a.m. the following morning. This intermittent fasting protocol is perhaps the easiest to follow. This plan is particularly good for beginners because of the relatively small fasting window. You can also opt to incorporate sleep in the fasting window, which means you'll be asleep for most of the fasting window. Apart from helping you lose fat and weight, this plan offers numerous benefits. First, it helps you break from the habit of binge eating or snacking at midnight mindlessly. Secondly, it helps in clearing inflammation as well as getting rid of damaged cells, thereby preventing cancer while also promoting healthy gut microbes. Fasting at night stimulates cell regeneration that has a positive effect on cancer, dementia, heart attacks, and dementia.

When you go for the 12:12 fasting plan, caution must be taken when choosing food so that you only take low-fat food with high protein and low carbohydrates. Most importantly, stay away from processed food. When followed to the latter, the 12:12 plan yields incredible results that include improved brain health, reduced inflammation, enhanced detoxification, and weight loss. To incorporate the 12:12 plan in your day, make sure that you leave 12 hours between your evening and morning meal. You can, however, take water and unsweetened tea.

16:8 Intermittent Fasting Plan

The 16:8 intermittent fasting plan limits your consumption of foods and beverages containing calories to 8 hours a day while abstaining from eating for the remainder of the 16 hours. You can repeat this cycle frequently from once to twice a day or even make it your daily routine depending on what you prefer. This plan is common among those looking to burn fat and lose weight. There are no strict regulations and rules, making it easy to follow and see the result with so little effort. It's also flexible and less restrictive hence can fit into just about any lifestyle. Apart from weight loss, the 16:8 will also help to improve blood sugar control, enhanced longevity, and boost brain function.

Getting Started With 16:8

The 16:8 plan is safe, simple, and sustainable. To begin, you need to pick an appropriate eating window within which you limit your food intake. Most people prefer eating between noon and 8 p.m. so that they skip breakfast. You may also have your eating window between 9 a.m. and 5 p.m. allowing you plenty of time for healthy breakfast, a normal lunch and a light dinner or snack. Since everyone is different, you can experiment with different timings and see what works for your lifestyle and schedule. Regardless of what you choose to eat, make sure you space out to have several small meals and snacks throughout the day. This is important in stabilizing your blood sugar levels and keeping hunger under control. To maximize the potential of health benefits, make sure you're only consuming nutritious whole beverages and foods during your eating.

Having nutrient-rich foods helps in rounding out your diet so that you reap the rewards of this eating plan. While at it, make sure you're drinking calorie-free beverages such as water and unsweetened coffee and tea to keep your appetite in check. The 16:8 plan is easy to follow since it cuts down the time you spend preparing food and cooking every week. Some of the benefits associated with this plan include improved blood sugar control, increased weight loss, and enhanced longevity. On the flipside, this plan also has drawbacks. Restricting your food consumption to eight hours can cause you to eat more during the eating window in a bid to make up for the time spent fasting. This can lead to weight gain, development of unhealthy eating habits, and digestive weight gain. You may also experience some short-term negative side effects like weakness, fatigue, and hunger when starting out. Some research findings suggest that intermittent fasting affects women differently and could interfere with reproduction and fertility. Therefore, make sure you consult your doctor before you start.

5:2 Intermittent Fasting Plan

The 5:2 intermittent fasting plan is also referred to as The Fast Diet. This plan, which was popularized by British journalist Michael Mosley, lets you have five days of normal eating and two days of restricted calories to a quarter of your daily needs, usually 500-600 per day. The plan doesn't spell out the specific days you should eat or fast. You're at liberty to make this decision. For instance, you can decide to fast on Mondays and Thursdays where you eat two to three small meals and eat normally for the rest of the days. Even then, you need to know that eating normally doesn't imply eating anything, including junk or even binge eating because then you won't lose weight but instead gain.

A study on the 5:2 diet found that this diet has the potential of causing weight loss that is similar to regular restriction of calories. This plan was also effective in the reduction of insulin levels as well as improving insulin sensitivity.

The 5:2 plan can be effective when done in the right manner because it lets you consume fewer calories. Thus, you shouldn't compensate for the fasting days by eating more than you'd normally eat when you're not fasting. There's no rule on when and what you should eat on the days when you're fasting. One of the side effects you'll experience at that beginning of this program is extreme episodes of hunger accompanied by feelings of weakness and sluggish. However, this tends to fade with time, especially when you're busy with other things. Eventually, they find it easier to fast. Should you notice that you're repeatedly feeling unwell or faint, be sure to talk to your doctor. The 5:2 plan, just like any other plan is not suitable for everyone. Some of the people who should avoid this plan include people who experience drops in blood sugar levels, people with an eating disorder, and people who are malnourished and underweight with known nutrient deficiencies.

Alternate Day Intermittent Fasting

With this plan, you fast on one day and eat the next day. This means that you're restricting what you'll be eating half the time. When you're fasting, you can drink calorie-free beverages like unsweetened tea, coffee, and water. Studies on alternate day fasting reveal that you can lose 3-8% of your body weight between 2 and 12 weeks. You can also consider modified alternate fasting that lets you have 500 calories on fasting days and is more tolerable because of the decreased amounts of hunger hormones and an increase in the satiety hormones. Alternate day fasting will not only help you to lose weight but also help in lowering insulin levels in type 2 diabetes patients. Type 2 diabetes makes up 90-95% of diabetes cases in the US.

Moreover, more than two-thirds of Americans are considered to be pre-diabetic, which means they've higher blood sugar levels that can't be categorized as diabetes. Restricting calories and losing weight is an effective means of improving or reversing the symptoms of type 2 diabetes. Alternate day fasting also contributes to mild reductions in risk factors for type 2 diabetes in obese and overweight individuals.

Most importantly, alternate day fasting is especially effective in reducing insulin resistance and lowering insulin levels with a minor effect on blood sugar control. Excessive insulin levels have been linked to obesity, cancer, heart disease, and other chronic diseases. Thus, insulin resistance and a dip in insulin levels can lead to a significant decline in type 2 diabetes. Evidence suggests that alternate day fasting is a great option for weight loss and reducing risk factors for heart disease. Other common health benefits of alternate day fasting are:

- Decreased blood triglycerides
- Lower LDL cholesterol concentration
- Decreased blood pressure
- Reduced waist circumference
- Increased number of large LDL particles and reduction in dangerous small, dense LDL particles.

One of the common effects of alternate day fasting is its ability to stimulate autophagy. This gives you the added advantage of having parts of old cells degraded and recycled. This process is crucial in preventing diseases like cancer, neurodegeneration, cancer, and infections. In addition, it also contributes to delaying aging as well as reducing the risk of tumors.

Warrior Fasting Diet

The warrior diet was created by Ori Hofmekler, who was a former member of the Israeli Special Forces. This intermittent fasting plan is based on the eating patterns of ancient warriors that feasted at night and ate little during the day. This plan is designed to improve the way we feel, eat, look, and perform by stressing the body through reduced consumption of food hence triggering survival instincts. According to Ori Hofmekler, this diet is not based on science but on personal observations and beliefs. When you follow this diet, you're required to under eat for at least 20 hours a day, that is considered to be the fasting period but eat as much food at night. You should aim at eating small amounts of foods such as hard-boiled eggs, dairy products, vegetables and fruits, and non-caloric fluids. You then have a four-hour feeding window. It is recommended that you stick to healthy, organic, and unprocessed food choices. Like other intermittent fasting plans, warrior fasting helps you burn fat, boost your energy levels, improve concentration/brain health, decrease inflammation, control blood sugar, and stimulate cellular repair.

Despite all these health benefits that the warrior diet promises, it also has some potential downfalls that include the following:

It's inappropriate for most people. This diet is inappropriate for most people, including expectant women, children, extreme athletes, people with diseases such as type 1 diabetes, and underweight people.

It can be difficult to stick to for some people. This is an obvious limitation of this diet because it restricts the time that you can eat substantial meals to just four hours. This can be difficult to maintain, especially if you desire to go out for lunch or breakfast.

Warrior fasting can cause disordered eating. This plan emphasizes on overeating that can be problematic for most people. However, Ori argues that you should know when you're satisfied and stop eating.

It can result in negative side effects. Some of the negative side effects that the warrior diet can potentially cause some of which can be severe include dizziness, fatigue, anxiety, low energy, insomnia, lightheadedness, constipation, fainting, hormonal imbalance, irritability and weight gain among others. Additionally, health professionals hold the opinion that this fasting plan can result in nutrients deficiency. However, you can take care of this by making sure you're eating nutrient-dense food.

Unlike other intermittent fasting plans, the warrior fasting plan has three phases:

Phase 1 - Detox. Start by under eating for 20 hours daily. You can eat anything from the clear broth, vegetable juices, hard boiled eggs, raw fruits, and vegetables. In your four-hour eating window, include whole grains, plant proteins, cooked vegetables, salads, and cheese. You can also take water, small amounts of milk, tea, and coffee throughout the day. The whole idea is to detox.

Phase 2. This week, your focus should be on high fat. Therefore, you shouldn't consume any starches or grains but instead focus on eating foods like vegetable juices, dairy, clear broth, raw fruits, hard boiled eggs lean animal protein as well as cooked vegetables.

Phase 3. This is the phase where you conclude your fat loss. Thus, it cycles between periods of high protein and high carb intake. This would mean 1-2 days of high carbs, followed by 1-2 days of high protein and low cards.

Eat Stop Eat Intermittent Fasting

The Eat stop eat intermittent fasting regimen involves fasting for 24 hours once or twice weekly. This method was made popular by Brad Pilon, a fitness expert and has been quite popular over the past few years. You fast from dinner one day to dinner the next day amounting to 24 hours of being in the fasted state. This means that if you finish dinner at 8 p.m., you don't eat anything until 8 p.m. the next day to make a full 24-hour fast. This fasting plan is not restricted to dinner alone; you can also fast from breakfast to breakfast or better still lunch to lunch and get the same end result. Like other intermittent fasting plans, you can take coffee, water, and other beverages with zero calories during the fast. However, no solid food is allowed. If your goal of doing the 24-hour weekly fast is to lose weight, make sure you're eating normally during your eating period. That is, just consume the same amount of food you'd be normally consuming without keeping the fast in mind. The challenge with this 24-hour fast is that it's fairly difficult for many people because of the length of the fasting window. Thus, you don't have to go all the way at the beginning. You can begin with 14-16 hours of fasting, increasing the duration with time. Generally, the first few hours of the fast will be easy before you become ravenously hungry. However, with discipline and taking enough fluid during the fasting duration, you can be sure to pull through. Soon, you'll get used to doing these fasts.

Spontaneous Meal Skipping

You don't have to stick to a specific intermittent fasting plan to reap the benefits. You could actually consider meal skipping. You can opt to skip meals from time to time when you're too busy to cook, or you don't feel hungry. Skipping one or two meals whenever you feel inclined basically means you're doing a spontaneous intermittent fast. It is simple; you can skip your lunch and have an early dinner. Alternatively, if you eat a large dinner, you can skip breakfast instead. Skipping meals can boost your metabolism Skipping meals is a good place to start your intermittent fasting experience, especially if the idea of going for long periods without food intimidates you. This intermittent fasting plan bursts the myth that you need to eat after every few hours; otherwise, your body will get into starvation mode or even lose muscle. The truth is that the human body is equipped very well to handle extended periods of famine, let alone having to do without a meal or two from time to time. Therefore, if there's a day you're really not hungry, you can skip breakfast so that you have healthy lunch and dinner. This fast is also convenient if you're traveling somewhere but just can't find something you can eat. You just must sure that you eat healthy foods.

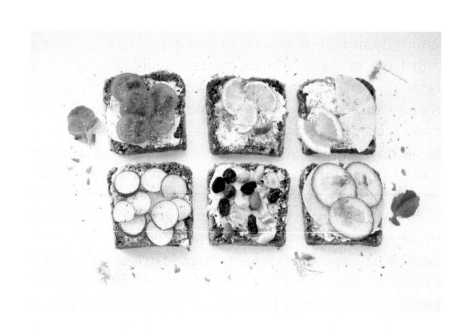

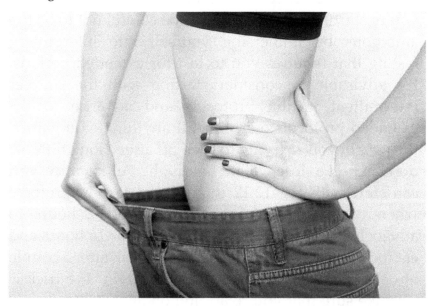

Preparation is the key to succeeding in intermittent fasting. When you prepare well, you can be sure to stay in control so that you're not feeling lost and out of place. If you want to reap the benefits of intermittent fasting quickly, you must be keen to make the right move when getting into this practice. Your body is accustomed to eating after 2-3 hours; therefore, you need to immerse yourself into fasting systematically. Although this sounds simple in principle, it's actually not easy when you start out. However, when you take caution and come up with a good plan, you'll have a smooth transition that will contribute to the success of your intermittent fasting quest. Here are some cautions you can consider while making the transition to intermittent fasting:

Transition slowly. It's okay to be ambitious about going without food for several hours. However, as you're starting out, you need to be careful not to be too ambitious by immersing yourself into intermittent fasting that requires you to fast for extended periods. It's advisable to consider starting with the simpler intermittent fasting protocols and advance to the extended protocols over time. If anything, you gained the weight you're trying to shed off after a long time, so don't expect to lose weight overnight. For instance, you can start with the 12:12 intermittent fasting protocol where you have a fasting window of 12 hours to advancing on to 16:8 that lets you fast for 16 hours and eat for 8 hours. You can even take a break after a couple of days or weeks before attempting again. The trick is to make sure that you're adding on another day every week until you're able to stick to your intermittent fasting plan. Only then can you consider trying intermittent fasting protocols that require you to fast for extended periods of between 18 and 24 hours like 5:2 or warrior depending on how comfortable you're. Don't hesitate to tailor the fasting protocol to your preference, even if it means not doing it every day.

Take your schedule into account. It's very important to keep your schedule in mind while planning for the intermittent fasting protocol that's right for you. Your choice of an intermittent fasting protocol should not be influenced by peer pressure rather, by what is suitable for you in relation to your schedule. Don't go for an extreme plan in the beginning just because your friends are doing it. If there's no way you can have your meals within an 8-hour window because your schedule is erratic, then the LeanGains 16:8 protocol is not appropriate for you. However, if you are sure you can't go for 24 hours without food, then this intermittent plan might be the most suitable for you. Ultimately, you must think about your schedule, your preferences, and if the plan will affect the other people that you live with before deciding what is best for you. This will make your transition to intermittent fasting smooth.

Don't start intermittent fasting alongside a new diet. If your goal is to lose weight and you're also interested in taking on a new diet like low-calorie diet or keto, make sure you're not starting it alongside intermittent fasting. This is because it takes time for your body to adjust to the new meals and foods included in your diet. Moreover, whether you're cutting down on meat on your vegetarian diet or you're simply reducing your carbs dramatically, it will have a huge effect on your body when combined with intermittent fasting. Therefore, to succeed with intermittent fasting, make sure that you stick to your diet for up to two weeks before adding intermittent fasting. This way, you will have a great understanding of your body, hence a smooth transition.

Eliminate snacks. Snacks refer to anything that will add empty calories to your system and cause cravings. Before beginning intermittent fasting, make sure you prepare your body to stay without food for longer periods than usual. The first step towards this is eliminating snacks. Although not evident, snacks are your biggest enemies because they're not nutritious; rather, they're only full of salt, sugar, flours, and refined oil. Thus, you must learn to avoid them in order to stay in shape. Snacks often cause your blood sugar levels to spike while loading your system with empty calories and provide very little to your gut. Make sure you eliminate snacks from your routine. You also need to avoid carbonated beverages that add empty calories and are full of sugar.

Most importantly, keep in mind that intermittent fasting is not based on restricting your calorie intake so you can consume calories within a limit that is reasonable. Rather, your calorie intake will automatically reduce since your eating windows are short. Remember, intermittent fasting is based on when you eat and not what you eat. One of the best ways to avoid processed foods is staying away from foods that are served at fast food chains, including salads that have various dressings. Instead, make it a habit to cook your own food. This will ensure you're only eating healthy food.

Stay true to your purpose. There's definitely a reason why you're getting into intermittent fasting. Staying true to this reason is the only way you'll stay grounded to the cause. Therefore, make sure you have defined the reason why you're going into fasting. This may be losing weight; fasting will reduce the level of hormones like insulin while increasing the human growth hormone and norepinephrine that make the stored body fat more accessible hence making it possible for you to burn fat and effectively lose weight. Fasting also helps in the prevention of heart disease, diabetes, as well as reduce inflammation. Most importantly, fasting will also offer protection against cancer, Alzheimer's while increasing longevity.

Face your fears. It's normal to feel nervous and even harbor doubts before beginning intermittent fasting, especially because we have been cultured to believe that breakfast is the most important meal of the day. However, you need to know that when unaddressed these worries can cause you to stop. Therefore, face them. It's important to know that breakfast is a neutral meal hence can be skipped. In fact, the reality is that skipping breakfast will not make you gain weight while eating breakfast will not rave up your metabolism. You also need to keep in mind that fasting will increase your metabolic rate and help you lose weight while retaining more muscle.

Begin with 3 meals. Intermittent fasting is all about a total lifestyle change. Therefore, you need to start by taking three meals. This may be surprising, and you may be wondering whether the fact that you're already skipping a meal means you are doing intermittent fasting. Well, the answer is no. Here's why; while you don't have time to consume three meals on any given day, you somewhat take improper meals in the course of the day. This kind of munching counts for intermittent fasting. Thus, we must consider starting off with a balanced breakfast, eat moderate lunch, and finish with a light dinner. When you get to a point where you're able to sustain without difficulty with the three meals you'll be ready to move on to intermittent fasting.

Be consistent with your intermittent fasting protocol. It's likely that you will be excited to make a change and transition to the next intermittent fasting protocol after some time. This is especially the case when you begin seeing results. Even then, you must remember that intermittent fasting mustn't be rushed. Make sure you stay on a single fasting protocol for at least two weeks before moving on to the next. Keep in mind that each of the intermittent fasting protocols presents its own unique results and advantages. Only when you get comfortable should you consider moving on to the next one.

No fasting protocol is superior. It's a common misconception that you can only get better results when you go for the tougher regimen. While there's some degree of truth in this belief, it's important to focus on individual capacity. Everyone has their unique capabilities, thus imitating someone else is utterly meaningless. Some people may post impressive results with a 12-hour fasting protocol while for others, it will take another protocol to experience similar results. So don't go for the toughest protocol but instead find a protocol that suits you.

Focus on eating healthy eating. One of the things that you're likely to ignore when starting intermittent fasting is the quality of food you're eating. Although your fast will generally involve cutting down on the number of calories you're consuming, it's equally important to be deliberate about your food choices. More specifically, focus on healthy eating, especially if you're aiming to make this a lifestyle. While you can eat unhealthy food while doing intermittent fasting, eating healthy foods contribute towards living a long and healthy life. Therefore, be sure to include fruits, nuts, vegetables, healthy fats, and lean proteins in your diet.

Know when to quit. It is important that you're flexible and adapts to your changing needs. For instance, if your plan is to fast for 16 hours, but you begin feeling tired, you might as well shorten your day. You may also be working out, but you generally feel you don't have enough energy, this is also a reason to break your fast early. You shouldn't aim to be perfect at the expense of your wellbeing. If you begin feeling sick during your fasting window, it's also a good reason to cut short your fasting and pay attention to you your health. It's better to be consistent than to be perfect.

Keep it simple. Unlike many other diets that are designed to help in losing weight, intermittent fasting doesn't require you to deviate from your usual meals to some sophisticated menus. Therefore, aim at eating your usual meals during your eating window. However, you can also consider combining your intermittent fasting regimen with a low carb-high fat diet comprising real whole foods.

Get enough rest. Fasting, by itself, is not enough if you want to embrace a healthy lifestyle. Make sure you're also getting enough sleep. Your body requires sleep to be able to carry out some of the important functions. Therefore, don't work at night unless it's important. We aren't wired as other nocturnal beings; thus, we need to follow through our circadian rhythm. When you get sound sleep at night, no doubt your body will be able to fight off the weight in a better way even as your stress and cholesterol levels improve. If anything, intermittent fasting puts emphasis on giving the body adequate sleep. Make sure you plan your day so that you free up some time for good sleep. Most importantly, make sure you rest more when you fast for extended periods.

Practice perseverance. It's unfortunate that most people that have a problem with their weight are also impatient. This is probably because they're already under pressure to lose weight, yet it's just not happening. Moreover, most people trying to lose weight have already tried other ways of shedding off excess fat unsuccessfully and are looking for quick results. Unfortunately, intermittent fasting is not an overnight success. It takes time and consistency before you can see the results. You must be ready to see the change happen after a while since you're correcting problems/weight that has accumulated over the years. Don't lose hope in the process because by quitting, you can't tell whether you had made any progress. You can stall hunger by laughing, running, or talking to friends or engage in activities that stall hunger.

Hydrate during fasting. It's extremely important always to make sure you're drinking up enough during intermittent fasting. Yet it's common to find beginners thinking that they should not actually consume anything during the fasting window. This is wrong because intermittent fasting allows you to take water, tea, or coffee as long as you don't use any cream, milk, or sugar. Staying hydrated is important in extending your feeling of satiety; thus drinking water will help you to get rid of that feeling of hunger.

Manage your fasting time properly. It's a common thing for people to mismanage time during the fasting window just as is with our normal schedules. You need to know that not managing your fasting time well is likely to be a cause of distress. This can make your journey of losing weight painful and difficult. Stop thinking about food the entire time you're in the fasted state. This will create problems since your gut will be confused. You can manage your fasting time by staying busy while making sure that you're engaged until the last leg of your fasting window. When you're idle, it's likely that you'll only be thinking about food. Think about ways of putting off hunger. After all, our bodies have ample energy reserves that can run without food for a long time.

Don't rush the process. We all want quick results, but with intermittent fasting, you have to follow through the process. Don't attempt to make quick jumps because the body doesn't work this way. The transition process of your body is quite slow. Thus, you need to allow more time to adjust to change that comes with intermittent fasting. To succeed with each of these processes, make sure you stay at every stage for some time. This gives your body time to adjust to the changes. Remember, you're trying to change habits that are decades old, so you need to be patient to make your body adjust to the process. The other thing you must remember is that fasting is different in men and women. While a man's system is rugged and doesn't get to be affected by periods of extended fasting, fasting can affect a woman's health adversely; hence, it takes time to normalize. Hence, the need to start small and advance with time.

Have realistic expectations. It's okay to have a goal and dreams about your weight loss goals. Even then, make sure that you're grounded in reality. This is a good place to start as you're able to accept facts and avoid lots of disappointments. Having unrealistic expectations often contributes to the failure to recognize the benefits you derive from the process. For instance, if your goal is losing weight, then you must really think about the amount of time, you'll put into fasting and your overall commitment. Not taking all the relevant factors into consideration will leave you feeling frustrated and difficult to achieve the results you desire.

Determine how long you want to fast/create a routine. Since intermittent fasting is more of a pattern of eating than a diet fad, you can only get the best results when you follow it in routine. This means that you will not get the results if you're only practicing fasting in a way that is unstructured. If anything, doing intermittent fasting in an irregular manner will not yield any results; rather, it'll leave you feeling hungry. Your gut releases the hunger hormone with so much accuracy. As such, the gut is able to sense the time when you eat so that you feel gurgling in your stomach around exactly the same time the next day. This means that if you're keeping a 14-hour fast regularly, you'll notice you feel hungry hunger just about the time you need to break your fast. This means that if you don't keep a regular routine, then this will not happen. Making intermittent fasting a usual routine will help you get over the hassle of being too conscious. After a while, this would be part of your lifestyle hence easy to follow.

Don't be greedy when it's time to breaking your fast. Food is the most alluring thing you can come across when you've been deprived of it for long hours. It's actually tempting. You need to make sure that you don't get greedy when breaking your fast, rather get off the fast in a proper manner. The biggest mistake you can make is eating a lot as it can lead to various problems among them poor digestion. Your gut can be dry after long periods of fasting. Thus, stuffing it with heavy food can result in problems. When breaking your fast start with liquid food, slowly transitioning to semi-solid and finally solid foods. You also need to check the quantity of food that you eat because the brain takes time to decode the leptin signals that you're full. When the brain finally signals you're full, you'll have overeaten. This means that you need to eat slowly so that your brain has enough time to determine your satiety levels. Alternatively, stop eating when you're at 80% full after which you're unlikely to feel hungry again.

You only require a few calories during intermittent fasting because your body is running on just a few calories or no food at all for a longer period than usual. This can result in having a hangover initially. You can train your body to come with the stress that is linked to food deprivation in order to get used to staying for long without food. If you realize that you can't cope with your intermittent fasting plan, then you can consider switching to another plan. You might have chosen a plan that is not suitable for your needs or lifestyle. Don't be discouraged if one plan doesn't work. Rather, make sure you work towards finding the right fasting protocol that you'll be comfortable with while getting the results you need.

By transitioning into intermittent slowly, you're giving your body a chance to self-regulate and gradually adapt to your eating pattern that is changing. It also helps in diminishing or avoiding symptoms of early transition that include dry mouth, insomnia, and digestive changes.

Chapter 10: Common Myths About Intermittent Fasting

Before joining the intermittent fasting bandwagon, it is important to have a clear picture of what it is you're getting into and the kind of results you should expect. Like with any other programs, there are several misconceptions and myths associated with the intermittent fasting lifestyle that is as popular as the benefits. Let's debunk some of the myths about this eating pattern so that you feel more confident embarking on this weight loss and wellness strategy:

You'll definitely lose weight. While one of the primary reasons why most people take on intermittent fasting is to lose weight, the results are not guaranteed. Several factors come into play. Thus, intermittent fasting will not always lead to weight loss. This is especially true if you're fasting faithfully while at the same time throwing down pizza, candy, and burgers. Intermittent fasting works well when you're on a healthy diet. Don't treat your eating window like a cheat day and expect to see positive results.

Intermittent fasting will slow down your metabolism. There's a general fear that when you go into intermittent fasting, your metabolism slows down. This is not actually true because intermittent fasting doesn't restrict the number of calories you take. Rather, it makes you wait for a few hours before you can have your first meal. This doesn't make a difference in your metabolic rate. Instead, changes in your metabolic rate will only come about when you're not eating enough, which is not the case with intermittent fasting.

You can eat as much food during your feeding window. It's not exactly true that you can eat as much as you want during your feeding window. Here's the thing. When you start intermittent fasting, your aim should be entering a healthier lifestyle. Unfortunately, most people only go into it to lose weight before going back to their reckless eating at the end of the fast. Experts warn that this is counterproductive to the results you've attained during your fasting window. The key to success with intermittent fasting is eating normally when you end your fast so that you don't negate the time spent fasting.

It's better to fast than snack for weight loss. Most conventional diet regimens recommend snacking in between meals. Those who opt for intermittent fasting think it should be a substitute for snacking. Ultimately, weight loss is occasioned by a constant deficit in calories. Whether those calories are consumed within a four to eight-hour window or spread throughout the day is not an issue. Instead, you should aim to do what is beneficial to your body.

Intermittent fasting for weight loss is far much better compared to other weight loss strategies. If you believe that intermittent fasting is the best strategy for your weight loss, you need to think again. It is important to keep in mind that intermittent fasting is simply about exercising caloric restriction in terms of when you take your food. If anything, there's no evidence to prove that intermittent fasting works better than the other methods and means of losing weight. It all boils down to your approach and discipline.

You can't skip breakfast. You must have heard this one even with other diets that are designed to help in weight loss. It's largely believed that breakfast if is the most important meal of the day hence must be taken even during intermittent fasting. In fact, this is part of the American tradition. Although you'll be told you need to consume a good breakfast to get fuel for the day, this is not necessarily true. If anything, it's likely that you don't have an appetite when they wake up. However, you can always listen to your body and have a small breakfast. Depending on the intermittent fasting protocol you choose, you can always have your meals at a time of day when its convenient.

Skipping breakfast makes you fat. It's believed that when you skip breakfast, you'll experience excessive hunger and cravings that lead to weight gain. While a number of studies have linked skipping breakfast to obesity, this is not the case with intermittent fasting. However, another 2014 study conducted between obese adults who skipped breakfast and those who didn't find any difference in weight. That is, there's no difference in weight loss whether you eat breakfast or not. Eating breakfast can have benefits, but it's not essential.

You can't work out when you're fasting. Contrary to popular belief that you can't work out when you're fasting, you can carry on with your work out routine when fasting. In fact, working out when fasting is a positive thing. It is believed that working out on an empty stomach, especially when it is the first thing you do in the morning is more rewarding. This is because you'll be burning stored fat instead of using up the calories from the food you just consumed. You can then eat your breakfast after working out to replenish your body.

All fasting is the same, and everyone gets the same results. There are many forms of intermittent fasting that you can follow. There's no official fasting protocol leaving the flexibility of choosing what works for you. Therefore, you can opt to fast daily while someone else fasts for on alternate days. Consequently, you can be sure that everyone will get results that are unique to them depending on the fasting protocol they're following and their goal.

Fasting makes you extremely fit and healthy. Intermittent fasting in itself is not a magic bullet to achieving health and fitness. You'll do well to combine your eating pattern with proper care and exercise. You must work to maintain health and fitness in your entire life. They should not be taken for granted. Fasting alone will not give you an ideal body overnight. Moreover, when you lose excess weight, you'll have to make sure you continue maintaining it with healthy eating habits that include regular exercise and a nutritious diet.

Intermittent fasting is productive because the body doesn't process food at night. Although it's a common misconception that your body doesn't process food at night, it's actually the reason you lose weight during intermittent fasting. Your body is wired to digest food no matter the time. However, when you allow the body a certain time, usually between 12 and 18 hours, the focus shifts to other metabolic processes like cellular repair and autophagy taking the attention from digestion. Your body will digest food even if you eat at 3a.m.

Intermittent fasting will decrease your training performance. One of the fears most people have when contemplating intermittent fasting is a decrease in training performance. This because of the possibility of having to skip or having a light pre-workout meal. The truth is that a closer look at athletes who train while in the fasted state have not experienced any hindrance to their performance due to nutrient deprivation. Moreover, it's important to keep in mind that intermittent fasting doesn't deprive the body of fluids and water.

Intermittent fasting will lead to loss of muscle mass. The fact that you've reduced the frequency of eating especially proteins doesn't mean your body is in the catabolic state as it is largely assumed. The idea that fasting reduces muscle mass is based on the idea that your body relies on a constant supply of amino acids to maintain, build, or repair muscle tissue. It is important to keep in mind that when you have a large meal of protein at your last meal prior to your 16-20 hour fast, your body is likely to be releasing the amino acids they need by the time you break the fast. It's common to have a complete meal that digests proteins slowly to the time you have your next meal. The thing is that fasting for extended periods will cause muscle loss only when you are not eating a large balanced diet during your feeding window.

Eating big meals with a lot of carbohydrates in the evening causes weight gain. Most fitness and nutrition experts will link carbs to insulin. While this is correct, there's a tendency to overgeneralize the psychological effects of insulin. The fear is that an increase in insulin, especially in the evening, will result in the conversion of nutrients to fats because insulin sensitivity is highest in the morning and lowest at night.

Fasting leads to glorified, binge eating, and bulimia disorders. This is another ridiculous claim that has been continually advanced about intermittent fasting by classifying it as disordered eating. The truth is that with intermittent fasting, the time you eat is not as important as meeting your daily macronutrient and calorie goals. What this means is that you're able to stick to your diet. Moreover, fasting presents a number of health benefits that disqualify the idea of promoting binge eating and bulimia. Besides, it's unrealistic to expect someone who is on an intermittent fasting protocol not to eat a large meal. Eating a large meal does not necessarily equal to binge eating, especially if you're staying within your nutrient needs.

Intermittent fasting has limited uses in limited populations. This myth in itself suggests that intermittent fasting is less applicable to the majority. This is not true because most of the people that have found success with intermittent fasting will attest to the fact that it's such a huge relief from having to constantly obsess about following the clock all day just to make sure that you're eating after every 3 hours. Intermittent fasting is most likely to work well with most people's routines, especially if you're working. Not many people like to have a large meal in the morning or at midday owing to the nature of their schedules.

Eating frequently will help reduce hunger. Some people, especially those that are keen on following conventional weight loss diets, believe that when you snack in between meals, you'll prevent excessive hunger and cravings. Well, knowing when to eat is far much better because you get to eat one large meal that is packed with nutrients; hence, you'll experience satiety for longer periods. If anything, there's no evidence to show that snacking will reduce hunger.

Fasting puts your body in starvation mode. A common argument against intermittent fasting is that it can activate the starvation mode. That is, failure to eat will make your body assume it's starving hence shut down metabolism and the ability to burn fat. Long term weight loss reduces the calories you burn, which can aptly be described as starvation mode. Even then, this tends to happen whenever you're trying to lose weight regardless of the method you're using. There's no evidence that this is more with intermittent fasting. Evidence points to the fact that fasting for short term can increase metabolic rate.

Intermittent fasting is not for people with diabetes. Findings of a recent study point to the fact that intermittent fasting will result in improved weight loss, fasting blood sugar, and stabilize blood sugar after dinner in group 2 diabetics. In some instances, prolonged fasting will restore your insulin sensitivity, especially in type 2 diabetes. When your insulin sensitivity is improved, your body will produce less insulin and experience less inflammation. This shows intermittent fasting is important for individuals with diabetes by reducing the risk of kidney and heart disease.

There are many myths about intermittent fasting. While some have merit, others are outrightly wrong. For most people, intermittent fasting presents real benefits. It's one of the best tools to lose weight.

Chapter 11: Common mistakes people make While Intermittent Fasting

Although it is billed as the most effective method of losing weight, you can easily have difficulty with intermittent fasting. Research has found intermittent fasting to have a 31% drop out rate. There are many mistakes people make when making a switch from your regular eating plan to intermittent fasting. This can jeopardize your expectations by influencing the results because you might not see the results everyone is raving about, resulting in giving up. Having a workable and realistic approach to intermittent fasting can be the difference between your success and failure. Here are some of the common pitfalls you're likely to be making in your intermittent fasting:

Having a wrong plan for your lifestyle. Intermittent fasting is flexible; hence, you have the liberty of selecting a plan that suits your lifestyle. You need to understand the dynamics of the different forms of intermittent fasting to make sure you choose what will work well with your lifestyle, needs, and schedule. By signing up for a plan that you can't keep up with, you're definitely setting yourself up for failure. For instance, if you're working in a full-time job, have an intense workout routine and an active family, the 5:2 plan will not be realistic instead of the 16:8 plan will be more sensible and easier to maintain because you'll have a reasonable feeding window. Therefore, take time to do your research and pick a plan that will work well for you, and you're able to stick with comfortably.

Getting into intermittent fasting too soon. One of the reasons most people give up on diets is because it presents a departure from the natural and normal way of eating. As such, you'll find it impossible to keep up with. This is often the case when you jump into intermittent fasting too fast. For instance, if you're accustomed to eating after every 2-3 hours, it's unrealistic to switch to a 24-hour fast suddenly. As a beginner, you can begin by fasting for 12 hours and have a 12-hour eating window. This comes close to your regular pattern. You can then extend your fasting window gradually until you reach your goal. It takes time to stop feeling hungry when you take on intermittent fasting. This way, you'll find better success. The secret is to be patient and see a lifestyle change

Eating too much during the eating window. Although you don't have to count calories as is typical with most diets, intermittent fasting requires discipline in terms of determining how much you should eat. While it's true that you may be too hungry from too many hours of fasting, caution must be taken so that you don't overeat during your eating window. In fact, you try not to be preoccupied with your next meal because this can lead to binge eating. Instead, consider sitting down to a larger meal that is more satisfying so that you're not completely famished when you enter your feeding window. When you do this correctly, you won't feel too hungry during the fasting window to want to eat everything.

Failure to hydrate adequately. Although your intermitted fasting plan alternates patterns of eating and fasting, you must make sure that you're taking in enough water. You actually need to have a bottle of water by your side because you're missing out on the water from veggies and fruits. Failure to stay dehydrated can results in headaches and cramps while worsening hunger pangs. You can also have tea or coffee but without sugar. You don't want to take any sweetened drink that can have an effect on your insulin levels and stimulate your appetite giving you the desire to eat. Avoid fluids that are filled with proteins since they can halt autophagy that you need to promote during fasting. If you find drinking up difficult, you can consider using an app to ensure you're sipping up in between your fasting and feasting windows.

Overlooking what you're while focusing on when you're eating. While it's true that intermittent fasting is more of time centered eating regimen with no specific rules on what you should eat, your goal should be to eat healthy, nutrient dense foods. Therefore, you should not dwell on milkshakes, French fries, and the likes in your diet as these can easily undo the gains of fasting. Shift your focus from treating yourself after hours of fasting to getting nutrient-dense foods that are nourishing. Generally, your meals should have a protein, complex carbs, fiber, and good fats. These will keep you feeling satiated and carry you through the fasting window while helping you to build muscle, feel energetic, and maintain a healthy brain.

Eating too little. While it is wrong to overeat during your feeding window, you should also not eat too little. Fasting affects the hormones that control your appetite leaving you feeling less hungry. Consequently, when you get to eat, you'll only eat a small portion of food and feel full. Even then, you need to be careful so that you don't consume too little because failure to eat enough will leave you feeling extremely hungry the next day so that you can end up feeling lethargic and unable to perform any work. Failure to eat adequate food will cannibalize your muscle mass, resulting in slowed down metabolism. Lack of metabolic muscle mass will sabotage your ability to maintain fat. Eventually, you may end up feeling the need to skip fasting or even give up on intermittent fasting altogether.

Leading a sedentary lifestyle. You may likely want to skip your workout session because you're used to having a pre-workout snack. Exercising when fasting will definitely seem foreign. Although it is advisable that you check with your doctor before exercising while intermittent fasting, it's safe to carry on with your exercise routine, albeit with some alterations. This is because your body has lots of stored energy in the form of stored fat that is used up when there's no food. Aim to keep up with your routine or consider low impact exercises like walking. For instance, if you're fasting overnight, you can exercise in the morning after which you can eat a protein-rich meal for better muscle build.

Obsessing over intermittent fasting. When your fasting, you might be inclined to decline invitations to parties or even opt out for dinner with friends. When this is the case, your intermittent fasting goal may not be sustainable. You can fix this by shifting your fasting schedule either backward or forward by a couple of hours on the days when you have a date with friends so that you can still enjoy your social life without being guilty or the fear of being left out. Remember, intermittent fasting as a lifestyle is flexible; hence, it has to fit in your special occasions.

INTERMITTENT FASTING FOR MEN

Introduction

In a world that desperately needs answers to fat loss questions, we seem determined to ignore the most obvious solution: based on my professional experience as a dietitian and my personal experience of trying fat, the time without food.

The strategy I recommend to my clients, intermittent fasting is a very effective way to lose weight and is also very beneficial to your health. It will save you a lot of money and time. If you can exercise, then Even better. This is so meaningful that there is almost no need to write an entire book on the subject. But you may have heard the famous saying:

"Breakfast is the most important meal of the day."

"If you don't eat, your metabolism will slow down, and you will eventually gain weight."

"If you don't eat every few hours, you will be very hungry and overeat the next meal."

" You must fuel your body (using carbohydrates) before training, otherwise you will not have the energy to exercise."

"If you don't eat every few hours, your blood sugar will drop and you will pass out and pass out. Weakness."

Most of us think that when we fast, something bad will happen to our body, probably because we have no experience in this area at all. However, fasting will not make you weak, tired, confusing your mind, or anything else that bothers you before people try. As part of religious or cultural practices, millions of people around the world fast regularly and benefit from improvements in physical and emotional health.

But fasting is almost forbidden in our society. The message we get from nutrition authorities (not to mention all health and fitness magazines) time and time again is that the body needs to eat more frequently throughout the day. It is recommended to eat snacks and not skip the main meal. As a result, we convinced ourselves to eat all the time to avoid weight gain. I think it hurt a lot of people a lot. I suspect you also doubt this, otherwise, you are not ready to try intermittent fasting.

The goal of this book is to show you that intermittent fasting is a very effective and safe way to lose weight, especially to burn fat while maintaining muscle mass. It is harmful to your body or makes you gain weight instead of losing weight. I will provide practical advice on how to integrate intermittent fasting into your life and how to make fasting smoother. Once you are convinced of the benefits of fasting and that you can easily practice fasting, please try it out within 24 hours before reading this book.

Chapter 1: What is Intermittent Fasting?

Intermittent fasting simply put is, not eating for a certain amount of time (fasting window) and then eating in another time window each window adds up to 24 hours. During your fasting hours, you are only allowed to drink water. Then when it comes to your eating window you may consume anything you want.

History of Intermittent Fasting

Fasting has been used to heal ailments and cure diseases for thousands of years.

Plutarch, an ancient Greek writer, also wrote: "Rather than taking medicine today, better fast." Fasting for better health was a popular belief among ancient Greek intellectuals. Fasting was one of the fundamental remedies given by many Biblical academics who believed in treating diseases/illnesses from the inside out. Their theory is that when you're unwell, you don't want to eat, which is an indication from your body that you should avoid eating. It is also true that the ancient Greeks felt it boosted brain function.

Consider the last time you ate a burger and pizza and experienced mental fog and fatigue as a result. These sensations are common when you overeat, and when you overeat, blood from your brain is moved to your intestines to deal with the meal, which is why people report mental fog after eating high-calorie foods. There were many other fasting adherents besides the Greeks. "The finest of all treatments is rest and fasting," as said by Benjamin Franklin, one of the United States' founding fathers.

As you know, many religions, such as Muslim, Christian, and Buddha, believed in the healing powers of fasting. They used it to cleanse and purify the soul, which makes sense since fasting has been shown to detoxify the body. Fast forward to 2006, when Martin Berkhan created intermittent fasting. The reason why he created it was simple; it was to save time and money cooking. This decision of his, made him lose body fat, balance out hormones and live an overall healthy lifestyle.

The method he used was the 16/8 method, which is the most popular method for intermittent fasting. Harvard University, which is one of the most renowned universities out there wrote an article on intermittent fasting. It stated all the benefits intermittent fasting brings with it, such as weight loss and hormone balance.

Numerous fitness professionals have now popularized intermittent fasting, and they say it is the best way to eat throughout the day. However, they don't realize that intermittent fasting has been here for a long time now. Many successful people live by intermittent fasting, and the reason is simple. When you start intermittent fasting, you will think and perform better. According to ancient Greek thinkers, it will help you heal from illness as well. So now you know the history of intermittent fasting.

How does It Work?

In this method of IF, you only eat within 8 hours and then fast for 16 hours. Most people will think this will cause them to experience extreme hunger. We usually eat all day, from the minute we wake up in the morning until we finally retire to our beds at night. That will average anywhere from 12 to 14 hours. This is called the fed state.

In this state, the body focuses more on digesting and absorbing recently eaten foods. These processes can take up to several hours. During the fed state, the body's fat-burning processes are at a minimum. It is hard for the body to burn stored fats during the fed state because it relies on the energy derived from recent food consumption.

Insulin levels are high during the fed state. This is a response to the influx of glucose from foods. This more elevated insulin level also hinders fat burning.

After the fed state, the body enters the post-absorptive state. In this state, the body is neither digesting nor processing food. This usually lasts for about 1 to 2 hours after you last ate a meal.

After the post-absorptive state, if you still haven't eaten or drank anything that contains calories, your body enters the fasted state.

During the fasting period, your digestive system does not actively digest solid foods. Instead, it concentrates on fully metabolizing and absorbing the nutrients from foods. This becomes an opportunity to utilize foods fully and turn these into readily usable energy. This energy is quickly used up by the body. Efficient energy use lessens the possibility of converting excess calories into fats.

In the fasted state, levels of insulin are low. The inhibitory effect of insulin on fat-burning is reduced; hence, the body can turn on its fat-burning processes at full force. This is why people who go on intermittent fasts burn fats and lose weight without changing their current diet. Even if they still eat the same kinds of foods every day, weight loss is evident.

Steady weight loss is achievable in the 16:8 intermittent fasting diet. This is because the cells burn glycogen stores for energy during the fasted state. When you eat again to break the fast, your body will turn energy into glycogen, instead of turning it into fat cells. This further enhances weight maintenance by reducing the amount of food that gets turned into and stored as fats.

One thing to keep in mind regarding intermittent fasting is that it is not a diet plan. It is, in reality, an eating pattern that demands you plan your meals to maximize the benefits to your fitness and health. The pattern consists of a cycle that alternates between eating and fasting intervals. So, in general, this eating pattern does not necessitate a change in your eating habits. What you need to do is adjust the way you eat now that you're on a rigorous diet.

You might be wondering if it's truly worth it to modify your eating habits. The answer is an emphatic yes. IF is an excellent option if you want to lose weight and keep it off without having to adhere to a strict diet plan or obsess about calorie tracking.

Most of the time, this eating pattern even demands you to maintain your calorie consumption while you're just getting started.

Furthermore, it is an excellent technique to maintain muscle mass while keeping your body lean. It's also the most straightforward technique for losing weight and staying inside your ideal weight range. You can do so without making drastic changes to your lifestyle. This makes intermittent fasting easy and simple in the sense that anyone can practice it while yet finding it important because it makes a real impact on your weight and health.

All our lives we heard our parents say, "Breakfast is the most vital meal of the day!", but were they right?

It's an awful tip, suggests the Leangains, the popular 16/8 hour method. With the Leangains, Martin Berkhan introduced the skipping of breakfast, extending the fasting period, and taking advantage of the natural fast during sleeping hours. The plan is to fast overnight and the first 6 hours of the day making a total of 16 hours, then eating all your calories in the remaining 8 hours.

For example; suppose you woke up at 6 am, waited for the next 6 hours until midnight, and from 12 pm to 8 pm you get to eat all your carbohydrates and proteins as large, fulfilling meals. You make this way of eating pattern your lifestyle, and the results are obvious.

Why skip breakfast is what you are wondering, right? The idea of 'skipping a morning meal is bad for you' began with studies sponsored by cereal companies to increase sales. This powerful message has been transferred on and has been engraved in the minds of people for so many years that it has become a proper belief. Now imagine... After taking your last meal, you fell asleep, and you woke up to a very low insulin level.

Trust me, the worst thing you can do to yourself right now would be having a high carbohydrate diet which will eventually increase your insulin level, depositing fat stores and shutting the fat burning process for nothing less than 12 hours minimum. Also, this will soon bring hunger growls in the stomach as the high insulin levels will result in low glucose levels.

Extension of fasting in the 16/8 process does wonders by triggering the metabolic phase, shifting the energy metabolism more onto ketones than on glucose. This time-restricted feeding can also decrease the abnormalities linked to obesity. During the 6 hours fast, you can have all the no-calorie liquids, the most important being mineral water. However, the water intake is advised as best at certain times. Similarly, snacking is allowed during the fed state, but it's better to have three full meals than nibbling all the time.

Have healthy food with more veggies, fruits, fiber, and protein, but no sugars and no snacking. This will give your body a rest and time to digest the food by breaking it and using it as energy photons to keep you active during the day.

This brings in the significance of exercise or at least staying active in the IMF (InterMittent Fasting) 16/8. If you cannot go to the gym, do weight lifting exercises such as pushups or squats at home. What matters is that you are not sitting idle. You can go swimming or to a park for cardio such as jogging or a brisk walk.

Fasting alone might burn your fat, but it will not help you achieve the desired goal. If we do not use the energy stored in our bodies, then our bodies end up storing this energy as fat, making us lazy. Therefore, exercise is vital for your general wellbeing, health, mental and physical strength, and it will also lighten your mood.

No doubt it worked for the bodybuilders, since the IMF 16/8 slows down the muscle tearing process, unlike in other diet programs, thus this is where its fame began. The weight loss encountered by the bodybuilders was tremendous, and the muscle growth was the best part. Many people have the wrong perception that fasting leads to burning muscle instead of burning fat.

However, this is not true. Instead, it activates the growth hormone. The hormone in combination with testosterone burns fat and consequently builds as much muscle as it can. It also keeps us focused and increases our level of alertness.

If you can lose weight, your insulin sensitivities will stay in control, especially in obese men and women, but again why do we need to increase our insulin sensitivity?

Insulin resistance is an omnipresent metabolic problem linked to obesity. Insulin is a peptide hormone secreted by the pancreatic Islets of Langerhans which maintains blood glucose levels. The adipose tissues and muscle insulin play an important role in weight loss.

In the muscles, during the fed state, insulin encourages glycogen synthesis through the stimulation of glycogen synthase. To enable energy to be anaerobically released through glycolysis, this activation is necessary, for example, during an intense muscular workout. Muscle cells are not dependent on glucose or glycogen for energy release during the basal state when insulin levels are low.

Therefore, low insulin levels divert the attention from burning glucose to finding other sources for energy, and this helps in building muscles as well as weight loss. Low insulin levels also promote the catabolism of protein, which is not healthy.

Starvation motivates this breakdown of protein molecules, while a diet routine with intermittent fasting done in the right terms and conditions, does not let the body reach this state.

Chapter 2: Intermittent Fasting and the Male Body

The Science of the Human Body

Have you ever wondered why it happens to be that you eat more when you're hungry than you're hungry for? Have you ever been curious about why you sometimes can't stop even when you know you're full? As someone coming to IF with goals of weight loss, you likely are very familiar with these frustrating feelings, but if you're coming to IF with goals other than weight loss, you might not be as familiar.

Regardless of your experience with hunger and whether or not you're able to stop eating when you feel you're full, there are scientific reasons why the saying "Your eyes were bigger than your stomach" exists. First on this list of reasons is the existence of hormones leptin and ghrelin. Both leptin and ghrelin seem to have a large effect on regulating appetite, and subsequently controlling fat storage and gain.

While leptin is secreted from fat cells in the stomach, heart, skeletal muscle, and placenta in females, ghrelin is secreted only from the lining of the stomach. Despite where the hormones come from, however, they both end up affecting the brain. Leptin decreases feelings of hunger, while ghrelin does the opposite. Leptin and ghrelin both end up communicating with the hypothalamus in the brain about stopping or starting to eat, but their effects are divergent.

Insulin is another hormone that our bodies produce that affects our health in several ways. For instance, insulin is produced in the pancreas, and it helps regulate the amount of glucose in our blood, but if someone's insulin levels are too high or too low, their weight is imminently affected. With low insulin levels, one can't help but lose weight, but too low of insulin levels can be dangerous because the body needs sugar to use as energy. The trick is finding a healthy balance while working to lose weight.

If you're overweight or working with IF, your hormones' signals to the brain become affected. If you're obese, for instance, the signals are interrupted and distorted, while for those working with IF, those signals are triggered not to go off as frequently through an altered pattern of eating.

One final element to note in this section would be the thyroid, whose function is essential in determining both health and ability with weight loss. The thyroid regulates hormones that affect the speed of your metabolism, and if your thyroid is over- or under-worked, your health, energy level, and weight will certainly be affected. To lose weight, you'll want to speed up your metabolism without hurting or overworking your thyroid, and that can be tricky to work out properly sometimes.

How the Male vs. Female Bodies React to Hunger

When it comes to the science of the human body, everything matters, from the foods we eat to how often we eat, what hormones we allow to produce, which ones we limit, and how well our thyroids are working.

When you're hungry, your body sends signals to the vagus nerve in your brain, and it communicates a lot of details. It reveals how empty (or full) your stomach happens to be, the nutrients that are processed in the intestines, and what deficiencies may be present in the body as a whole. After the stomach sits empty, it starts to grumble (a process called "borborygmus," which pushes any remaining food into the intestines to be digested fully), and then your stomach and intestinal walls begin producing that hormone, ghrelin, that makes you feel hungry.

If you're female and you tell yourself you're not hungry when you get this feeling, your brain often doesn't work in your favor. The hypothalamus and vagus nerve get triggered, making you feel hungry even if you keep telling yourself you can't eat yet or aren't mentally hungry. In the male body, however, the physical hunger sensations and hormone secretions can be limited in effect to the brain through inhibitive thoughts against hunger and eating.

Furthermore, a study on female versus male rats from 2013 revealed that when females (opposed to males) fast for a few days at a time, their abilities to control that hunger response become more fine-tuned than males' do, leading to their ability to lose more weight overall than the male rats could. This study applies to humans' experiences with intermittent fasting as well.

Reasons for Sex Distinction with IF

The primary reason why there is a separation of males and females in the study regarding IF is that the reproductive organs of males and females are different, making their responses to intermittent fasting dissimilar. With different reproductive organs and different reproductive capacities, these two sexes will have different sets of hormones being produced at different times and being sent to very diverse spaces in the body.

Ultimately, it is true that these two sexes will have different responses to fasting, in terms of weight loss potential and reproductive health. As the rat study from 2013 reminds us, females can lose weight faster through IF than males can, but they also have restricted abilities to have children during those times of IF (while males don't), which reaffirms the importance of sex distinction in studies of (and practice with) intermittent fasting in the human world. Different bodies respond differently to things that jolt the system like IF, and it's truer to say that each person's process with IF will be dissimilar. However, the first step is making distinctions based on sex and hormonal realities so that the individual comes out of the fast as healthy and energetic as possible.

When it comes down to it, noting sex differences, as it pertains to weight loss work with fasting, helps refine the process of IF for the individual. With these differences taken into account and planned for, the results of the fasting lifestyle change are better, meaning more productive, less restricting, and more beneficial for the health of the individual overall.

Sport & Fitness

As you consider getting started with the ketogenic diet and intermittent fasting, there are key factors that should be put into consideration. You should ensure that you stay within the macros for the keto diet as you also eat enough calories during the eating period. Fasting should be combined with optimal nutrition; sufficient sleep, and work with reduced stress if the desired benefits are to be realized. If you find the two to be challenging, then you can begin with the ketogenic diet and get keto-adapted before incorporating intermittent fasting.

When you are getting started, likely, the body is still dependent on the intake of high carbs and utilization of glucose so you are likely to feel hungry much faster which makes it difficult to stick with fasting. Once the body adapts to ketosis where ketones are seen as the source of energy, fasting then feels more natural and manageable. Starting the process gradually helps people to adapt well to the process, unlike jumping into change at once. You can begin the process by cutting on the regular intake of snacks, then gradually move to cut full meals.

Finding your macros is vital as you get started since you need to decide the number of calories, proteins, carbs, and fats that you should be eating each day. If your goal is to lose weight then defining your macros is a critical step. Once you have set the number of macros, you should then commit to eating the set amount of macronutrients. If you intend to lose weight, then a lot of emphases should be given to sticking with the required number of macros.

You must consume all the calories during the eating window as you also follow the approved intake of keto foods to ensure that your body stays on ketosis. There are endless options of healthy and nutritious ketogenic diet foods that you can choose from, but you have to decide to do away with high carbohydrate foods. Before the body adapts to a high-fat diet, there will be instances where you get to experience serious hunger cravings as you engage in intermittent fasting. Just ensure that you avoid any form of binging on carbs so that you don't get thrown out of ketosis.

During the feeding period, the number of meals that one gets to consume doesn't matter; all that matters is maintaining the caloric intake which should constitute the macronutrients and the calories that one gets to consume. If you want 1000 calories per day then you should ensure that you consume all the calories during the eating window. As a beginner, you can decide to maintain a wider feeding window like 8 hours within the day but that should reduce as you get acquainted with the fasting process and keto diet.

As the body gets accustomed to fasting and the keto diet, you should also be able to make the feeding window shorter for improved benefits. You can opt to skip breakfast then have some good lunch and dinner. Keep testing how short you can make the feeding window to be before your body begins to resist.

Being on the ketogenic diet and intermittent fasting puts the body into a prime primal state where one is completely self-sufficient and also capable of producing energy regardless of the time and the number of calories that one gets to consume. It's possible to fail even with the combination if you lack insight on what goes on psychologically and how you can sustain the process. When one is getting started, it's more likely that the body is not on ketosis and that's why they must take time and go through a period of keto-adaptation.

If you get started when the body is still geared towards burning sugar for fuel then it might take such a long time before you get into the ketosis state and the side effects might be very intense. Fasting on keto should follow several stages for the adaptation to take place.

The Plan to Build the Ultimate Body

The correct training, nutrition, and dedication to follow a tough training schedule designed to shock the muscles into growth can yield fantastic results. Now combine that with Intermittent Fasting and you move into a whole new world of gaining muscle and leaning up.

Do you want to move to the next level of physical performance?

1 - Training Frequency

Many people say you can only train a body part once a week. This theory is fast becoming obsolete. All we have to do is look to the past. Did you know many of the '60s and 70's bodybuilders were training the entire body 2-3 times a week? 3 times a week is extreme for a normal person who has to work and earn a living, etc. So like me, you want something high impact, time-friendly, and results-driven. The regime is spread over two weeks, training the body twice in the first week and once in the second, and repeat.

2 - Body Fat

There are several things you need to consider, to get the maximum out of your workouts. Your testosterone is utilized at its best when you have a lower body fat percentage. So this is the number one issue to deal with when beginning a new regime. A low body fat percentage gives you more utilization. This is also why the workouts are supersets. We are ramping up your intensity and effort to burn additional calories.

3 - Nutrition

Nutrition is regarded as the most crucial aspect of muscle development. You will not progress if your nutrition is incorrect, regardless of how good your training routines are. I'm sure you know something about nutrition, but I'm here to supplement your knowledge. You've heard of high-protein, high-carbohydrate, and high-healthy-fat diets, right? But what are the best foods to eat to get those vital nutrients? This equates to giving your muscles exactly what they require, implying that you will gain muscle mass. Last but not least is a high water intake. This cleans our systems, regulates body temperature, and keeps the entire body hydrated. So with heavy exercise, 3 liters a day is an ideal figure to aim for. This isn't part of intermittent fasting, you can drink as much water as you like.

Chapter 3: Breakfast Recipes

Recipe 1: <u>Almond Smoothie with Dates and Cinnamon</u>

Are you having a sweet craving but avoiding refined sugars? This almond-date smoothie is just the thing to satisfy that craving. The sweetness comes from the dates, but we slow down the blood sugar rise by combining it with the healthy fats and protein in almond butter and improve the insulin response with a generous addition of cinnamon.

Calories: 1056

Prep Time: 10 minutes

Cook Time: -

Serving Size: 1

Ingredients:

- 5 small to medium dates

- Hot water, for soaking the dates

- 1 cup unsweetened soy milk

- 1 banana

- ½ cup almond butter

- ½ teaspoon ground cinnamon, divided
- 1½ teaspoons maple syrup (optional)

Directions:

1. Place the dates in a small bowl and add enough hot water to cover. Let sit for about 3 minutes to soften. Drain. Remove and discard the pits.

2. In a blender, combine the softened dates, soy milk, banana, almond butter, and ¼ teaspoon of cinnamon. Blend until mixed. Taste and add the remaining cinnamon and maple syrup (if using).

Recipe 2:   Blackberry Cheesecake Smoothie

Blackberries might not be your first choice of berry, but perhaps that should change. Blackberries are extremely rich in fiber (about five grams in two-thirds of a cup) as well as vitamins C and K. Blackberry seeds are also a good source of protein, omega-3 fatty acids, and fiber. Because of the health benefits of the seeds and other berry components, whole berries are preferable to smooth strained purée for your recipes.

Calories: 377

Prep Time: 10 minutes

Cook Time: -

Serving Size: 2

Ingredients:

- 1 cup unsweetened almond milk
- ⅔ cup cream cheese
- ½ cup blackberries
- ½ cup shredded fresh baby spinach
- 1 scoop vanilla protein powder
- 1 tablespoon granulated erythritol

Directions:

3. Combine the almond milk, cream cheese, blackberries, spinach, protein powder, and erythritol in a blender and blend until smooth.

4. Pour the blended mixture into 2 glasses and serve immediately.

Recipe 3: <u>Breakfast Sandwich with Jalapeño Keto Mug Bread</u>

Almond flour is lower in carbohydrates and higher in fat than wheat flour and can be used in keto baking. This keto mug bread cooks in 90 seconds in the microwave and is a moist bread that resembles toast when fried. It can be flavored to complement the meal. In this recipe, we'll use jalapeño to do so.

Calories: 890

Prep Time: 10 minutes

Cook Time: 15 minutes

Serving Size: 2

Ingredients:

- 7 tablespoons butter, divided

- 3 large eggs, divided

- 5 tablespoons heavy (whipping) cream, divided

- 1 teaspoon baking powder

- ⅛ teaspoon salt

- 6 tablespoons superfine almond flour (no almond skins)

- ½ teaspoon finely diced jalapeño pepper

- 1 teaspoon finely minced fresh chives (optional)

- 2 breakfast sausage patties, cooked

Directions:

5. Put 1 tablespoon of butter in each of 2 similar-size microwave-safe mugs. Melt the butter for about 20 seconds on high power in the microwave. Swirl the mug to coat the sides with the melted butter.

6. In a small bowl, whisk 1 egg, 3 tablespoons of heavy cream, the baking powder, salt, almond flour, and jalapeño to blend. Evenly divide the batter between the buttered mugs. Microwave on high power for 90 seconds. Let sit for 1 minute. Remove the bread from the mugs and cut each "loaf" horizontally into 2 round bread disks.

7. In a skillet over medium heat, melt 2 tablespoons of butter. Add the bread disks and fry for about 2 minutes, until brown and toasty on one side. Flip the bread, add 2 tablespoons of butter to the skillet, and fry for about 2 minutes more, until brown on the other side. Remove and set aside.

8. In a small bowl, whisk the remaining 2 eggs, the remaining 2 tablespoons of heavy cream, and the chives (if using).

9. Place the skillet over medium heat with the remaining 1 tablespoon of butter. Pour the egg mixture into the pan. Cook, covered, for about 5 minutes, or until the liquid has evaporated.

10. On a platter, layer one piece of toasted keto mug bread, 1 cooked sausage, and half of the scrambled eggs. Add a second slice of toasted bread on top. Carry on with the second sandwich in the same manner.

Recipe 4:   Cheddar Ham Frittata

Tastes very good.

Calories: 226

Prep Time: 4 minutes

Cook Time: 9 minutes

Serving Size: 2

Ingredients:

- Ham, chopped – 1 2/3 cups

- Cheddar, shredded – 1 tbsp

- Spinach – about 1/6 cup or 80 g

- Chestnut mushrooms, diced – 2/3 cup

- Medium egg – 4

- Oil – 1 tsp

Directions:

11. Set the grill to the highest setting and leave it to heat up. Subsequently, in an ovenproof frying pan, heat the oil over a medium flame.

12. Fry the mushrooms in the pan for 2 minutes or until they soften. Add in the spinach and the ham and keep stirring them 1 minute longer after the spinach has wilted.

13. Spice with a pinch of salt and black pepper after the vegetables are cooked.

14. Lower the flame to pour in the beaten eggs and let them evenly spread and cook uninterrupted for 3 minutes – just enough time to let them set.

15. Put the cooked meal under the grill for 2 minutes after spritzing it with cheese. Serve it either hot or cold, your choice.

Recipe 5:   Cheesy Egg Rounds with Spicy Broccolini

These rounds are a delicious way to get a portion of low-carb veggies in. If you have a waffle iron, you can use this recipe to make chaffless (cheese waffles). Just use the same mixture to make 2 waffles instead of rounds. It will take about 3 minutes per chaff. This recipe also works with any cheese that  melts well or any vegetables that don't contain lots of moisture. The rounds are good for dipping into your favorite sauce like sweet chili, ketchup, or spicy mustard.

Calories: 549

Prep Time: 5 minutes

Cook Time: 15 minutes

Serving Size: 2

Ingredients:

- 2 large eggs

- 1 cup grated Cheddar cheese

- 2 tablespoons coconut flour

- 2 garlic cloves, crushed

- 14 stalks of Broccolini

- Salt

- Freshly ground black pepper

- 1 tablespoon unsalted butter

- 1 tablespoon extra-virgin olive oil, divided

- Juice of ½ lemon

- ½ red chile, thinly sliced

- 1 tablespoon sesame seeds

Directions:

16. Crack your eggs into a large bowl and lightly whisk. Add the cheese and coconut flour and mix well. Add the garlic and mix well.

17. Finely chop the Broccolini stems and add to the egg mixture, reserving the tops for later. Season with salt and pepper and mix well.

18. Melt the butter along with half the olive oil in a large sauté pan or skillet over medium heat

19. Place a heaping tablespoon of the egg mixture in the pan. Repeat, adding the rounds until the pan is full but the rounds are not running together. You are aiming for 6 to 8 rounds in total and will need to do these in batches. Cook each round for 2 minutes per side. Flip with a spatula and transfer to a plate when ready.

20. Prepare a steamer for the Broccolini tops or in a boiling pot. Whichever method you prefer, cook the Broccolini for 2 to 3 minutes before draining.

21. Divide the rounds between two serving plates. Add the Broccolini tops on the side and finish with a squeeze of lemon juice, slices of red chile, sesame seeds, and the remainder of the olive oil.

Recipe 6: Chicken-Avocado Omelet

Omelet-making is a valuable skill, and it pays to learn the secrets. The trick to fluffy omelets is to move the beaten eggs continually in your skillet. As the eggs firm up, use the spatula to move the uncooked eggs while continuing to swirl. Say hello to the perfect omelet.

Calories: 200

Prep Time: 15 minutes

Cook Time: 10 minutes

Serving Size: 2

Ingredients:

- 4 large eggs

- ¼ cup heavy (whipping) cream

- 2 teaspoons chopped fresh cilantro

- Pinch red pepper flakes

- 2 tablespoons extra-virgin olive oil

- ½ cup chopped cooked chicken

- 1 tomato, coarsely chopped

- 1 avocado, diced

- Sea salt

- Freshly ground black pepper

- ¼ cup crumbled feta cheese

Directions:

22. In a medium bowl, mix the following: eggs, heavy cream, cilantro, and red pepper flakes until well combined.

23. Put olive oil in a large skillet and heat over medium.

24. Pour the egg mixture into the skillet and cook until just barely set, lifting the edges with a spatula to let the uncooked egg flow underneath, about 6 minutes.

25. When the egg mixture is firm, scatter the top with the chicken, tomato, and avocado.

26. Season with salt and black pepper.

27. Fold one edge of the omelet over, cut in half, and transfer to 2 plates.

28. Serve topped with feta cheese.

Recipe 7:   Cinnamon Blueberry Pancakes

Who doesn't love a pancake? These whole-food pancakes fill that pancake-shaped void we all have from time to time, but without the harmful sugar. The key to capturing the balance right is using frozen berries, as these pack a much bigger flavor punch than fresh berries.

Calories: 428

Prep Time: 5 minutes

Cook Time: 15 minutes

Serving Size: 2

Ingredients:

- 2 large eggs
- ½ cup cream cheese
- ⅔ cup plus 1 tablespoon almond flour
- 1 teaspoon baking powder
- 1 teaspoon ground cinnamon
- 1 teaspoon honey
- 1 tablespoon water
- 1 tablespoon unsalted butter, divided
- 1 cup unsweetened frozen blueberries

Directions:

29. Except for the butter and blueberries, combine all ingredients in a blender. Blend on high for 30 seconds or until smooth, making sure the lid is secure. While you prepare the blueberry topping, let the mixture sit for a few minutes.

30. Combine the blueberries with a splash of water in a medium saucepan over medium heat. Remove from heat after bringing to a low simmer. Cook for another 2 minutes with the lid ajar. Remove from the heat and place on a cooling rack.

31. Half the butter is melted in a nonstick sauté pan or skillet over medium heat. After the butter has melted, pour 3-4 tablespoons of the pancake batter into each pancake pan. As you begin the second batch, add the remaining butter. In total, you'll be able to make about 6 pancakes.

32. After about 3 minutes of cooking, when small bubbles appear in the pancakes, flip and cook for another 2 minutes on the other side. Continue until you've used up all of the pancake batters.

33. To serve, pour the blueberry topping into a jug. Use an immersion blender before decanting if you prefer a smooth texture. With your hot pancakes, serve.

Recipe 8: Creamy Keto Broccoli Soup

Broccoli is one of the most nutritious vegetables, packed with fiber, vitamins C and K, folate, and a powerful anti-cancer compound called sulforaphane. For this creamy soup recipe, I use the entire broccoli head, not just the florets.

Calories: 549

Prep Time: 20 minutes

Cook Time: 30 minutes

Serving Size: 4

Ingredients:

- 2 tablespoons extra-virgin olive oil

- 1 small onion, finely chopped

- 2 tablespoons butter

- 2 garlic cloves, minced

- 1 head broccoli, florets finely chopped, and stems peeled and finely grated

- 2 tablespoons Bone Broth (optional)

- 4 cups no-salt-added chicken broth

- 1 tablespoon cornstarch

- ⅛ teaspoon cayenne pepper

- 2 tablespoons grated full-fat Parmesan cheese

- 2 tablespoons grainy mustard

- ½ cup heavy (whipping) cream

- 2 cups grated aged Cheddar cheese

- Salt

- **Freshly ground black pepper**

- **2 tablespoons pumpkin seeds, toasted (optional)**

Directions:

34. Heat the oil in a big pot on medium. To soften the onion, add it to the pan and cook for 5 to 8 minutes. Minimize the heat to low and then add the garlic and butter. Cook, stirring occasionally, for 2 to 3 minutes, or until the garlic is tender.

35. Cook for 3 minutes after adding the broccoli.

36. Combine the bone broth (if using), chicken broth, and cornstarch in a large mixing bowl. Raise the temperature to medium-high. The soup should be simmered for 10 minutes, or until the broccoli is soft.

37. Reduce the heat to a low setting. Combine the cayenne pepper, Parmesan cheese, mustard, heavy cream, and Cheddar cheese in a mixing bowl, and set aside to soften and melt the cheese.

38. Season to taste using salt and black pepper, if desired.

39. Serve topped with the toasted pumpkin seeds (if using).

Recipe 9:   Easy Tofu Scramble

One of the easiest recipes in this collection. It's low-fat, high in protein, and packed with great flavor. Tofu is made from soybeans, a complete protein. This scramble has 23 grams of protein per serving and both essential fatty acids — omega-6 and omega-3.

Calories: 249

Prep Time: 5 minutes

Cook Time: 10 minutes

Serving Size: 2 to 4

Ingredients:

- 1 teaspoon extra-virgin olive oil

- 1 pound firm tofu

- ⅛ teaspoon ground turmeric

- 1 tablespoon nutritional yeast flakes, plus more as needed

- ½ teaspoon salt, plus more as needed

- ⅛ teaspoon garlic powder, plus more as needed

- Freshly ground black pepper

Directions:

40. In a nonstick skillet over medium heat, heat the oil.

41. Roughly crumble the tofu with your hands (not too finely) and add it to the heated pan. Stir the tofu to coat with the oil.

42. Sprinkle in the turmeric and stir to get a consistent pale-yellow color throughout.

43. Stir in the nutritional yeast, salt, and garlic powder to incorporate. Taste and adjust the seasonings to suit. Add the pepper to taste.

44. Serve as you would scrambled eggs, with a side of salsa, sliced tomato, avocado, or toast, as desired.

Recipe 10: <u>Egg Salad</u>

You will enjoy this simple breakfast.

Calories: 331

Prep Time: 2 minutes

Cook Time: 10 minutes

Serving Size: 1

Ingredients:

- 160g trimmed French beans,

- 150g thickly sliced potatoes,

- 160g roughly chopped romaine lettuce

- 3 eggs

- 160g peas frozen

- For the dressing:

- 2 tsp. of cider vinegar

- 3 tbsp. of basil chopped

- 1 tbsp. of capers

- ½ tsp. mustard powder

- 1 tbsp. of olive oil

- 2 tbsp. of mint chopped

- 1 finely grated garlic clove

Directions:

45. Heat the potatoes for 5 minutes in a saucepan of boiling water. Insert the beans & cook for another 5 minutes, then scoop inside these peas & cook for 2 minutes before all vegetables are soft. In the meantime, cook the eggs for 8 mins in another cup. Drain and pass under the cool spray, then shell and halve carefully.

46. In a large cup, combine all the seasoning components with a strong black pepper smash, grinding the herbs & capers with a spoon back to enhance their flavors.

47. To cover, blend the warmed veggies into the seasoning, then apply the lettuce and put it all together. Place the eggs on the plates and sprinkle over some salt and pepper for serving.

Recipe 11: <u>Green Smoothie with Apple, Avocado, and Spinach</u>

This is a light but nutrient-packed smoothie, ideal for mornings on the go or to have on hand for whenever you break your fast.

Calories: 239

Prep Time: 3 minutes

Cook Time: -

Serving Size: 2

Ingredients:

- 1 small apple or pear, cored and roughly chopped
- Juice of 1 lemon or lime
- ½ avocado, peeled and pitted
- ½ small cucumber, roughly chopped
- 1 celery stalk, roughly chopped
- Handful of spinach
- Handful of ice
- Splash of water

Directions:

48. Put all ingredients in a blender.

49. Blend on full power until smooth, about 20 seconds.

50. Serve immediately.

Recipe 12: <u>Herbed Turkey Broth</u>

Sage, rosemary, and thyme are the herbs I use to make stuffing at Thanksgiving, so by using these as part of the poultry seasoning, it reminds me of eating a satisfying roast turkey meal with all the fixings! Enjoy the broth as a dirty fast, or have the soup as a low-carb dish.

Calories: 159

Prep Time: 15 minutes

Cook Time: 40 minutes

Serving Size: 4

Ingredients:

- 1 tablespoon extra-virgin olive oil
- 1 onion, diced
- 1 celery stalk, diced
- 2 carrots, diced
- 1 skin-on turkey leg (about 1 pound)
- 8 cups water, divided
- 1 teaspoon salt, plus more as needed
- 1 teaspoon dried rosemary leaves, crushed
- ½ teaspoon dried thyme
- ½ teaspoon dried sage

- Nutmeg

- Freshly ground black pepper

- Chopped fresh parsley, for garnish (optional)

Directions:

51. In a medium pot over medium-low, heat the oil. Add the onion, celery, and carrots. Increase the heat to medium and cook for about 5 minutes, stirring occasionally, or until the vegetables are softened.

52. Add the turkey leg. Cook for 3 to 5 minutes, until the vegetables and turkey stick to the pot. Pour in ¼ cup of water to deglaze the pot, stirring to scrape up any browned bits from the bottom. Turn the turkey leg a quarter turn and repeat the browning and deglazing with ¼ cup of water three more times. The turkey leg should appear browned all over.

53. Transfer the turkey leg to a cutting board and remove and discard the skin. Return the turkey leg to the pot.

54. Add the remaining 7 cups of water, increase the heat to medium-high, and bring to a boil. Reduce the heat to medium.

55. Stir in the salt, rosemary, thyme, sage, and a pinch of nutmeg. Cook for 10 minutes more, or until the turkey reaches an internal temperature of 165°F.

56. Strain the broth using a colander set over a heatproof bowl and enjoy the broth. Season with more needed salt and pepper. Top with the parsley (if using).

Recipe 13: <u>Layered Egg Bake</u>

This layered dish takes time to make, but the finished meal is worth it. To create tasty variations, mix up your vegetable choices or use ground poultry instead of beef. Just hold the quantities and bake time constant to ensure your casserole comes out correctly.

Calories: 541

Prep Time: 15 minutes

Cook Time: 50

Serving Size: 6

Ingredients:

- 3 tablespoons extra-virgin olive oil, divided, add more for greasing

- 8 ounces ground beef

- 1 cup sliced mushrooms

- ½ onion, chopped

- 2 teaspoons minced garlic

- 2 cups chopped fresh baby spinach

- 1 zucchini, chopped

- 1 red bell pepper, chopped

- 8 large eggs

- 1 cup heavy (whipping) cream

- ½ teaspoon salt

- ½ teaspoon freshly ground black pepper

- 2 cups shredded Swiss cheese

Directions:

57. Preheat the oven to 350°F. Lightly grease a 10-by-10-inch casserole dish with olive oil and set aside.

58. Heat 1 tablespoon of olive oil in a large skillet over medium-high heat.

59. Sauté the ground beef until cooked through, breaking it up, about 6 minutes.

60. Transfer the meat to the casserole dish, spreading it out evenly.

61. Place the skillet back on the heat and add 1 tablespoon of oil.

62. Sauté the mushrooms, onion, and garlic until softened, about 5 minutes. Spread the mushroom mixture over the meat.

63. Place the skillet back over the heat and add the remaining 1 tablespoon of oil. Sauté the spinach, zucchini, and bell pepper until softened, about 5 minutes, and then spread it over the mushroom mixture.

64. In a medium bowl, whisk together the eggs, heavy cream, salt, and black pepper and pour the egg mixture over the casserole ingredients. Tap the dish to disperse the mixture to the bottom.

65. Sprinkle the Swiss cheese over the eggs and bake until the eggs are cooked through and the top is golden for about 35 minutes.

Recipe 14: Lettuce Huevos Rancheros

Huevos rancheros, or "rancher's eggs," is a Mexican breakfast dish beloved by people far and wide. This variation of the spicy dish includes avocado as a pretty topping. Avocado is high in both nutrients and healthy monounsaturated fat. This monounsaturated fat, called oleic acid, helps fill you up and is a fabulous choice for a fasting diet.

Calories: 418

Prep Time: 20 minutes

Cook Time: 5 minutes

Serving Size: 4

Ingredients:

- 1 tablespoon extra-virgin olive oil
- 8 large eggs
- ½ jalapeño pepper, finely chopped
- 8 large Boston lettuce leaves
- ½ cup salsa
- ½ cup sour cream
- 1 cup shredded Cheddar cheese
- 1 avocado, diced

- 4 teaspoons chopped fresh cilantro

Directions:

66. Heat the olive oil in a large skillet over medium-high heat.

67. Add the eggs and jalapeño pepper and scramble until they form light and fluffy curds, about 4 minutes in total. Remove the skillet from the heat.

68. Arrange the lettuce leaves on a serving plate and evenly divide the eggs, salsa, sour cream, Cheddar cheese, avocado, and cilantro among the leaves. Serve.

Recipe 15: <u>Mediterranean Egg Casserole</u>

Eggs are versatile, it can be used to create savory or sweet dishes. But watch out: When eggs get overcooked, they become rubbery and unpalatable. This is because the water in the egg gets squeezed out, the yolk solidifies, and the whites become too tight. The trick is to watch your casserole and use a  thermometer (if you have one) to bake the casserole to 160°F.

Calories: 252

Prep Time: 15 minutes

Cook Time: 35 minutes

Serving Size: 6

Ingredients:

- 1 tablespoon extra-virgin olive oil, add more for greasing
- ½ onion, chopped
- 1 red bell pepper, seeded and diced
- 1 tablespoon minced garlic
- 8 large eggs
- ½ cup heavy (whipping) cream
- 1 cup halved cherry tomatoes
- ¼ cup sliced black olives

- 1 cup crumbled goat cheese

- 2 tablespoons chopped fresh basil, for garnish

Directions:

69. Preheat the oven to 375°F.

70. Lightly grease a 10-by-10-inch baking dish with olive oil and set it aside.

71. Put 1 tablespoon of olive oil in a large skillet and heat over medium-high and sauté the onion, bell pepper, and garlic until softened for about 4 minutes.

72. Transfer the vegetables to the baking dish and spread them out.

73. In a medium bowl, whisk both eggs and heavy cream until blended and pour over the vegetables in the baking dish.

74. Scatter the tomatoes, olives, and goat cheese over the top of the eggs and bake until the top is puffed and golden brown, about 30 minutes.

75. Serve topped with basil.

Recipe 16: Peanut Chicken Lettuce Wraps

This is a fun meal for entertaining. Just increase all the quantities based on the number of guests you're feeding, and rather than assemble the wraps, put the ingredients on the table and let your guests assemble their own. My kids love this meal for this reason.

Calories: 256

Prep Time: 10 minutes plus 20 minutes to marinate

Cook Time: 15 minutes

Serving Size: 2 to 4

Ingredients:

- 1 boneless, skinless chicken breast, cut into finger-length strips

- ½ cup plus 1 tablespoon peanut sauce, divided

- 8 large lettuce leaves, such as iceberg

- 1 cup enoki mushrooms (see tip)

- ½ red bell pepper, thinly sliced

- 1 (3-inch) piece cucumber, cut into slices

- ½ cup shredded carrot

- 6 to 12 cilantro sprigs

- 6 to 12 fresh mint leaves

Directions:

76. In a shallow bowl, combine the chicken and ½ cup of peanut sauce. Cover and let marinate at room temperature for 20 minutes.

77. Preheat a grill to medium heat or the oven to 350°F.

78. Remove the chicken from the marinade and place it on the grill. Cook for around 7 minutes per side, until the chicken is cooked through and the juices run clear. Alternatively, place the chicken on a baking sheet and bake for 25 to 30 minutes, until cooked through. Discard the marinade.

79. Place a lettuce leaf on a plate. Add 1 to 3 pieces of chicken, 4 to 9 mushrooms, 1 or 2 red pepper slices, 2 or 3 cucumber slices, 1 tablespoon shredded carrot, 2 or 3 cilantro sprigs, and 2 or 3 mint leaves. Roll up the lettuce leaf, folding in the ends as you roll.

80. Serve the remaining 1 tablespoon of peanut sauce in a small bowl for dipping.

Recipe 17: <u>Savory Bowl Oats</u>

A classic breakfast, nothing beats a bowl of oats! This has a savory twist on it

Calories: 460

Prep Time: 1 minute

Cook Time: 30 minutes

Serving Size: 1

Ingredients:

- 1 tsp. of salt

- 8 oz. of halved Brussels sprouts

- 16 oz. of butternut squash cubed

- 1 tbsp. of olive oil

- ½ cup of coarsely chopped onion,

- 1 tsp. black pepper

- 2 cups of oats

- 1 tbsp. of butter

- 4 eggs

- 2 cups of water

- 2 strips cooked and crumbled turkey bacon

- ½ cup of Cheddar cheese shredded Sharp

Directions:

81. Oven preheats to 400°F. Lay a broad parchment baking sheet.

82. Assemble the Brussels sprouts, butternut squash, sliced onion, olive oil, ½ teaspoon salt & ½ teaspoon black pepper in a wide cup, add to the baking sheet and move to it.

83. Bake 20 to 22 minutes, or until tender and golden brown vegetables are available.

84. The butter is melted over medium heat as the vegetable roast in a medium bath. Attach the oats, then prepare a toast for 30 seconds. Set the temperature, and get it to a simmer. Switch the heat to low and enable the oats to cook for 8 to 10 minutes until they achieve a dense consistency, adding more water as required. Stir in melted cheese, then season with salt and black pepper leftover. Keep wet.

85. Cook eggs sunny-side up or over easy in a big greased non-stick saucepan.

86. In a cup, spoon oats, cover with vegetables, an egg, then cover with crumbled bacon.

Recipe 18: Scrambled eggs with Berries

A great recipe that you can easily make.

Calories: 303

Prep Time: 5 minutes

Cook Time: 10 minutes

Serving Size: 2

Ingredients:

- Egg – 1

- Egg whites - 3

- Whole wheat toast – 2 slices

- Vegetables (any according to your taste like spinach, kale, or cherry tomatoes)

- Berries – 1 cup

- Oil (filled in a spray jar)

Directions:

87. Switch on the stove - gas or electric - and keep it maintained at a medium flame.

88. Spray just enough oil in a stainless-steel pan to cook the vegetables. Heat the oil in the pan for a few seconds before adding them.

89. Keep stirring the vegetables until they soften. Then, pour in the beaten egg and egg whites and scramble them.

90. While they are cooking, toast the 2 slices of bread.

91. Place the scrambled eggs on top of the toast and serve alongside the berries (strawberries, raspberries, and blueberries).

Recipe 19: <u>Soft-boiled Eggs with Avocado and Bacon</u>

Crispy, crunchy bacon, and fresh avocado, perfect for dipping into gooey, unctuous eggs: This is a definite breakfast treat, ideal for those days when time is on your side. For a super-speedy version, make this in advance by hard-boiling the eggs, crumbling the bacon, dousing the avocado in  lemon juice, and putting all the ingredients on a bed of baby spinach in your favorite lunch box, ready to go.

Calories: 309

Prep Time: 5 minutes

Cook Time: 20 minutes

Serving Size: 2

Ingredients:

- 6 slices of American bacon
- 4 large eggs
- 1 firm avocado
- Pinch chili powder
- Salt
- Freshly ground black pepper

Directions:

92. Preheat the oven to 375°F.

93. Lay the bacon on a grilling pan or baking sheet and cook in the oven for 15 minutes.

94. In the meantime, heat a large pot of water on the stove. When the water begins to boil, lower your eggs in gently with a spoon. Switch off the heat. For softboiled eggs, leave for 6 to 8 minutes before removing the eggs and setting them aside. For hardboiled, leave for 10 minutes.

95. Return to your bacon, turn it over, and leave for another 5 minutes or until it is golden and crispy. Remove from heat and set aside.

96. Cut the avocado in half and remove the pit. From top to bottom, segment the flesh into 4 to 6 slices per side depending on the size and firmness of your avocado. Using a spoon, remove the outer skin.

97. Divide the bacon and avocado slices onto two serving plates. Sprinkle the avocado with chili powder. Put the eggs into egg cups. Serve immediately with salt and pepper on the side.

Recipe 20: Sour Cream and Onion Egg Salad Lettuce Wraps

My favorite potato chip flavor is sour cream and onion. If you're with me on that, you'll love this recipe. This is such a flavorful, dare I say, decadent egg salad, you won't miss the bread.

Calories: 265

Prep Time: 25 minutes

Cook Time: -

Serving Size: 1

Ingredients:

- 2 large hard-boiled eggs, peeled

- 3 tablespoons full-fat sour cream

- 1 tablespoon dried onion flakes

- 2 scallions, finely diced

- Salt

- Freshly ground black pepper

- 2 to 4 large lettuce leaves

- Paprika, for seasoning (optional)

Directions:

98. In a medium bowl, smash the hard-boiled eggs with a fork until lumpy, not smooth.

99. Stir in the sour cream, onion flakes, scallions, and salt and pepper to taste. Spoon the egg salad into the lettuce leaves.

100. Garnish with the paprika (if using).

Recipe 21: <u>Spicy Sausage and Egg-Stuffed Zucchini</u>

If you wish, use tomatoes, pumpkin, squash, or bell peppers instead of zucchini as vehicles for your filling. Simply scoop out the centers, fill, and bake for the same amount of time in the same temperature oven. Pro tip: Double the filling part of the recipe to create a satisfying meal for extra-hungry guests.

Calories: 544

Prep Time: 15 minutes

Cook Time: 35 minutes

Serving Size: 4

Ingredients:

- 4 medium zucchini

- 1 tablespoon extra-virgin olive oil, divided

- 8 ounces Italian sausage (hot or mild)

- 1 scallion, white and green parts, finely chopped

- 4 large eggs

- ½ cup heavy (whipping) cream

- Sea salt

- Freshly ground black pepper

- 1 cup shredded sharp Cheddar cheese

Directions:

101. Preheat the oven to 400°F.

102. Cut a slice off each zucchini lengthwise and scoop out the insides, leaving the outside shell intact. Lightly oil a 9-by-9-inch baking dish with 1 teaspoon of olive oil and set the zucchini in the dish, hollow-side up.

103. Lightly oil the outside of the zucchini with 1 teaspoon of olive oil.

104. Place a small skillet over medium-high heat and add the remaining oil.

105. Sauté the sausage and scallion until the meat is cooked through and browned, about 6 minutes. Then fill each zucchini with equal amounts of the sausage mixture.

106. In a small bowl, whisk the eggs and heavy cream and season with salt and pepper.

107. Fill each zucchini with equal amounts of the egg mixture and top with the Cheddar cheese.

108. Bake until the eggs are firm, the zucchini is softened, and the cheese is lightly browned for about 30 minutes.

Recipe 22: <u>Super Spinach Egg Scramble</u>

This scramble is a surefire way to start the day off with lots of the good stuff. Make it your own with different spice combinations.

Calories: 234

Prep Time: 1 minute

Cook Time: 5 minutes

Serving Size: 2

Ingredients:

- 4 large eggs
- Splash of heavy cream
- 1 teaspoon extra-virgin olive oil
- 1 cup baby spinach leaves
- ¼ teaspoon smoked paprika
- 1 tablespoon finely chopped chives
- Salt
- Freshly ground black pepper

Directions:

109.　　In a medium mixing bowl, crack your eggs. Lightly whisk in the heavy cream. Remove from the equation.

110. In a nonstick sauté pan or skillet, heat the olive oil over medium heat. Combine the spinach and paprika in a mixing bowl.

111. Sauté for 2 minutes, stirring occasionally until the spinach has wilted

112. Pour the egg mixture into the pan. Stir as the mixture comes together and the eggs look cooked. You are aiming for a rough rather than a fine scramble. This should take about 1 minute.

113. Remove from the heat and divide eggs between two serving plates.

114. Sprinkle the chives over the scramble and season with salt and pepper, to taste. Serve and eat immediately while hot.

Recipe 23: Vegan Bulletproof Coffee Latte

Bulletproof Coffee was invented by Dave Asprey, the founder of Bulletproof. Feel free, however, to use non-Bulletproof ingredients. Vegan Bulletproof Coffee Latte is less thick than the original (no butter!) but still contains MCT oil, or medium-chain triglycerides. This easily metabolized fat is thought to help burn fat, promote mental clarity, and curb sugar cravings.

Calories: 278

Prep Time: 5 minutes

Cook Time: -

Serving Size: 1

Ingredients:

- 1½ cups hot brewed coffee

- ½ cup unsweetened almond milk

- 2 tablespoons MCT oil

- ¼ teaspoon vanilla extract

Directions:

115.   Combine the coffee, almond milk, MCT oil, and vanilla in a blender and blend until smooth and creamy. Serve immediately.

Recipe 24: Watermelon Pink Smoothie

The watermelon flavor that you will surely love in the morning.

Calories: 143

Prep Time: 5 minutes

Blending Time: 5 minutes

Serving Size: 4

Ingredients:

- Seedless watermelon, cut into cubes – 8 cups

- 2% Reduced-fat plain Greek yogurt – 4/3 cup

- Mint, chopped – 8 tbsp

Directions:

116.   Firstly, blend the watermelon chunks with the yogurt.

117.   Add the mint and mix until the smoothie is creamy and smooth.

Recipe 25: Zucchini Chocolate Bread

Let's be honest. This chocolatey bread is pretty much a dessert for breakfast. When eating one meal a day, you might combine a couple of slices of this bread with an omelet or frittata to reach 900 to 1,000 calories. This recipe uses zucchini, which can aid the digestive process following a fast.

Calories: 286

Prep Time: 15 minutes

Cook Time: 1 hour

Serving Size: 8

Ingredients:

- ½ cup coconut oil, melted, plus more for greasing the loaf pan
- 1 cup almond flour
- 1 cup granulated erythritol
- ½ cup coconut flour
- ¼ cup cocoa powder
- 1½ teaspoons baking powder
- 1 teaspoon ground cinnamon
- ½ teaspoon baking soda
- ¼ teaspoon salt

- 4 large eggs

- 2 teaspoons vanilla extract

- 2 cups finely grated zucchini

Directions:

118.   Preheat the oven to 350°F.

119.   Lightly grease a 9-by-4-inch loaf pan with coconut oil and set aside.

120.   In a large bowl, stir together the almond flour, erythritol, coconut flour, cocoa powder, baking powder, cinnamon, baking soda, and salt until well blended.

121.   In a medium bowl, whisk the following: eggs, coconut oil, and vanilla until mixed.

122.   Add the wet to the dry ingredients then stir until just combined.

123.   Stir in the zucchini.

124.   Spoon the batter into the prepared loaf pan and bake until a knife inserted in the center comes out clean, about 1 hour.

125.   Let the bread cool completely.

126.   Store wrapped in the refrigerator for up to 4 days or in the freezer for up to 1 month.

Chapter 4: Lunch Recipes

Recipe 26: <u>Arugula Salad with Tuna</u>

Peppery arugula pairs well
with the tuna and lemon
dressing in this recipe, and
olives and capers add a nice
saltiness. If you normally eat
the entire can of tuna yourself,
then consider this a "serves
one" recipe.

Calories: 386

Prep Time: 15 minutes

Cook Time: -

Serving Size: 1 or 2

Ingredients:

- 2 cups baby arugula leaves

- 1 (5-ounce) can water-packed tuna, drained

- 1 tomato, diced

- 1 cup diced cucumber

- 20 pitted black olives

- 2 teaspoons capers, drained

- 2 tablespoons freshly squeezed lemon juice

- 1 tablespoon extra-virgin olive oil

- ½ teaspoon dried oregano

- Salt

- Freshly ground black pepper

Directions:

128.   Place 1 cup of arugula leaves in each of two serving bowls.

129.   Place ½ can of tuna on the arugula in each bowl. Evenly divide the tomato, cucumber, olives, and capers between the bowls.

130.   In a small bowl, whisk the following: lemon juice, oil, oregano, and salt and pepper to taste to blend. Drizzle the dressing over each salad.

Recipe 27: Bacon and Egg Salad

Bacon and eggs are a staple keto meal. If you add a bacon fat-based dressing, cheese, and crisp romaine, you have a culinary sensation. To avoid overcooking the hardboiled eggs, start them in a pot of cold water (about 1 inch above the eggs), bring the water to a boil, remove the  pot from the heat, and let the eggs stand, covered, for 12 minutes. Cool them in cold running water and store them in the refrigerator until needed.

Calories: 297

Prep Time: 20 minutes

Cook Time: -

Serving Size: 6

Ingredients:

- 4 tablespoons melted bacon fat or extra-virgin olive oil

- 2 tablespoons apple cider vinegar

- Freshly ground black pepper

- 8 cups chopped romaine lettuce

- 8 cooked bacon slices, chopped

- ¼ cup grated Parmesan cheese

- 4 large hardboiled eggs, chopped

Directions:

131. In a large bowl, whisk the bacon fat and apple cider vinegar until emulsified. Season with pepper.

132. Add the lettuce, bacon, and Parmesan cheese to the bowl and toss to coat.

133. Top with the hardboiled eggs and serve. Transfer pâté into a small bowl and the crudités onto a plate.

134. Serve immediately.

Recipe 28: <u>Bacon Cheeseburger Soup</u>

Dill pickle in your soup? Yes, the briny flavor complements the bacon, Cheddar, and beef broth in this recipe. Feel free also to add mustard. This tastes great the next day, too.

Calories: 536

Prep Time: 15 minutes

Cook Time: 35 minutes

Serving Size: 6

Ingredients:

- 3 tablespoons extra-virgin olive oil, divided

- 8 ounces ground beef

- 1 onion, chopped

- 2 celery stalks, chopped

- 1 carrot, shredded

- 1 tablespoon minced garlic

- 4 cups low-sodium beef broth

- 1 (15-ounce) can of low-sodium diced tomatoes

- 1 cup heavy (whipping) cream

- 1 cup shredded sharp Cheddar cheese

- 8 cooked bacon slices, chopped

- 2 tablespoons chopped dill pickles, for garnish

- 2 tablespoons chopped fresh parsley, for garnish

Directions:

135.   Heat 2 tablespoons of olive oil in a large stockpot over medium-high heat.

136.   Sauté the ground beef until browned and cooked through about 6 minutes. With a slotted spoon, remove to a plate.

137.   Add the remaining 1 tablespoon of oil and sauté the onion, celery, carrot, and garlic until softened for about 6 minutes.

138.   Stir in the beef broth, tomatoes, and reserved beef and bring the soup to a boil.

139.   Reduce the heat to low and simmer until the vegetables are tender, about 15 minutes.

140.   Add the heavy cream, Cheddar cheese, and bacon and stir until the cheese is melted for about 3 minutes.

141.   Serve topped with the chopped pickle and parsley.

Recipe 29: Caprese Salad with Avocado

This pretty red-white-and-green salad works just as well for a fancy lunch as a speedy lunch box. Spend time on the plating for something a bit more sophisticated, or just throw it into a bowl and lightly toss for a quicker version. For an extra Mediterranean hit, throw in a few black or green olives.

Calories: 525

Prep Time: 5 minutes

Cook Time: -

Serving Size: 2

Ingredients:

- 1 full-fat mozzarella cheese ball (4 to 5 ounces)

- 2 or 3 large tomatoes

- 1 large avocado

- ½ cup stemmed fresh basil

- 1 cup arugula

- 3 tablespoons extra-virgin olive oil

- 1 tablespoon balsamic vinegar

- Salt

- Freshly ground black pepper

Directions:

142.   Cut the mozzarella and tomatoes into ¼-inch slices.

143.   Cut the avocado in half, remove the pit, cut into ¼-inch-thick slices and scoop them out with a spoon.

144.   Place a slice of tomato and a basil leaf on a plate, then overlap them with a slice of mozzarella and a slice of avocado. Repeat until all the ingredients have been plated.

145.   Add the arugula to a pile in the center of the plate.

146.   Drizzle with olive oil and balsamic vinegar and season with salt and pepper to taste. Serve immediately or cover and place in the refrigerator for up to 24 hours.

Recipe 30: <u>Cheesy Tuna Sandwich</u>

Enjoy munching on the cheesy goodness of this tuna recipe.

Calorie: 198

Prep Time: 5 minutes

Cook Time: 10 minutes

Serving Size: 4

Ingredients:

- Toasted whole wheat bread – 4 slices
- Light tuna chunks, fresh preferred – 2-5 ounces
- Low-fat mayonnaise – 2 tbsp
- Flat-leaf parsley, chopped – 1 tbsp
- Minced shallots, medium size – 2 tbsp
- Lemon juice – 1 tbsp
- Cheddar cheese, grated – ½ cup
- Hot sauce – a dash
- Tomatoes, sliced – 2
- Salt – 1/8 tsp
- Grounded pepper – to taste

Directions:

147.   Let the broiler preheat while you prepare everything.

148.   In a medium bowl, mix the shallots, tuna, mayonnaise, lemon juice, parsley, pepper, and hot sauce.

149.   On one side of each of the 4 toasts, spread ¼ cup of the mayonnaise tuna spread. Top them with slices of tomato and 2 tbsp of shredded cheese.

150.   Line a baking tray with foil and broil the sandwiches for 3 to 5 minutes - just until the cheese turns golden and then serve.

Recipe 31: Chicken Chow Mein

This chow mein is missing the base noodles but is nonetheless close to the classic dish. If you want to add noodles, toss in konjac noodles along with the sauce. This extra ingredient doesn't change the macros much, only adding about 25 calories per portion.

Calories: 406

Prep Time: 20 minutes

Cook Time: 25 minutes

Serving Size: 4

Ingredients:

FOR THE SAUCE

- ½ cup low-sodium chicken broth

- 2 tablespoons coconut amino

- 2 tablespoons rice vinegar

- 1 tablespoon fish sauce

- 1 tablespoon granulated erythritol

- 1 tablespoon coconut oil

- 1 tablespoon almond flour

FOR THE CHOW MEIN

- 3 tablespoons extra-virgin olive oil

- 12 ounces boneless, skinless chicken breast, diced

- 1 tablespoon sesame oil

- 1 teaspoon minced garlic

- 2 cups shredded Napa cabbage

- 2 cups bean sprouts

- 1 carrot, shredded

- 1 cup snow peas, stringed and julienned

- 2 scallions, green parts only, chopped

Directions:

TO MAKE THE SAUCE

151.   Stir the chicken broth, coconut amino, rice vinegar, fish sauce, erythritol, coconut oil, and almond flour together in a small bowl until well combined. Remove from the equation.

TO MAKE THE CHOW MEIN

152.   In a large skillet, put the olive oil and heat over medium-high.

153.   Sauté the chicken for about 8 minutes, or until it is just cooked through. Remove the chicken to a platter with a slotted spoon and set aside.

154.   Add the sesame oil to the skillet and sauté the garlic until softened for about 2 minutes.

155.   Stir in the cabbage, bean sprouts, and carrot, and sauté until tender-crisp, about 6 minutes.

156.   Sauté for 4 minutes after adding the snow peas and scallions.

157.   Move the vegetables to one side of the skillet; then pour the sauce on the other side and cook until it thickens, about 2 minutes.

158.   Return the chicken to the skillet and toss everything together. Serve.

Recipe 32: <u>Chicken Jalfrezi</u>

A great recipe that you can add to your list.

Calories: 252

Prep Time: 20 minutes

Cook Time: 20 minutes

Serving Size: 1

Ingredients:

For the sauce

- 1 tsp. of turmeric
- 1 tbsp. of coriander ground
- 1 finely chopped green chili
- ½ roughly chopped large onion
- Vegetable oil
- 1 tbsp. of cumin ground
- 400g of can tomatoes
- 2 chopped garlic cloves,

For the meat & veg

- 2 finely chopped red chilies
- ½ large sliced onion,
- 2-3 diced chicken breasts,
- 1 tsp. of coriander ground
- Chopped fresh handful coriander leaves

- 1 tsp. of turmeric

- 1 tsp. of cumin ground

- 1 chopped red pepper,

- Naan bread/basmati rice to serve

- 2 tsp. of garam masala

Directions:

159.   Take 2-3 sliced chicken pieces & cover in 1 tsp. of cumin, 1 tsp. of coriander, & 1 tsp. of turmeric, then put in the fridge to marinate before preparing the sauce.

160.   In a big skillet with just a little veg oil, fry 1/2 loosely cut up large onion, 2 minced garlic cloves as well as 1 finely minced green chili for around 5 minutes until golden brown.

161.   Add the onion mix with 300ml of water and boil for about 20 minutes.

162.   In the meantime, place in a blender the 400g jar plum tomatoes & make a quick beat (strive for a nice accuracy).

163.   Steam another big saucepan and cook for around a minute 1 tbsp. of coriander, 1 tbsp. of cumin & 1 tsp. of turmeric in the dash of oil. In this sauce, add the tomatoes and cook for about 10 minutes.

164.   Then, beat the blender with the onion mix & put it in the spicy tomato sauce. Season thoroughly, whisk, boil for 20 minutes, and then simmer. You should produce and preserve large amounts of this sauce for later usage.

165. In vegetable oil, fry the marinated meat, and mix continuously. Switch the fire down after several minutes, then incorporate the remaining 1/2 chopped onion, 1 cut red pepper & 2 finely minced red chilies. Remove until pepper and onions weaken.

166. Put in the cooked meat the sauce you made earlier, and boil for about 10-20 mins, adding a dash of liquid if it becomes too thick.

167. Whisk together 2 tsp. of garam masala & handfuls of minced coriander leaves right before you serve it out. Serve with rice basmati or bread naan.

Recipe 33: Coconut Noodle Crab Salad

Festive zucchini noodles, bright carrot, and red pepper, and deep green cilantro dance in a creamy citrus-infused sauce in this visually stunning salad. Cilantro has a pungent, assertive flavor and adds vitamins A, C, and K as well as potassium, calcium, iron, and manganese to the dish.

Calories: 314

Prep Time: 30 minutes

Cook Time: -

Serving Size: 4

Ingredients:

FOR THE DRESSING

- ½ cup coconut milk

- 2 tablespoons coconut oil

- Juice and zest of 1 lime

- 1 tablespoon erythritol

- 1 teaspoon coconut amino

- ½ teaspoon minced garlic

- ½ teaspoon grated fresh ginger

FOR THE NOODLES

- 4 cups spiralized zucchini

- 1 red bell pepper, julienned

- 1 carrot, shredded

- 1 jalapeño pepper, seeded and minced

- 2, thinly sliced, scallions of white and green parts,

- 8 ounces crabmeat

- ½ cup shredded unsweetened coconut

- 2 tablespoons chopped fresh cilantro, for garnish

Directions:

TO MAKE THE DRESSING

168.   In a small bowl, whisk together the coconut milk, coconut oil, lime juice and zest, erythritol, coconut amino, garlic, and ginger until well blended. Set aside.

TO MAKE THE NOODLES

169.   In a large bowl, **put** the zucchini, bell pepper, carrot, jalapeño, and scallions until well mixed.

170.   Add the dressing and toss to coat.

171.   Arrange the salad on 4 plates and evenly divide the crab and shredded coconut among them.

172.   Serve topped with cilantro.

Recipe 34: <u>Fish Avocado Tacos</u>

Fish tacos are hot these days. Why? Because they're delicious! Cumin is the most prominent flavor in this recipe and its peppery flavor pairs well with the salmon. Cumin is high in iron and also contains calcium, manganese, and magnesium—key minerals for supporting bone health.

Calories: 498

Prep Time: 20 minutes

Cook Time: 15 minutes

Serving Size: 4

Ingredients:

- 4 (4-ounce) salmon fillets

- 1 teaspoon ground cumin

- ⅛ teaspoon cayenne pepper

- Sea salt

- 2 tablespoons extra-virgin olive oil

- ½ cup avocado oil mayonnaise

- ¼ cup sour cream

- 1 teaspoon sriracha sauce

- Juice of 1 lime

- 1 cup shredded cabbage

- 1 carrot, shredded

- 1 cup shredded celery root

- 4 large lettuce leaves

- 1 avocado, diced

- 1 tablespoon finely chopped fresh cilantro

Directions:

173.   Preheat the oven to 350°F.

174.   Pat the salmon fillets dry with paper towels and place them in a single layer in a 9-by-9-inch baking dish.

175.   Season the fish lightly with cumin, cayenne, and salt.

176.   Drizzle the fish with the olive oil and bake until just cooked through 12 to 15 minutes.

177.   While the fish is baking, stir together the mayonnaise, sour cream, sriracha sauce, and lime juice in a medium bowl until well blended.

178.   Stir in the cabbage, carrot, and celery root until mixed.

179.   When the fish is cooked, arrange the lettuce leaves on your work surface and place a fish fillet in the center of each.

180.   Top with the slaw, avocado, and cilantro and serve.

Recipe 35: Fish Curry with Cauliflower Rice

I used to reserve ordering curry for when I visited restaurants because I thought it was too difficult to make at home. But this recipe couldn't be easier and more delicious, thanks to that little bottle of green curry paste. This is a restaurant-quality meal that you can easily make at home.

Calories: 320

Prep Time: 20 minutes

Cook Time: 15 minutes

Serving Size: 4

Ingredients:

- 12 ounces white fish, such as bass, halibut, or sole

- Salt

- Freshly ground black pepper

- 1 (14-ounce) can of full-fat coconut milk

- 2 tablespoons green Thai curry paste

- (optional) 2 tablespoons chopped fresh cilantro, add more for garnish

- 1 small head cauliflower, washed, leaves removed, head broken into florets

- 4 tablespoons butter

Directions:

181.   Preheat the oven to 375°F.

182.   Season the fish with salt and pepper and place it in a baking dish.

183.   In a small bowl, whisk together the following: coconut milk, curry paste, and cilantro to blend. Pour the liquid over the fish.

184.   Bake for around 20 minutes, or until the fish flakes easily with a fork.

185.   While the fish bakes, in a food processor, process the cauliflower just until it's the size of rice.

186.   In a large pan over medium heat, melt the butter. Add the cauliflower, cover the pan, and cook for 5 to 8 minutes, or until your desired doneness. Taste and season with salt, as desired.

187.   Serve the in shallow bowls and top with the fish and curry sauce. Garnish with fresh cilantro (if using).

Recipe 36: <u>Fluffy Parmesan Omelet</u>

This recipe takes your eggs from fine to the divine. The soft fluffy omelet center contrasts beautifully with the crisp outer layer, and it makes a perfect lunch for one. The fresher the eggs, the fluffier the finish. Choose this recipe on days when you can take the time to sit at a table and savor the result.

Calories: 516

Prep Time: 5 minutes

Cook Time: 10 minutes

Serving Size: 1

Ingredients:

- 3 large eggs, separate yolk, and white

- 3 tablespoons unsalted butter, divided

- Salt

- Freshly ground black pepper

- Freshly grated Parmesan cheese, for garnish

Directions:

188.　　Put the egg whites in a large bowl then whisk until fluffy with stiff peaks. In a separate bowl, whisk the egg yolks until combined. Tip egg yolks into egg whites and gently fold them together with a metal spoon.

189.　　Melt 1 tablespoon of butter in a sauté pan or skillet over medium-low heat. When the butter starts bubbling, pour the egg mixture into the pan. Cook for around 5 minutes until the bottom is a pale brown and the sides start to pull away from the pan.

190.　　Divide the remaining 2 tablespoons of butter in half, and using a spatula, gently lift one side of the omelet and drop the butter into the pan underneath the omelet. Repeat on the other side. Cover the pan and leave for 3 to 4 minutes or until the top of the omelet looks set.

191.　　While it is still in the pan, fold the omelet in half. Season with salt and pepper and sprinkle some Parmesan over to taste.

192.　　Tip onto a plate and serve hot. Simmer the soup for about 7 minutes after adding them so that the corn and the noodles are cooked. Serve into bowls, garnish with parsley and mint.

Recipe 37: <u>Greek Village Salad</u>

This is my favorite salad recipe, and the not-so-secret ingredient is white wine vinegar, not balsamic. Trust me on this one. My second secret is thinly sliced red onion. I've perfected this to get a paper-thin slice — that way, the onion doesn't overpower the other flavors in the salad.

Calories: 207

Prep Time: 15 minutes

Cook Time: -

Serving Size: 2

Ingredients:

- 2 tomatoes, cut into large cubes

- 2 mini cucumbers, cut into slices

- 10 paper-thin slices of red onion

- 2 ounces Greek feta cheese

- 2 tablespoons black Kalamata olives, pitted

- 1 tablespoon extra-virgin olive oil

- 1 tablespoon white wine vinegar

- ¼ teaspoon dried oregano

- ¼ teaspoon dried basil, or 1 tablespoon finely minced fresh basil leaves

- Salt

- Freshly ground black pepper

Directions:

193.   In a medium bowl, combine the tomatoes, cucumbers, and red onion. Top with the feta cheese and olives.

194.   In a small bowl, whisk together the oil, vinegar, oregano, basil, and salt and pepper to taste to blend. Pour the dressing and gently toss to coat.

195.   If you are eating carbs, enjoy this salad with a slice of crusty bread to soak up the dressing.

Recipe 38: <u>Kale and Chard Shakshuka</u>

It's made of inexpensive ingredients such as tomatoes, eggs, greens, herbs, and cheeses. Tomatoes are the base of most shakshuka, including this recipe. Tomatoes contain lycopene, a potent antioxidant that may support heart health. And get this: When you cook tomatoes, you increase the lycopene content!

Calories: 407

Prep Time: 15 minutes

Cook Time: 20 minutes

Serving Size: 4

Ingredients:

- ¼ cup extra-virgin olive oil

- ½ onion, diced

- 1 tablespoon minced garlic

- 4 cups chopped kale

- 4 cups chopped Swiss chard

- ½ cup chopped fresh parsley

- 1 (15-ounce) can of low-sodium diced tomatoes

- Juice from 1 lemon

- 1 teaspoon ground cumin
- ½ teaspoon red pepper flakes
- 8 large eggs
- 1 cup shredded Parmesan cheese

Directions:

196.   Heat the olive oil in a large skillet over medium-high heat.

197.   Sauté the onion and garlic until softened, about 3 minutes.

198.   Stir in the kale, Swiss chard, and parsley and sauté until the greens are wilted for about 8 minutes.

199.   Stir in the tomatoes, lemon juice, cumin, and red pepper flakes, and bring the mixture to a simmer.

200.   Use the back of a spoon to make 8 wells in the tomato mixture, and then crack an egg into each well. Cover the skillet with a lid and let cook until the egg whites are no longer translucent, 4 to 5 minutes.

201.   Remove from the heat and serve topped with the Parmesan cheese.

Recipe 39: <u>Keto Meatballs with Zucchini Pasta in Tomato Cream Sauce</u>

This recipe was a real meal changer for us. We all love these decadent meatballs and tomato cream sauce, and we are now devoted zucchini pasta lovers. This recipe might just change your life, too!

Calories: 649

Prep Time: 60 minutes

Cook Time: 15 minutes

Serving Size: 4

Ingredients:

For the meatballs

- 8 ounces ground beef

- 2 bacon slices, cut into small pieces

- 1 large egg

- ¼ cup full-fat grated mozzarella cheese

- ½ small onion, finely diced

- 2 garlic cloves, minced

- 1 tablespoon minced fresh parsley

- 1 tablespoon grated full-fat Parmesan cheese

- 1 teaspoon dried basil

- 1 teaspoon dried oregano
- ½ teaspoon freshly ground black pepper
- 2 tablespoons extra-virgin olive oil

For the sauce

- 1 tablespoon extra-virgin olive oil
- ½ onion, finely diced
- 2 garlic cloves, minced
- 1 cup canned diced tomatoes, with juices
- 2 tablespoons basil pesto
- 1 tablespoon Parmesan cheese, plus more for garnish
- 1 cup heavy (whipping) cream
- ⅛ teaspoon salt
- Fresh parsley, for garnish (optional)
- Red pepper flakes, for seasoning (optional)

For the zucchini pasta

- 2 zucchini, ends removed
- 2 tablespoons extra-virgin olive oil

Directions:

To make the meatballs

202.　　In a large bowl, mix the ground beef, bacon, egg, mozzarella cheese, onion, garlic, parsley, Parmesan cheese, basil, oregano, and pepper. Form the meat mixture into 8 meatballs.

203.   In a large skillet over medium-high heat, heat the oil. Add the meatballs. Cook for 4 minutes per side.

To make the sauce

204.   In a medium pot over medium heat, heat the oil. Add the onion and sauté for 3 to 4 minutes, until soft. Reduce the heat and add the garlic. Cook for 2 to 3 minutes, stirring frequently.

205.   Add the tomatoes and their juices. Use an immersion blender to puree the tomatoes, leaving some texture, if you prefer. Increase the heat and bring the mixture to a simmer. Cook for about 2 minutes.

206.   Stir in the pesto, Parmesan cheese, heavy cream, and salt to combine. Reduce the heat to keep warm.

To make the pasta

207.   Using a vegetable peeler, peel thick strips off the zucchini, including the skin. Continue until you can no longer peel, then cut the remaining core into thin strips. If you have a spiralizer, spiralize the zucchini into noodles.

208.   In a large skillet over medium heat, heat the oil. Add the zucchini and pan-fry for about 5 minutes, until soft.

209.   Serve the zucchini and meatballs on the plate and top with the tomato cream sauce. Sprinkle with fresh parsley (if using), red pepper flakes (if using), and Parmesan cheese.

Recipe 40: <u>Lamb Scouse</u>

A nice meal that you would want.

Calories: 564

Prep Time: 10 minutes

Cook Time: 2 hours

Serving Size: 1

Ingredients:

- 250ml of chicken stock

- 1 tbsp. of plain flour

- 500g of chunked potatoes

- 350g of chunked turnip

- 1 large chopped onion,

- 500g of neck fillet of lamb

- 4 chunked carrots

- 2 sprigs of thyme

- 250ml of bitter ale

- 3 tbsp. of vegetable oil

- 2 of bay leaves

- Cooked beetroot or red cabbage pickled to serve

- 2 cubes beef stock

Directions:

210.   Put the bits of the lamb into flour, and season properly.

211.   Heat 1 tbsp. of oil over high heat in a big, heatproof casserole pan. Working in lots, golden the meat on all parts, put more oil if appropriate, then put away on a large plate.

212.   Switch the heat to normal and dump in 2 tbsp. of oil, tip the turnips, carrots, & onion, add a little salt & simmer until soft & darkened for 8 minutes.

213.   Return meat & the stock, ale & herbs to the oven. Crumble in the cubes of supply & season properly.

214.   Place the potatoes over top of the stew, get to boil, then decrease the heat to simmer. Cook till the meat is soft & the potatoes soft for 2 hrs.

215.   Serve with beetroot or pickled cabbage, if you prefer.

Recipe 41: <u>Lemony Chicken Soup</u>

This recipe is versatile—strain it and enjoy the broth as part of your dirty fast, or leave the vegetables and cube the chicken for a low-carb meal (see tip). It's satisfying and flavorful and comes together quickly.

Calories: 166

Prep Time: 10 minutes

Cook Time: 35 minutes

Serving Size: 4

Ingredients:

- 1 tablespoon extra-virgin olive oil
- 1 onion, diced
- 2 carrots, diced
- 1 celery stalk, halved lengthwise and diced
- 2 garlic cloves, minced
- 3 skin-on chicken legs
- 4 cups chicken broth or water, add more if needed
- ½ teaspoon dried thyme
- Juice of 1 lemon, plus more as needed
- ½ teaspoon salt
- Freshly ground black pepper

Directions:

216.   In a large pot over medium heat, heat the oil. Add the onion and then cook for 3 to 4 minutes, stirring, until softened.

217.   Add the carrots, celery, and garlic. Cook for around 6 to 8 minutes while stirring occasionally, until the vegetables are soft and caramelized.

218.   Add the chicken legs. Cook the chicken for 3 to 5 minutes, until browned and they stick to the pot. Turn the chicken a quarter turn and pour in ¼ cup of chicken broth to deglaze the pot, stirring to scrape up any browned bits from the bottom. Continue to brown the chicken and deglaze the pot with ¼ cup of broth at each turn, until the chicken is browned all over.

219.   Add the remaining 3 cups of broth, increase the heat to medium-high and bring to a boil. Cook the chicken for 10 to 15 minutes more, until the chicken is cooked through. Add more broth if the soup starts getting too thick.

220.   Stir in the thyme and lemon juice. Taste and add more lemon juice if desired, and the salt and pepper to taste.

Recipe 42: <u>Lemony Mackerel Pâté with Crudités</u>

This is a crunchy and satisfying lunch you can eat one-handed, ideal for multitasking days. It's easy to make ahead of time so you can grab and go. It also makes a great sharing starter or canapé for days or nights when you are entertaining.

Calories: 513

Prep Time: 10 minutes

Cook Time: -

Serving Size: 1

Ingredients:

- 4 ounces smoked mackerel fillets
- ½ cup plain full-fat cream cheese
- Zest of 1 lemon
- Juice of ½ lemon
- A handful of fresh parsley
- Pinch nutmeg
- Salt
- Freshly ground black pepper
- 5 small celery sticks
- 2 carrots

- 1 red bell pepper

Directions:

221.   For the pâté, remove the skin of the mackerel fillets and discard. Flake the fish into a medium bowl.

222.   Add cream cheese, lemon zest, lemon juice, parsley, and nutmeg. Stir and gently mash with a fork to combine. You are looking for a rough texture rather than a completely smooth one. Season with salt and pepper.

223.   For the crudités, slice the celery, carrots, and bell pepper into batons roughly ½ inch thick and 4 inches long.

224.   Transfer pâté into a small bowl and the crudités onto a plate.

225.   Serve immediately.

Recipe 43: <u>Loaded Cauliflower Soup</u>

This loaded soup is . . . well . . . loaded with vegetables, cream, bacon, and cheese. Every spoonful is filled with flavor. Instead of leaving the cauliflower florets whole, you can also purée the soup in a food processor or blender before adding the cream. If you like crispy bacon, don't add it directly to the soup, but  instead use it as a topping along with the cheese and scallions.

Calories: 429

Prep Time: 15 minutes

Cook Time: 25 minutes

Serving Size: 6

Ingredients:

- 3 tablespoons extra-virgin olive oil

- 1 onion, chopped

- 2 teaspoons minced garlic

- 6 cups chopped cauliflower

- 6 cups low-sodium chicken broth

- 2 cups heavy (whipping) cream

- 1 cup cooked chopped bacon

- 1 teaspoon ground nutmeg

- Sea salt

- Freshly ground black pepper

- 1 cup shredded Cheddar cheese

- 1 scallion, white and green parts, chopped

Directions:

226.   Heat the olive oil in a large stockpot over medium-high heat.

227.   Sauté the onion and garlic until softened, about 3 minutes.

228.   Add the cauliflower and chicken broth to the stockpot.

229.   Bring the soup to a boil, then reduce the heat to low and simmer until the vegetables are tender, about 20 minutes.

230.   Stir in the heavy cream, bacon, and nutmeg.

231.   Season with salt and pepper and serve topped with the Cheddar cheese and scallions.

Recipe 44: <u>Low-Carb Buffalo Chicken Casserole</u>

I love the flavor of buffalo chicken wings but hate the mess. This recipe will remind you of the flavor of buffalo wings, but it uses two parts cauliflower for everyone part chicken.

Calories: 325

Prep Time: 15 minutes

Cook Time: 25 minutes

Serving Size: 4

Ingredients:

- ½ cup cream cheese, at room temperature
- ⅓ cup chopped scallions
- ¼ cup buffalo wing sauce
- ¼ cup blue cheese salad dressing
- 4 cups grated cauliflower
- 2 cups cubed cooked chicken
- ½ cup grated Emmental cheese or cheese of choice
- Paprika, for seasoning

Directions:

232.   Preheat the oven to 400°F.

233.   In a medium bowl, stir together the cream cheese, scallions, buffalo wing sauce, and blue cheese dressing.

234.   Add the grated cauliflower and cooked chicken and toss to combine and coat. Pour the mixture into a 9-by-11-inch casserole dish. Sprinkle with the Emmental cheese.

235.   Bake for 25 minutes, until hot and bubbly. Sprinkle with the paprika before serving.

Recipe 45: Quick Lentil Curry with Sweet Potatoes

I love how quickly this recipe comes together and that it has so many great things going for it. Sweet potatoes and carrots are high in beta-carotene, and lentils are a good vegetarian protein source. The spices in the curry paste (I use Patak's brand Madras flavor) also add to the health benefits of this dish. If
the curry is too spicy for you, use a generous amount of yogurt to help cool the heat.

Calories: 177

Prep Time: 15 minutes

Cook Time: 30 minutes

Serving Size: 6

Ingredients:

- 1 cup lentils, rinsed

- 1 tablespoon extra-virgin olive oil

- 1 small yellow onion, chopped

- 1 carrot, chopped

- 1 garlic clove, minced

- 1 tablespoon curry paste

- 4 cups vegetable broth

- 1 sweet potato, peeled and chopped

- ½ cup unsweetened plain yogurt (optional)

- 1 tablespoon chopped fresh cilantro (optional)

Directions:

236.   Combine the lentils in a medium mixing basin with enough water to cover them by 2 inches or more. Allow soaking until required.

237.   Heat the oil in a big pot over medium Cook, stirring occasionally, for 4 to 6 minutes, until the onion and carrot are softened.

238.   Reduce the fire to low and add the garlic. Cook, stirring occasionally, for about 3 minutes, or until soft. Add the curry paste and mix well.

239.   Add the vegetable broth and sweet potato, increase the heat to high and bring the mixture to a boil. Reduce the heat to a simmer and cook for about 10 minutes, or until the sweet potato is soft enough to puree with an immersion blender.

240.   Using an immersion blender, puree half to three-fourths of the sweet potato to create a creamy consistency.

241.   Drain the soaking lentils and add them to the pot. Cook for about 10 minutes, until soft.

242.   Serve topped with yogurt (if using) and cilantro (if using).

Recipe 46: Quinoa Salad with Honey-Spiced Pecans and Roasted Beets

Filling and comforting, this wholesome salad soothes the soul with earthy flavors and warming spices. The caramelized pecans add a surprising texture, giving this dish some real personality. A cup of herbal tea with cinnamon, ginger, or cacao would make an ideal drink for afterward.

Calories: 713

Prep Time: 10 minutes

Cook Time: 25 minutes

Serving Size: 2

Ingredients:

- 1 cup chopped raw beets
- 3 tablespoons extra-virgin olive oil, divided
- Salt
- Freshly ground black pepper
- ⅔ cup dried quinoa
- 1 teaspoon cumin
- 1 tablespoon unsalted butter
- 1 tablespoon honey

- ½ teaspoon cayenne pepper

- 2 ounces whole pecans

- Juice of ½ lemon

- Handful finely chopped fresh **parsley**

Directions:

243.   Preheat the oven to 350°F.

244.   Place beets on a baking sheet and drizzle with 1 tablespoon of olive oil and season with salt and pepper. Shake to coat, then bake for 25 minutes. Check and shake the sheet every 7 or 8 minutes.

245.   As the beets bake, bring 1 cup of water to boil in a saucepan. Add the quinoa, cumin, and a pinch of salt. Turn the temperature to low, cover, and simmer for 15 minutes. You will know the quinoa is cooked as it will be soft, and a white or transparent ring will appear around the outside of each grain. Turn off the heat and set it aside.

246.   In a small sauté pan or skillet, melt the butter and honey over medium heat until it bubbles and turns a nice dark caramel color. This will take about 2 minutes. Do not touch the pan during this time. Add the cayenne pepper and the pecans and gently toss to coat. Be very careful as the caramel will be incredibly hot. Remove from heat, and tip the mixture onto a plate to cool.

247.   Make a dressing by mixing the remaining olive oil, lemon juice, and salt and pepper to taste.

248.   Put the quinoa in a large bowl. Add the beets and the dressing and mix. Top with the parsley and the pecans. Serve in 2 bowls.

Recipe 47: Simple Muffuletta Salad

Created by Italian immigrants, the muffuletta is a meat and cheese–a packed sandwich made on a whole loaf of bread. This salad skips the bread, of course, but still is flavored with traditional olives, garlic, and fresh herbs.

Calories: 627

Prep Time: 25 minutes

Cook Time: -

Serving Size: 4

Ingredients:

FOR THE DRESSING

- ½ cup extra-virgin olive oil
- 3 tablespoons balsamic vinegar
- 1 teaspoon chopped fresh oregano
- ½ teaspoon minced garlic
- ¼ teaspoon minced fresh basil
- Sea salt
- Freshly ground black pepper

FOR THE SALAD

- 4 cups chopped romaine lettuce
- 1 red bell pepper, chopped

- ½ red onion, chopped
- 1 cup giardiniera salad, drained and chopped
- 4 ounces sliced provolone cheese, chopped
- 3 ounces sliced spicy capicola, chopped
- 3 ounces sliced Genoa salami, chopped
- 3 ounces sliced mortadella, chopped
- 3 ounces sliced prosciutto, chopped
- ½ cup sliced black olives
- ¼ cup shredded mozzarella cheese

Directions:

TO MAKE THE DRESSING

249.   In a small bowl, whisk the following: olive oil, balsamic vinegar, oregano, garlic, and basil until well combined.

250.   Season with salt and pepper and set aside.

TO MAKE THE SALAD

251.   In a large bowl, put the following: the lettuce, bell pepper, onion, giardiniera salad, provolone cheese, capicola, salami, mortadella, and prosciutto.

252.   Add the dressing and toss to coat.

253.   Serve topped with olives and mozzarella cheese. For the pâté, remove the skin of the mackerel fillets and discard. Flake the fish into a medium bowl.

254.   Add cream cheese, lemon zest, lemon juice, parsley, and nutmeg. Stir and gently mash with a

fork to combine. You are looking for a rough texture rather than a completely smooth one. Season with salt and pepper.

255.   For the crudités, slice the celery, carrots, and bell pepper into batons roughly ½ inch thick and 4 inches long.

256.   Transfer pâté into a small bowl and the crudités onto a plate.

257.   Serve immediately.

Recipe 48: <u>Spicy Cauliflower Soup</u>

This soup is a warming but calorie-light lunch that leaves lots of room for adding sides to suit your preferences and dietary goals. Also, it's a great recipe to use to break your fast. Have a batch whipped up and ready to go in the refrigerator for when the time comes.

Calories: 99

Prep Time: 10 minutes

Cook Time: 30 minutes

Serving Size: 4

Ingredients:

- 1 tablespoon ghee
- 1 head cauliflower, with leaves, removed, roughly chopped
- 1 medium white onion, finely chopped
- 3 garlic cloves, minced
- 1 tablespoon garam masala
- 4 cups vegetable stock
- 1 cup baby spinach leaves
- Salt
- Freshly ground black pepper

- 4 tablespoons full-fat plain yogurt

- Juice of ½ **lemon**

Directions:

258.   Warm the ghee in a stockpot over medium heat and add the cauliflower and onion. Sauté for 10 minutes, stirring occasionally until caramelized.

259.   Add the garlic to the pan and cook for 1 minute, until fragrant. Then add the garam masala and cook for 1 minute. Stir.

260.   Add the stock and bring it to a boil. Lower the heat and simmer for 20 minutes, adding the spinach in for the last 2 minutes.

261.   Take the pot off the heat. Decant into a blender — or use an immersion blender in the pot — and blend until smooth. Season with salt and pepper to taste.

262.   Ladle soup into bowls and serve each with a tablespoon of plain yogurt, a squeeze of lemon juice, and an extra twist of black pepper.

Recipe 49: Turmeric Ginger Soup

This turmeric and ginger soup will make you feel energized after working in the morning.

Calorie: 223

Prep Time: 10 minutes

Cook Time: 10 minutes

Serving Size: 4

Ingredients:

- Ginger, shredded – 4 tbsp

- Turmeric – 4 tsp

- Large carrots – 12

- Wholemeal bread – 80 g

- Sour cream – 4 tbsp + extra for serving

- Cayenne pepper – 2-3 pinches + extra for serving

- Vegetable stock – 4 cups or 800 ml

Directions:

263.   Peel and dice the carrots.

264.   Put them in a blender along with all the other ingredients. Blend until the mixture is smooth.

265.   In a pan or a microwave, heat until it becomes piping hot. Garnish with the extra sour cream and the extra cayenne pepper and serve.

Recipe 50: <u>Vermicelli Veggie Soup</u>

A great vegetable recipe for your body.

Calories: 288

Prep Time: 15 minutes

Cook Time: 1 hour 30 minutes

Serving Size: 8

Ingredients:

- Large carrots, diced – 2

- Corn on the cobs with corn kernels removed – 2

- Large leeks, trimmed and thinly sliced – 2

- Vermicelli noodles – 200 g

- Parsley and mint, chopped finely – a small bunch of both

Ingredients for the stock:

- Onions, cut into quarters – 2

- Carrots, sliced thickly - 2

- Leek, diced – 1

- Bay leaves – 1

- Celery sticks, roughly sliced – 4

- Black peppercorns – 6

- Chicken – 1.3 kg

- Vegetable stock cube – 1

Directions:

266. In a very large saucepan, put all the ingredients of the stock and the chicken and cover everything with 3 liters of cold water.

267. After it boils, bring it to a simmer and cook for about 1 hour or 1 hour 30 minutes. Remove any froth that forms every 20 minutes or so.

268. Take out the chicken and try to remove as much fat as you can from the stock by straining it through a sieve.

269. Pour the stock back into the pan – rinse it first – and leave it to simmer until the stock is about 2 liters. Then, add in the leeks and the carrots and reduce the stock for 10 minutes.

270. While it simmers down, shreds the chicken and throws away its skin and bones. Add the shredded chicken to the pan along with the sweetcorn and the vermicelli noodles.

271. Simmer the soup for about 7 minutes after adding them so that the corn and the noodles are cooked. Serve into bowls, garnish with parsley and mint.

Chapter 5: Snack and Sides Recipes

Recipe 51: Avocado Deviled Eggs

A fun snack that has a bit of a notorious name.

Calories: 184

Prep time: 10 minutes

Cook time: 6 minutes

Serving Size: 6

Ingredients

- Eggs - 6

- Avocado, pitted and meat scooped - 1

- Garlic powder - ¼ teaspoon.

- Paprika, smoked - ¼ teaspoon.

- Cilantro, chopped - 3 tablespoons.

Directions:

272.   Place the eggs in the Instant Pot and add 1½ cups of water.

273.   Close the lid and make sure that the vent points to "Sealing."

274.   Select the "Manual" option and cook for 6 minutes.

275.   Do quick pressure release.

276.   Allow the eggs to completely cool before cracking and peeling off the shells.

277.   Beat the eggs and remove the yolk.

278.   In a bowl, mix the yolk, paprika, avocado, and garlic powder. Sprinkle with pepper and salt.

279.   Stuff the avocado-yolk mixture into the hollow egg whites.

280.   Garnish with cilantro.

Recipe 52: <u>Baked Fennel</u>

You will enjoy every bite.

Calories: 75

Prep time: 10 minutes

Cook time: 50 minutes

Serving Size: 6

Ingredients:

- Fennel bulbs - 3

- Chicken broth - 1 cup

- Gorgonzola cheese, crumbled - ¼ cup

- Panko bread crumbs - ¼ cup

- Salt

- Pepper

Directions:

281.   Cut the fennel bulbs in half lengthwise through the root end.

282.   Put the fennel cut-side down in a skillet and add the chicken broth. Cover and simmer for 20 minutes.

283.   Preheat oven to 375°F. Place cooked fennel bulbs in a baking dish, cut sides up.

284.   Mix the Gorgonzola with the bread crumbs and divide the mixture evenly on the top of each fennel bulb.

285. Bake for 25 minutes, season with salt and pepper and serve hot.

Recipe 53: <u>Cabbage Chips</u>

A snack for those who are craving vegetables, it is low-calorie too!

Calories: 35

Prep time: 10 minutes

Cook time: 20 minutes

Serving Size: 10

Ingredients:

- 1-pound cabbage
- 1 oz Parmesan, grated
- 1 tsp ground paprika
- 1 tsp sesame oil

Directions:

286.   Separate the cabbage leaves into the petals.

287.   Tear the petals and sprinkle with ground paprika and grated Parmesan. Shake the torn leaves.

288.   Heat the instant pot on sauté mode for 3 minutes.

289.   Then place the cabbage petals in one layer in the instant pot.

290.   Cook the chips for 2 minutes from each side.

291.   Then cook the cabbage chips for 2 minutes more from each side or until they are light crunchy.

292.   Repeat the same steps with the remaining
     torn cabbage petals.

Recipe 54: Cauliflower Turmeric Buns

Wonderful Turmeric and cauliflower recipe.

Calories: 65

Prep time: 30 minutes

Cook time: 30 minutes

Serving Size: 6

Ingredients:

- ¾ cup plain yogurt

- 2 tablespoons chia seeds

- ½ teaspoon almond extract

- 2 tablespoons dried sour cherries

- 2 tablespoons almonds, chopped and toasted

Directions:

293. Preheat the oven to 400F. Line a baking sheet with parchment paper.

294. Pulse the cauliflower in the processor until riced.

295. Add the riced cauliflower into a bowl with a tsp. of water, then cover with a plastic wrap with some holes on top.

296. Place the cauliflower bowl into the microwave and heat for 4 minutes.

297.   Remove the plastic wrap and cool the cauliflower for 5 minutes. Then transfer into paper towels and squeeze out all excess moisture.

298.   Pour the squeezed cauliflower into a bowl. Add eggs, flour, turmeric, salt, pepper, and mix.

299.   Mold the mixture into 6 buns, then arrange on top of the baking sheet and fit into the oven.

300.   Bake for 25 to 30 minutes.

301.   Serve.

Recipe 55: <u>Cheese Spinach Crackers</u>

A good combination that you can dip on the sauce.

Calories: 126

Prep time: 15 minutes

Cook time: 25 minutes

Serving Size: 16

Ingredients:

- 1 ½ cups almond flour

- 5 cups (150g) fresh spinach

- ½ cup flax meal

- ¼ cup coconut flour

- ½ tsp. ground cumin

- ¼ cup butter

- ½ cup parmesan cheese, grated

- ½ tsp. flaked chili peppers, dried

- ½ tsp. salt

Directions:

302.   Bring water to a boil in a saucepan.

303.   Add spinach and cook for 1 minute.

304.   Add cooked spinach leaves into a cold water bowl to stop the cooking process.

305.   Squeeze out the water from the spinach leaves and drain.

306.   Process the spinach in a food processor and process until a smooth consistency is reached.

307.   In the meantime, add almond flour, coconut flour, flax meal, cumin, chili flakes, salt, and parmesan cheese into the bowl and mix well.

308.   Add softened butter and spinach into the flour mixture and mix to combine well.

309.   Transfer dough into a refrigerator. Wrap in foil and keep for 1 hour.

310.   Preheat oven to 400F.

311.   Remove the foil wrapping and transfer the dough to a parchment paper-lined baking sheet.

312.   Top dough with a second parchment paper piece and roll dough with a rolling pin until the dough is ¼ inch thick.

313.   Slice dough into 16 even pieces, using a pizza cutter.

314.   Transfer the baking sheet into the preheated oven and bake the dough for 18 to 20 minutes.

315.   For a crunchier texture, adjust oven temperature to 260F and bake for 15 to 20 minutes more.

Recipe 56: <u>Cheesy Breadsticks</u>

A Cheesy snack you can have.

Calories: 399

Prep time: 10 minutes

Cook time: 20 minutes

Serving Size: 5

Ingredients:

- 2 cups shredded mozzarella cheese

- 2 tbsp coconut flour

- 2 whole eggs

- 1 pinch of salt

Toppings:

- ½ cup shredded parmesan cheese

- 1 tbsp Italian seasoning

- ½ tsp garlic powder

Directions:

316. Preheat the oven to 350F.

317. Line a baking sheet with parchment paper.

318. Add salt, eggs, coconut flour, and mozzarella to the food processor.

319. Process until smooth.

320.   Scoop mix onto the lined baking sheet and flatten to 1-inch thickness, forming a square.

321.   Bake for 15 minutes.

322.   Remove from the oven, sprinkle with parmesan cheese, garlic powder, and Italian seasoning.

323.   Remove from the oven and let sticks cool for 10 to 15 minutes.

324.   Slice and serve.

Recipe 57: <u>Cheesy Meatballs</u>

Something to eat while you are training.

Calories: 492

Prep time: 10 minutes

Cook time: 35 minutes

Serving Size: 6

Ingredients:

- 1 pound 75% lean ground beef

- 1 pound 72% lean ground pork

- 1/3 cup shredded Parmesan cheese

- 1 tsp granulated garlic

- 1 tsp granulated onion

- 1 tsp salt

- 1 tsp black pepper

- 8 oz. mozzarella cheese, sliced into small cubes

- 1 tbsp olive oil

Directions:

325.   Preheat the oven to 350F.

326.   In a bowl, combine pork, beef, parmesan, onion, garlic, salt, and pepper. Mix well.

327.   Divide the meat mixture into 24 portions and shape it into balls.

328.   Push a cube of mozzarella cheese into the center of each meatball. Cover the cheese well.

329.   Heat olive oil in a skillet. Add meatballs in hot oil and brown on all sides.

330.   Arrange the meatballs on a baking sheet and bake for 30 minutes, turning once.

331.   Serve.

Recipe 58: <u>Cherry-Almond Chia</u>

If you had a chia pet as a kid, you know all about chia seeds. But instead of sprouting them on a clay pot, you'll soak these seeds in yogurt overnight. These water-loving seeds absorb up to twelve times their weight in liquid to form a gel. Chia is a complete protein and an abundant plant source of  omega-3s. In a study that compared plain yogurt to yogurt plus chia as a morning snack, yogurt plus chia resulted in better satiety, reduced hunger, and eating a smaller lunch.

Calories: 399

Prep time: 10 minutes, plus overnight to rest

Cook time: -

Serving Size: 1

Ingredients:

- ¾ cup plain yogurt

- 2 tablespoons chia seeds

- ½ teaspoon almond extract

- 2 tablespoons dried sour cherries

- 2 tablespoons almonds, chopped and toasted

Directions:

332.   In a lidded container, stir together the yogurt, chia seeds, and almond extract. Cover and

refrigerate overnight. The next morning, add the dried cherries and toasted almonds.

Recipe 59: <u>Corn and Edamame Salad with Ginger Dressing</u>

Edamame is generally sold frozen, either in the shell or loose. They take only 3 minutes to prepare and are great on their own as a snack with a little salt or soy sauce. Like other forms of soy, they have benefits for heart health, immune function, and cancer protection.

Calories: 143

Prep time: 10 minutes

Cook time: 10 minutes

Serving Size: 4

Ingredients:

For the dressing

- 1 tablespoon freshly squeezed lime juice

- 1 tablespoon low-sodium tamari

- 1 tablespoon rice vinegar

- 1 teaspoon high-oleic sunflower oil, safflower oil, or canola oil

- 1½ teaspoons minced peeled fresh ginger

- 1 garlic clove, minced

For the salad

- 2 cups shelled frozen edamame

- 1 cup fresh or frozen corn

- 4 scallions, thinly sliced

- 1 sheet nori seaweed, crumbled

Directions:

To make the dressing

333.　　In a small bowl, whisk the following: lime juice, tamari, vinegar, oil, ginger, and garlic to blend. Set aside.

To make the salad

334.　　Bring a medium pot of water to a boil over high heat. Add the frozen edamame and corn and boil for 3 minutes. Drain. Transfer the edamame and corn to a serving bowl and add the scallions.

335.　　Add the dressing and toss to coat.

336.　　Top with crumbled nori.

Recipe 60: Cream Mussels with Blue Cheese

Try this unique snack.

Calories: 412

Prep time: 5 minutes

Cook time: 10 to 15 minutes plus 20 minutes for chill

Serving Size: 2

Ingredients:

- 1 1/3 lb. mussels in the shells, fresh or frozen

- 3 ½ oz. Dorblu Cheese

- juice of ½ orange

- ½ - 2/3 cup (100-150 ml) cream, 33% fat

- 2 tbsp mustard with grains

- 2 tbsp hot chili sauce

Directions:

337.   For fresh mussels, wash the mussels and remove the "beards" attached to the shells.

338.   For frozen mussels, defrost. As a rule, these have already been cleaned.

339.   Preheat oven to 350 °F. Put the mussels on a large baking sheet or in a deep pan.

340.   Put a small piece of Dorblu cheese in each shell with mussel and cover them with cream.

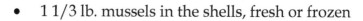

341.   Mix the mustard and orange juice. Top the shells with this mixture.

342.   Bake in the oven for 10-15 min.

343.   Remove from the oven, arrange the mussels on a plate, and add a little hot chili sauce to each mussel or sprinkle with a small number of chili flakes.

Recipe 61: Creamy and Crunchy Egg Balls

A wonderful recipe.

Calories: 67

Prep time: 40 minutes

Cook time: -

Serving Size: 6

Ingredients:

- 2 medium hard-boiled eggs

- 2 tbsp cream cheese

- 1 tbsp coconut oil, melted

- 2 slices prosciutto, cooked and crumbled

Directions:

344. In a food processor, place eggs, cream cheese, and coconut oil, and pulse until well mixed.

345. Refrigerate until the mixture solidifies, about 30 minutes.

346. Remove from refrigerator and shape into 6 balls.

347. Place crumbled prosciutto on a plate and roll balls in it to coat.

348. Serve.

Recipe 62: <u>Creamy Mushrooms with Garlic and Thyme</u>

An amazing snack that is low in calories.

Calories: 98

Prep time: 5 minutes

Cook time: 5 minutes

Serving Size: 4

Ingredients:

- 4 tbsp unsalted butter

- ½ cup onion, chopped

- 1 pound button mushrooms

- 2 tsp garlic, diced

- 1 tbs fresh thyme

- 1 tbsp parsley, chopped

- ½ tsp salt

- ¼ tsp black pepper

Directions:

349.   Melt the butter in a pan. Place the mushrooms and onion into the pan. Add salt and pepper. Cook the mushroom mix for about 5 minutes until they're browned on both sides.

350.   Add the garlic and thyme. Additionally, saute the mushrooms for 1-2 minutes. Top them with parsley.

Recipe 63: <u>Dijon Mustard Deviled Eggs</u>

It looks very pretty, you would want it.

Calories: 84

Prep time: 10 minutes

Cook time: 10 minutes

Serving Size: 6

Ingredients:

- Hard-boiled eggs, peeled – 6

- Dijon mustard – ½ tsp

- Black pepper, grounded – 1/8 tsp

- Salt – ¼ tsp

- Mayonnaise – 2-3 tbsp

- Paprika for garnishing

Directions:

351.   Bisect the peeled eggs into two halves and remove the yolk. In a bowl, mash the yolk with a fork.

352.   Stir in the mayonnaise, mustard and salt, and pepper.

353.   Spoon the egg yolk mixture into the whites and sprinkle with paprika to serve.

Recipe 64: <u>Keto Zucchini Toast</u>

Very great Keto recipe, you will love zucchini even more.

Calories: 399

Prep time: 10 minutes, plus overnight to rest

Cook time: -

Serving Size: 1

Ingredients:

- ¼ cup almond flour
- 1 cup zucchini, shredded and boiled
- ¼ tsp. garlic powder
- 1 egg
- 1 tbsp flax meal
- 1 pinch black pepper
- ¼ tsp oregano
- 1 pinch salt
- ¼ tsp basil

Directions:

355.   Preheat the oven to 450F. Line a baking sheet with parchment paper.

356.   Whisk ingredients in a bowl to form a batter.

357.   Divide the batter into 4 equal parts and lay each on the baking sheet.

358.   Transfer the sheet to the oven and bake for 20 minutes.

359.   Remove, cool, and serve.

Recipe 65: <u>Lemon and Coconut Cookies</u>

Every bite is a delight. The lemon and coconut cookie combination is a keto recipe that has low calories for a cookie!

Calories: 118

Prep time: 10 minutes

Cook time: 15 minutes

Serving Size: 24

Ingredients:

- 1 cup butter, softened
- ½ cup granulated sugar substitute
- 1 ½ cups coconut flour
- 4 eggs
- ½ tsp. salt
- ¼ cup chopped almonds
- 2 tsp. lemon extract

Directions:

360.   Preheat the oven to 375F.

361.   Line two cookie sheets with parchment paper.

362.   In a bowl, combine the sugar substitute, lemon extract, salt, and butter and beat well together.

363.   Add the eggs one at a time, beating well after each addition.

364.   Stir in the coconut flour.

365.   Drop spoonfuls of the mix onto the prepared sheets, flatten with a fork.

366.   Top with a sprinkle of chopped almonds and bake for 12 to 15 minutes.

367.   Turn the cookies after 8 minutes to brown evenly.

368.   Remove and serve.

Recipe 66: <u>Lemon-Lavender Muffins</u>

With no butter or oil and only one egg, these low-fat muffins are still full of flavor, thanks to the lemon and complimentary lavender flavor. Although we often associate lavender with soap, perfume, and aromatherapy, culinary-grade lavender buds are edible and they add a mild floral bouquet to the muffins.

Calories: 129 per muffin

Prep time: 20 minutes

Cook time: 16 minutes

Serving Size: 12 small muffins

Ingredients:

For the muffins

- ⅔ cup granulated sugar

- 2 teaspoons culinary-grade lavender buds

- 2 cups barley flour or all-purpose flour

- 1 teaspoon baking powder

- ½ teaspoon salt

- 1 large egg

- 3 tablespoons freshly squeezed lemon juice

- 1 tablespoon lemon pulp

- 1 teaspoon grated lemon zest

- ⅔ cup plus 2 tablespoons soy milk

- ½ cup unsweetened applesauce

For the glaze (optional)

- ½ cup confectioners' sugar

- 1 tablespoon freshly squeezed lemon juice

- 2 teaspoons grated lemon zest, divided

Directions:

To make the muffins

369. Preheat the oven to 375°F. Using paper liners, line the cups of a regular muffin tin.

370. In a food processor, blend the granulated sugar and lavender buds for 3 to 4 minutes. Strain the mixture through a fine-mesh sieve into a bowl. If making the glaze, reserve any larger buds for garnish.

371. In a large bowl, whisk the barley flour, baking powder, and salt to combine. Set aside.

372. Add the egg to the lavender sugar. Using a handheld mixer, blend on low speed for about 3 minutes, until fluffy. Stir in the lemon juice, lemon pulp, lemon zest, soy milk, and applesauce.

373. Combine the wet and dry ingredients in a mixing bowl and stir to combine. Evenly distribute the batter into the prepared muffin tin.

374.   Bake for 14 to 16 minutes, or until a toothpick inserted into the center of a muffin comes out clean. Let the muffins cool until warm.

To make the glaze (if using)

375.   In a small bowl, stir the following: confectioners' sugar, lemon juice, and 1 teaspoon of lemon zest. Top each muffin with 1 teaspoon of glaze (if using).

376.   Sprinkle the muffins with the remaining 1 teaspoon of zest and garnish with the reserved lavender buds.

377.   Refrigerate leftovers in an airtight container for up to 3 days.

Recipe 67: <u>Low Carb Guacamole</u>

Low carb and easy on the stomach, a perfect snack!

Calories: 96

Prep time: 15 minutes

Cook time: 5 minutes

Serving Size: 2

Ingredients:

- Ripe avocado, diced – 1 large
- Fresh cilantro, roughly chopped – ¼ cup
- Zucchini, diced into ½ inch cubes – 1 large
- Garlic cloves, ground – 2
- Hot sauce (e.g. Tabasco) – ½ tsp
- Lime juice – 2 tbsp
- Salt – ¼ tsp
- Onion, finely diced – ¼ cup

Directions:

378.   Set the microwave on a high power level. Then, cover the Zucchini with a damp towel in a microwave-safe dish and microwave for 4 to 5 minutes so that the zucchini becomes tender.

379.   In a sieve, drain any water from the microwave dish and lightly squeeze the zucchini to free it of water.

380. Add zucchini, cilantro, avocado, lime juice, garlic, onion, salt, and hot sauce to a large bowl. Mesh everything roughly until all the ingredients are combined.

381. You can eat it seasoned with lemon or even spread it on bread.

Recipe 68: <u>Mini Cheesecakes</u>

Enjoy these mini treats and get yourself to work.

Calories: 166

Prep time: 10 minutes

Cook time: 15 minutes

Serving Size: 9

Ingredients:

For the cheesecakes

- 2 tbsp butter
- 8 ounces cream cheese
- 3 tbsp coffee
- 3 eggs
- 1/3 cup swerve
- 1 tbsp sugar-free caramel syrup

For the frosting

- 3 tbsp sugar-free caramel syrup
- 3 tbsp butter
- 8 ounces mascarpone cheese, softened
- 2 tbsp swerve

Directions:

383.   In a blender, mix cream cheese with 1/3 cup swerve, 1 tbsp. caramel syrup, coffee, 2 tbsp. butter, and eggs and blend well.

384.   Spoon into a cupcake pan, place in the oven at 350F, and bake for 15 minutes.

385.   Cool and freeze for 3 hours.

386.   In a bowl, mix 3 tbsp. butter, with 3 tbsp. caramel syrup, 2 tbsp. swerve, mascarpone cheese, and blend well.

387.   Spoon this over cheesecakes and serve.

Recipe 69: <u>Party Meatballs</u>

A good snack that you can also share with other people.

Calories: 223

Prep time: 5 minutes

Cook time: 15 minutes

Serving Size: 8

Ingredients:

- 1 ½ lb. ground beef
- ½ cup finely chopped bacon
- ½ cup almond flour
- 1 tsp garlic powder
- ½ tsp parsley flakes
- Salt freshly ground black pepper (to taste)
- 1 ½ cups sugar-free ketchup
- ½ cup sugar-free steak sauce
- 2 cups filtered water
- ¼ cup shredded parmesan cheese

Directions:

388.   Except for ketchup, steak sauce, water, and cheese add all the ingredients to a bowl and mix well.

389.   Make equal-sized meatballs from the mixture.

390.   In another bowl, add ketchup, steak sauce, and water, and mix well.

391.   In the bottom of the Instant Pot, please meatballs and top with ketchup mixture.

392.   Secure the lid and press Manual. Cook under High Pressure for 5 minutes.

393.   Press Cancel and do a quick release.

394.   Remove the lid and sprinkle with cheese.

395.   Serve.

Recipe 70: Peppermint Patties

A great combination that you'll snack on.

Calories: 126.4

Prep time: 20 minutes plus 3 hours for cooling

Cook time: 5 minutes

Serving Size: 1

Ingredients:

- ½ cup coconut oil (slightly softened)

- 2 tbsp. coconut cream

- ½ cup Erythritol-based Sweetener

- 1 tsp. peppermint extract

- 3 oz. chopped dark chocolate (sugarless)

- 1 tbsp. coconut oil or ½ oz. cacao butter

Directions:

396.   Beat the coconut cream and coconut oil using an electric bowl in a medium bowl until smooth.

397.   Add the peppermint extract and sweetener and keep beating.

398.   Line a baking sheet with parchment or wax paper. Drop a heaping spoonful of the mixture on the parchment or wax paper. Make a circular shape about 1½ inches in diameter.

399.   Refrigerate for 2 hours until it becomes firm.

400.   Melt the cacao butter and chocolate together and put them inside a bowl and place them over a pan containing water that just started simmering. Keep stirring the mixture to make sure it is well mixed. Remove from heat. Cool a little.

401.   Position the patties on the baking sheet. Drizzle with chocolate mixture. Then allow it to set.

Recipe 71: <u>Sherry Vinegar Arugula</u>

A great snack recipe that you can prepare in just 15 minutes.

Calories: 72

Prep Time: 15 minutes

Serving Size: 4

Ingredients:

- Arugula – 8 cups

- Olive oil – 4 tsp

- Sherry vinegar (you can use another type as well) – 4 tsp

- Salt – a pinch

- Sunflower seeds, salted and roasted – 8 tsp

- Parmesan, grated – 4 tbsp

Directions:

402.   Season the arugula with salt, oil, and vinegar in a large bowl.

403.   Sprinkle 1 tsp of the sunflower seeds and toss to mix.

404.   Toss again after adding the Parmesan so that it combines well with the other ingredients in the bowl.

405.   Drizzle on the 1 tsp of seed that is left, serve, and enjoy.

Recipe 72: <u>Summer Swiss Chard</u>

Colorful and taste very good, pairs well with your routine.

Calories: 132

Prep time: 5 minutes

Cook time: 15 minutes

Serving Size: 4

Ingredients:

- Swiss chard - 1 pound.

- Olive oil - 3 tablespoons.

- Onion, diced - 1 cup.

- Salt

- Oregano - ½ teaspoon.

- Red-wine vinegar - 3 tablespoons.

- Salt

- Pepper

Directions:

406.　　Chop the chard and set it aside.

407.　　Put olive oil in a skillet and heat over medium.

408.　　Add the diced onion, a pinch of salt, and oregano and cook until the onions are tender.

409.　　Add the chopped chard and sauté for a few minutes and then remove from heat.

410.   Stir in the vinegar and season with salt and
    pepper.

Recipe 73: <u>Swedish Buns</u>

Great to taste. Try this if you want to have a snack

Calories: 257

Prep time: 15 minutes

Cook time: 25 minutes

Serving Size: 4

Ingredients:

- ¾ cup almond flour

- 1 tbsp. whole flax seeds

- 2 tbsp. psyllium husk powder

- 1 tbsp. shelled sunflower seeds

- ½ tsp. salt

- 1 tsp. baking powder

- 2 eggs

- 2 tbsp. avocado oil

- ½ cup sour cream

Directions:

411.   Preheat the oven to 400F. In a bowl, add almond flour, seeds, psyllium husk powder, salt, and baking powder. Mix well.

412.   Add eggs, avocado oil, and sour cream into the mixture and mix until fully combined.

413.   Let dough sit for 5 minutes then cut into 4 portions.

414.   Shape each dough portion into a ball and transfer onto a parchment paper-lined 9″ round cake pan.

415.   Place the cake pan into the preheated oven. Bake for 20 to 25 minutes or until browned.

416.   Cool, slice, and serve.

Chapter 6: Dinner Recipes

Recipe 74: <u>Almond Zucchini Noodles</u>

A nice dinner recipe that will satisfy you.

Calories: 190

Prep Time: 15 minutes

Cook Time: 30-35 minutes

Serving Size: 4

Ingredients:

- Red pepper flakes, crushed – ¼ tsp

- Almond flour – 1 tbsp

- Garlic, ground – 2 cloves

- Coconut oil – ½ tsp

- Zucchinis, cut with julienne peeler – 4 will make 4 cups

- Extra-virgin olive oil – 2 tbsp

- Fresh parsley – ¼ cup Black pepper and salt – to taste

Directions:

417.   Gently toss the zucchini noodles along with salt after putting them in a colander so that the noodles are slightly coated with the salt.

418.   Leave them to sit for 20 to 30 minutes so that excess water is removed. Then, wash them with running water, drain thoroughly, and pat dry by using paper towels.

419.   Meanwhile, add coconut oil in a heated skillet above medium-high. Allow it to melt for 2 minutes and then mix in a pinch of salt and almond flour and sauté them. Cook until it's a toast brown color – approx. 2 minutes - and save the crumbs in the pan for garnishing.

420.   Again, place the pan on a medium-high flame, put in the zucchini noodles, and sauté to make them tender – 1 to 2 minutes.

421.   Adjust the heat to low and push the noodles to one side. Stir the added olive oil, red pepper flakes, and garlic for almost 20 seconds or until the garlic is fragrant.

422.   Mix and stir the noodles to coat them with spiced oil. After switching off the flame, add in the salt, black pepper, and parsley. Dust the noodle with almond flour crumbs and serve.

Recipe 75: <u>Beef Bacon Burgers</u>

These are bacon cheeseburgers—yes—but with cheese inside the meat, not melted on top. There's just something fun about biting into a pocket of Cheddar. Freeze these patties raw or cooked and store for up to 3 months. Try freezing them on a baking sheet so that you won't have to chisel away at a solid hunk of beef.

Calories: 315

Prep Time: 10 minutes

Cook Time: 15 minutes

Serving Size: 8

Ingredients:

- 1 pound grass-fed ground beef
- 8 ounces bacon, chopped
- ¼ cup ground pecans
- ¼ cup chopped onion
- 1 large egg
- 2 ounces Cheddar cheese, diced
- ¼ teaspoon sea salt
- Pinch freshly ground black pepper
- 1 tablespoon extra-virgin olive oil

- Favorite keto-friendly burger toppings

Directions:

423.   Preheat a grill to medium-high. (Or preheat an oven to 450°F.)

424.   In a medium bowl, combine the beef, bacon, pecans, onion, egg, Cheddar cheese, salt, and pepper until well mixed.

425.   Form the beef mixture into 8 equal patties and brush them with olive oil.

426.   Grill the burgers, turning once until cooked through, 13 to 15 minutes in total. (If using an oven, place the patties on a baking sheet lined with parchment paper and bake until cooked through, turning once, about 20 minutes in total.)

427.   Serve with your favorite toppings.

Recipe 76: <u>Cajun Shrimp</u>

Its miniature size is fun to look at.

Calories: 127

Prep time: 10 minutes

Cook time: 5 minutes

Serving Size: 2

Ingredients

- Tiger shrimp - 16

- Corn starch - 2 tablespoons.

- Cayenne pepper - 1 teaspoon.

- Old bay seasoning – 1 teaspoon.

- Salt

- Pepper

- Olive oil – 1 teaspoon.

Directions

428.   Rinse the shrimp. Pat dry.

429.   In a bowl, combine corn starch, cayenne pepper, old bay seasoning, salt, pepper. Stir.

430.   In a bowl, add the shrimp. Drizzle olive oil over shrimp to lightly coat.

431.   Dip the shrimp in seasoning, shake off any excess.

432.   Preheat fryer to 375°F. Lightly spray cook basket with non-stick Keto cooking spray.

433.   Transfer to the fryer. Cook 5 minutes shake after 2 minutes until cooked thoroughly.

434.   Serve on a platter.

Recipe 77: <u>Chicken Pot Pie Soup</u>

Chunks of tender chicken, oodles of chopped vegetables, and pinches of fragrant herbs combine with creamy, cheesy broth to create this mouthwatering soup. For a real treat, spoon it into an oven-safe bowl, top with Swiss or mozzarella cheese, broil until melted and golden brown, and serve.  This charming presentation adds just over 100 calories and 8 grams of fat and protein per serving.

Calories: 336

Prep Time: 20 minutes

Cook Time: 35 minutes

Serving Size: 6

Ingredients:

- 2 tablespoons extra-virgin olive oil, divided

- 1 pound skinless chicken breast, cut into ½-inch chunks

- 1 onion, chopped

- 1 cup quartered mushrooms

- 2 celery stalks, chopped

- 2 carrots, diced

- 1 tablespoon minced garlic

- 5 cups low-sodium chicken broth

- 1 cup heavy (whipping) cream

- ¼ cup cream cheese

- 1 cup chopped green beans

- 1 tablespoon chopped fresh thyme

- Salt

- Freshly ground black pepper

Directions:

435.   In a large stockpot over medium-high heat, heat 1 tablespoon olive oil and sauté the chicken breasts for about 10 minutes, or until just cooked through.

436.   Place the chicken on a platter and set it aside with a slotted spoon.

437.   Sauté the onion, mushrooms, celery, carrots, and garlic in the remaining 1 tablespoon of oil for 6 to 7 minutes, or until softened.

438.   Bring the soup to a boil, stirring in the chicken broth and saved chicken. Reduce to low heat and cook for about 15 minutes, or until the vegetables are soft.

439.   Simmer for 3 minutes after incorporating the heavy cream, cream cheese, green beans, and thyme.

440.   Serve immediately after seasoning with salt and pepper.

Recipe 78: <u>Chicken Tenders with Creamy Almond Sauce</u>

To mix things up, serve the tenders without creamy almond sauce as a lettuce wrap base or in a salad. These tenders can be prepared and frozen (raw or cooked) for up to three months.

Calories: 555

Prep Time: 12 minutes

Cook Time: 20 minutes

Serving Size: 4

Ingredients:

FOR THE ALMOND SAUCE

- ½ cup heavy (whipping) cream
- 2 tablespoons almond butter
- Juice of 1 lime
- 1 teaspoon coconut amino

FOR THE CHICKEN TENDERS

- 2 large eggs, beaten
- 1½ cups almond flour
- 12 ounces boneless chicken, cut into ½-inch wide strips
- 3 tablespoons extra-virgin olive oil

Directions:

TO MAKE THE ALMOND SAUCE

441.   In a small bowl, whisk the following: heavy cream, almond butter, lime juice, and coconut amino until well blended. Set aside.

TO MAKE THE CHICKEN TENDERS

442.   Preheat the oven to 400 degrees Fahrenheit.

443.   Set aside a baking sheet lined with parchment paper.

444.   Place the beaten eggs in a small bowl in your work area.

445.   In a separate small bowl, put the almond flour and set it next to the egg mixture.

446.   Dredge the chicken in almond flour, then in the egg mixture, and finally in the almond flour again.

447.   Brush all sides of the breaded tenders with olive oil before placing them on the prepared baking sheet.

448.   Bake for 15 to 18 minutes, rotating once until the chicken is cooked through and brown.

449.   Serve with a dollop of almond sauce on top.

Recipe 79: Classic Eggplant Parmesan

Bring the sunny flavors of southern Italy to your table with a crowd-pleaser of a dish, ideal for families or casual dinners with friends. Add a simple green side salad to cut through the richness of the dish.

Calories: 481

Prep time: 15 minutes

Cook time: 45 minutes

Serving Size: 6

Ingredients

- 4 medium eggplants
- Salt
- 4 tablespoons extra-virgin olive oil
- 2 tablespoons tomato paste
- 4 garlic cloves, crushed
- 1 large bunch of fresh basil, stemmed and divided
- 1 large (28-ounce) can tomato purée
- 14 ounces mozzarella cheese, cut into ¼-inch-thick slices
- ¾ cup grated Parmesan cheese
- Freshly ground black pepper

Directions

450.   Preheat the oven to 350°F.

451.   Cut the eggplants into ¼-inch-thick slices. Brush the slices with olive oil and add a sprinkling of salt. Heat a griddle, sauté pan, or skillet over high heat and cook the eggplant slices in a single layer until they begin to soften and brown on one side, then flip and brown on the other, about 5 minutes total. Add the next batch until all slices are cooked. Remove from heat and set aside.

452.   Heat a medium saucepan over medium heat and add the tomato paste and the garlic and stir. Add half the basil. After 2 minutes add the tomato purée, stir, and bring it to a simmer. Turn the flame down to low, cover, and leave to simmer for 10 minutes gently. Once done, remove from heat.

453.   Add a spoonful of tomato sauce to the bottom of a 7-by-11-inch oven-proof dish. Add a layer of the eggplant, then a layer of the mozzarella and some torn basil leaves, and top with another layer of sauce. Repeat until all the eggplant and mozzarella are placed. Top with a thin tomato sauce layer with some of the mozzarella poking through. Sprinkle with Parmesan and a generous seasoning of black pepper and a few leftover basil leaves.

454.   Bake for around 20 minutes or until the top is bubbling and golden. Serve immediately.

Recipe 80: <u>Cream-Poached Trout</u>

If you've never had poached fish with cream, you're in for a treat. The leeks pair well with the sweetness of the cream in this dish but don't overpower the flavors as an onion might. Leeks contain kaempferol, a flavonoid that researchers believe may benefit the

heart. Take the time to clean your leeks after slicing them because they are often filled with grit.

Calories: 449

Prep Time: 10 minutes

Cook Time: 20 minutes

Serving Size: 4

Ingredients:

- 4 (4-ounce) skinless trout fillets

- Sea salt

- Freshly ground black pepper

- 3 tablespoons butter

- 1 leek, white and green parts, halved lengthwise, thinly sliced, and thoroughly washed

- 1 teaspoon minced garlic

- 1 cup heavy (whipping) cream

- Juice of 1 lemon

- 1 teaspoon chopped fresh parsley, for garnish

Directions:

455. Preheat the oven to 400°F.

456. Pat the trout fillets dry with paper towels and lightly season with salt and pepper. Place them in a 9-by-9-inch baking dish in one layer. Set aside.

457. Place a medium saucepan over medium-high heat and melt the butter.

458. Sauté the leek and garlic until softened, about 6 minutes.

459. Add the heavy cream and lemon juice to the saucepan and bring to a boil, whisking.

460. Pour the sauce over the fish and bake until the fish is just cooked for 10 to 12 minutes.

461. Serve topped with parsley.

Recipe 81: <u>Crispy Baked Tofu, Broccoli, and Mushroom Stir-Fry with Peanut Sauce</u>

The next time I'm invited to an event that serves cocktails and appetizers, I'll bring these—they're a great little appetizer on their own, even without the stir-fry.

Calories: 313

Prep Time: 20 minutes

Cook Time: 35 minutes

Serving Size: 4

Ingredients:

For the baked tofu

- 2 tablespoons low-sodium or regular tamari
- 1½ teaspoons extra-virgin olive oil
- 1 teaspoon garlic powder
- 1 pound firm or extra-firm tofu, cubed
- 1½ tablespoons cornstarch

For the peanut sauce

- ¼ cup peanut butter
- ¼ cup water
- 1½ teaspoons soy sauce

- 1 teaspoon honey

- 1 teaspoon freshly squeezed lime juice

- ⅛ teaspoon red pepper flakes

For the stir-fry

- 1 tablespoon high-oleic sunflower oil, safflower oil, or canola oil

- 1 bunch scallions, cut on the diagonal into 1-inch slices

- 1 or 2 garlic cloves, minced

- 1 (½-inch) piece fresh ginger, peeled and grated

- 4 cups broccoli florets

- 2 cups mushrooms, quartered

Directions:

To make the baked tofu

462.　　Preheat the oven to 400°F. Line a baking sheet with parchment paper.

463.　　In a small bowl, stir together the tamari, oil, and garlic powder. Place the tofu in a shallow bowl and pour the sauce over it. Stir to coat. Let sit for 5 to 10 minutes to absorb the liquid.

464.　　Sprinkle the tofu with the cornstarch and stir to coat. Evenly distribute the bowl's contents onto the prepared baking sheet.

465.　　Bake for 10 minutes, flip the tofu, and bake for 10 minutes more, until browned and crispy on the outside.

To make the peanut sauce

466.   While the tofu bakes, in a small bowl, whisk together the peanut butter, water, soy sauce, honey, lime juice, and red pepper flakes until smooth. Set aside.

To make the stir-fry

467.   In a large pan over medium heat, heat the oil. Add the scallions, garlic, and ginger. Cook for 2 to 3 minutes, being careful that the garlic does not burn.

468.   Add the broccoli and mushrooms. Increase the heat to high and cook for about 3 minutes, stirring constantly.

469.   Reduce the heat to medium, add water, 2 tablespoons at a time, if the pan is dry, and cover the pan. Cook for 3 to 4 minutes and check the broccoli for doneness. When the broccoli is almost done, stir in the peanut sauce to coat. Serve with the baked tofu.

Recipe 82: <u>Fried Shrimp Rice</u>

Very nice, eating this makes you feel like a boss.

Calories: 205

Prep Time: 5 minutes

Cook Time: 10 minutes

Serving Size:1

Ingredients:

- ¼ cup of soy sauce
- Pinch pepper flakes
- 6 cups of cauliflower rice
- 1 tbsp. of honey
- ½ lb. of deveined thawed & peeled shrimp
- ½ cup of peas frozen
- ½ tsp. ginger grated
- ½ cup of cubed carrots
- 1 tbsp. of sesame oil
- 1 bunch chopped green onions
- 3 beaten eggs

Directions:

470.   Slice the cauliflower into pieces and put it in a food processor. Throb to finely cut and put aside until it matches rice.

471.   Whisk san-j tamari, ginger, honey, and red pepper flakes together in a small bowl; set aside.

472.   Warm sesame oil in a wide skillet or wok, on medium-high flame. Place in the onions white portion and sauté for around a minute. Mix in frozen peas and carrots, then simmer for around 2 minutes to heat through. Shift vegetables to 1 end of the wok and apply them to beaten eggs. Place the eggs on 1 edge of the plate, then transfer the mixture while it heats until it is cooked completely. Attach shrimp, and fry, until they have turned pink for around 2 minutes.

473.   Merge in riced cauliflower and whisk. Add the tamari sauce solution over the plate, ensuring that the mixture is uniformly spread throughout, and continue to cook for another 4 minutes until the cauliflower has smoothed but has an al dente consistency. Switch off the fire, scatter green onions, cap to soften, and serve after a minute.

Recipe 83: <u>Grilled Flank Steak with Bacon Onion Jam</u>

Flank steak is a lean cut of beef. You need to add fat to hit your keto macros. To this end, this recipe uses a simple vinaigrette marinade, heavy on olive oil. You can choose to broil the steak in the oven if you do not have a grill. Broil until desired doneness, about 7 minutes per side for medium-rare, and let rest 10 minutes.

Calories: 598

Prep Time: 10-30 minutes

Cook Time: 10 minutes

Serving Size: 4

Ingredients:

- 2 tablespoons extra-virgin olive oil
- 2 tablespoons balsamic vinegar
- 1 (1-pound) flank steak
- 1 cup Bacon Red Onion Jam
- Sea salt
- Freshly ground black pepper
- 1 teaspoon chopped fresh parsley

Directions:

474.   In a medium bowl, stir both the olive oil and balsamic vinegar and add the steak, turning to coat. Let stand at room temperature for 20 minutes.

475.   Let the Bacon Red Onion Jam come to room temperature.

476.   Preheat the grill to medium-high heat.

477.   Remove the steak from the marinade and season the steak with salt and pepper. Discard the marinade.

478.   Grill the steak until your desired doneness, about 5 minutes per side for medium-rare.

479.   Remove the steak and then let it rest for 10 minutes before slicing the meat across the grain.

480.   Serve with the Bacon Red Onion Jam. Serve with your favorite toppings.

Recipe 84: <u>Jerk Pork Tenderloin</u>

Pork tenderloin is a lean cut of meat, so it's not the first choice for keto. Nonetheless, it's still a nutritious protein source. Plus pork tastes so mild, it goes with nearly anything.

Calories: 287

Prep Time: 15 minutes

Cook Time: 20 minutes

Serving Size: 6

Ingredients:

- 1 tablespoon granulated erythritol
- ½ tablespoon garlic powder
- ½ tablespoon ground allspice
- ½ tablespoon dried thyme
- 1 teaspoon ground cinnamon
- ¼ teaspoon salt
- ¼ teaspoon freshly ground black pepper
- ⅛ teaspoon cayenne pepper
- 1 (1-pound) pork tenderloin, cut into 1-inch rounds
- ¼ cup extra-virgin olive oil
- ½ cup sour cream
- 2 tablespoons chopped fresh cilantro, for garnish

Directions:

481.   In a medium bowl, stir together the erythritol, garlic powder, allspice, thyme, cinnamon, salt, pepper, and cayenne.

482.   Rub the pork pieces generously on all sides with the seasoning mixture.

483.   Heat the olive oil in a large skillet over medium-high heat.

484.   Panfry the pork until just cooked through, turning once, about 20 minutes in total.

485.   Serve topped with sour cream and cilantro.

Recipe 85: <u>Lamb Kebabs with Roasted Vegetables</u>

Bring the flavors of the Greek taverna to your dinner table for a hearty and nutritious dinner. If you don't want to make the accompanying dip, buy a Greek-style dip such as tzatziki instead.

Calories: 651

Prep time: 15 minutes

Cook time: 25 minutes

Serving Size: 2

Ingredients

- 1 medium zucchini, diced

- 2 medium red onions, diced

- 1 small head cauliflower, diced

- 1 red bell pepper, diced

- 1 teaspoon dried oregano

- 2 tablespoons extra-virgin olive oil, divided

- 1 pound cubed lamb leg (or chicken if preferred)

- ½ teaspoon allspice

- Salt

- Freshly ground black pepper

- 2 garlic cloves, peeled

- 3 fresh mint sprigs

- 1 cup full-fat plain yogurt

- Juice of ½ lemon

Directions

486.	Preheat the oven to 350°F.

487.	Arrange the zucchini, onion, cauliflower, and red pepper on a baking sheet. Sprinkle with the oregano and drizzle with 1 tablespoon olive oil. Shake to coat and bake for 25 minutes. Check and shake the sheet every 7 or 8 minutes.

488.	Put the lamb, allspice, and remaining 1 tablespoon olive oil in a large bowl and season with salt and pepper. Mix the ingredients, ensuring all the lamb is coated.

489.	If you are using wooden skewers, soak them in water for a few minutes to prevent them from burning during cooking. Once the wooden skewers are ready (or right away if you are using metal skewers), thread the diced lamb onto the skewers, aiming for 4 big or 6 medium chunks depending on the size of skewers.

490.	At the vegetables' 10-minute mark, place the kebabs on top of the roasting vegetables to cook for the final 15 minutes.

491.	Make the dip by crushing the garlic, tearing the mint leaves, and mixing them with the yogurt in a small bowl. Stir in the lemon juice.

492.   Divide the kebabs and roasted vegetables between two plates and serve with the dip.

Recipe 86: <u>Lentil and Sweet Potato Tacos with Fresh Guacamole and Pico de Gallo</u>

This is a great meal for Meatless Monday with the family. Everything is the same as a taco meal, except you use lentils and sweet potato in place of meat. I've made this dish with just lentils, but the sweet potato adds a nice flavor and texture.

Calories: 549

Prep Time: 20 minutes

Cook Time: 25 minutes

Serving Size: 4

Ingredients:

For the tacos

- 1 cup lentils, rinsed

- 2 cups water

- 1 small to medium sweet potato, peeled and cut into ½-inch cubes

- 2 teaspoons extra-virgin olive oil or preferred cooking oil

- 1 tablespoon taco seasoning, plus more as needed

- 8 (6-inch) taco shells or (8-inch) soft tortillas

- ¾ cup shredded sharp Cheddar cheese or other cheese of choice

- ½ cup sour cream

For the guacamole

- 1 tablespoon finely diced onion

- 1 tablespoon fresh cilantro

- 1½ teaspoons freshly squeezed lime juice

- 1 teaspoon finely diced jalapeño pepper

- ⅛ teaspoon salt

- 1 avocado, halved, pitted, and peeled

For the pico de gallo

- 1 tomato, finely diced

- 1 tablespoon finely diced onion

- 1 tablespoon finely minced fresh cilantro

- 1 teaspoon finely diced jalapeño pepper

- Salt

Directions:

To make the tacos

493.	Combine the lentils and water in a medium pot over high heat. Bring the water to a boil. Reduce the heat to keep the mixture at a low simmer for 15 minutes. It's best if the lentils are tender. Drain. Place in a medium mixing basin.

494.	In a small pot, add the sweet potato and enough water to submerge it while the lentils simmer completely. Bring the water to a boil in a large pot over high heat. Cook for about 10 minutes, or until soft, then drain and combine with the lentils in a mixing dish.

495.　　Add the oil and taco seasoning to the lentils and sweet potato and stir to incorporate. Taste and add more seasoning, if needed.

To make the guacamole

496.　　In a medium bowl, stir the onion, cilantro, lime juice, jalapeño, and salt.

497.　　In a small bowl, mash the avocado with a fork, keeping it lumpy. Add the avocado to the other ingredients and mix just enough to incorporate the avocado.

498.　　To make the pico de gallo

499.　　In a small bowl, stir the tomato, onion, cilantro, jalapeño, and salt to taste.

To assemble the tacos

500.　　Fill the taco shells with the lentil and sweet potato mixture. Top with Cheddar cheese, sour cream, guacamole, and pico de gallo, as desired.

Recipe 87: Mediterranean Grilled Chicken with Lemon Aioli and Homemade Caesar Salad

There are ways to minimize the formation of carcinogens when meat is cooked at high temperatures or over a flame. By marinating the meat in antioxidant-rich ingredients (olive oil, lemon juice, garlic, oregano, and rosemary), you minimize the formation of these compounds. It's protective

to not cook directly over the flame. This is a delicious way to enjoy grilled chicken.

Calories: 984

Prep Time: 35 minutes

Cook Time: 15 minutes

Serving Size: 2

Ingredients:

For the chicken

- 3 tablespoons extra-virgin olive oil

- 3 tablespoons freshly squeezed lemon juice

- 1 garlic clove, minced

- 1 teaspoon dried rosemary, crushed

- ½ teaspoon dried oregano

- ¼ teaspoon salt

- ¼ teaspoon freshly ground black pepper
- 2 (4-ounce) boneless, skinless chicken breasts

For the aioli

- ½ cup full-fat mayonnaise
- 1 garlic clove, crushed
- 4 teaspoons freshly squeezed lemon juice

For the salad

- 2 large egg yolks (see tip)
- 3 tablespoons grated full-fat Parmesan cheese
- 2 tablespoons extra-virgin olive oil
- 2 tablespoons freshly squeezed lemon juice, add more as needed
- 2 anchovy fillets, finely chopped
- ¼ teaspoon Worcestershire sauce, plus more as needed
- ⅛ teaspoon garlic powder, plus more as needed
- 4 cups torn romaine lettuce pieces
- 3 bacon slices, cooked and crumbled

Directions:

To make the chicken

501.　　In a large bowl, whisk together the oil, lemon juice, garlic, rosemary, oregano, salt, and pepper to blend.

502.　　Make ¼-inch-deep cuts into the chicken breasts about 1 inch apart. Place the chicken breasts in the marinade and turn to coat. Let marinate at room temperature for at least 20 minutes, or up to several hours in the refrigerator.

To make the aioli

503.　　In a small bowl, stir together the mayonnaise, garlic, and lemon juice. Cover and refrigerate until needed.

To make the salad

504.　　In a large bowl, whisk the following: egg yolks, Parmesan cheese, oil, lemon juice, anchovies, Worcestershire sauce, and garlic powder until smooth. Taste and adjust the seasonings, as desired. Add the lettuce and bacon and toss to coat and combine.

505.　　Preheat the grill: Turn off the heat in the center section of the grill and turn the other sections to medium heat.

506.　　Remove the chicken from the marinade and set it on top of the middle section without heating it. Cook for 5 to 7 minutes per side, until the chicken, is cooked through and the juices run clear.

507.　　Alternatively, if you don't have a grill, preheat the oven to 350°F. Bake for 25 to 30 minutes, or until the internal temperature of the chicken reaches 165°F.

508.　　Serve the chicken with the Caesar salad on the side and lemon aioli for dipping.

Recipe 88: <u>Mussels with White Wine and Leeks</u>

If you want an elegant meal on a budget, look no further. I purchased two pounds of mussels at my local fish market for $6 — now that's an affordable protein! Although cleaning the mussels is a bit of work, cooking the dish is a snap. Traditionally these mussels would be served with  crusty bread used to soak up the broth, but if you're following a low-carb diet, just enjoy this wonderful broth with a spoon after your mussels are finished.

Calories: 632

Prep Time: 30 minutes

Cook Time: 15 minutes

Serving Size:2 to 4

Ingredients:

- 2 pounds mussels
- 8 cups cold water
- 2 tablespoons sea salt
- 1 small leek
- 1 tablespoon extra-virgin olive oil
- 1 tablespoon unsalted butter
- 2 garlic cloves, minced

- 4 thyme sprigs

- 1 cup dry white wine

- 1 tablespoon Bone Broth (optional)

- 1 tablespoon chopped fresh parsley

Directions:

509.   Place the mussels in a clean sink full of water. Scrub them with a brush to remove their beards. Rinse and soak again if still gritty. Drain.

510.   In a large pot or bowl, combine the mussels, cold water, and salt. Let soak for 10 minutes. Discard any open mussels. Rinse the remaining mussels.

511.   Cut the leek lengthwise, remove the greens, and clean well. Chop the white parts medium-fine. Set aside.

512.   In a large pot over medium-low heat, heat the oil and melt the butter. Add the chopped leek to the pot and cook for 4 to 6 minutes, until softened.

513.   Add the garlic and reduce the heat to low. Remove the thyme leaves from the stems and add them to the pot along with the white wine and bone broth (if using). Increase the heat to medium-high.

514.   Add the mussels and cover the pot. Steam for 5 to 7 minutes; if the mussels are open, they're ready. Discard any mussels that don't open. Stir in the fresh parsley. Spoon the mussels and broth into shallow bowls and serve.

Recipe 89: <u>Pasta Carbonara</u>

Carbonara was created in Italy during World War II. Powdered eggs and bacon (the two main ingredients) were stapled wartime rations. After the war, returning GIs brought carbonara back to the United States, and it soon caught on in restaurants and kitchens everywhere. Carbonara sauce might not be in your usual keto repertoire, but it's quick and delicious, so you should make the leap.

Calories: 329

Prep Time: 10 minutes

Cook Time: 15 minutes

Serving Size: 6

Ingredients:

- 8 bacon slices, chopped

- 1 tablespoon minced garlic

- ½ cup dry white wine

- 4 large egg yolks

- 2 large eggs

- ½ cup heavy (whipping) cream

- 2 tablespoons chopped fresh parsley

- 2 tablespoons chopped fresh basil

- ½ cup grated Parmesan cheese, divided

- Sea salt

- Freshly ground black pepper

- 4 medium zucchini, spiralized

Directions:

515.   Cook the bacon in a large skillet over medium-high heat, about 6 minutes.

516.   Add the garlic and sauté for 3 minutes.

517.   Stir in the white wine to deglaze the skillet, about 2 minutes. While the bacon is cooking, whisk the egg yolks, eggs, heavy cream, parsley, basil, and ¼ cup of Parmesan cheese in a small bowl until well mixed.

518.   Season the egg mixture with salt and pepper and set aside.

519.   Add the zucchini noodles to the skillet with the bacon, reduce the heat to low, and sauté for 2 minutes.

520.   Add the egg mixture to the skillet and toss until well combined and the egg sauce is cooked through and thick, about 4 minutes.

521.   Serve topped with the remaining ¼ cup of Parmesan cheese.

Recipe 90: <u>Pesto-Crusted Salmon with Crunchy Arugula Salad</u>

The generous crust on this fish is full of crunch and vibrant flavors that the whole family will love. If you can't squeeze it all on, any leftover pesto is great stirred into zucchini noodles. If you'd rather pop the salmon in the oven and forget about it  for 15 minutes, you can. The only thing you forgo is crispy skin.

Calories: 840

Prep time: 10 minutes

Cook time: 5 minutes

Serving Size: 2

Ingredients

For the salmon

- 2 (5-ounce) salmon fillets, skin on
- 3 tablespoons chopped walnuts
- 1 small bunch of fresh basil
- 4 tablespoons extra-virgin olive oil
- 1 ounce fresh Parmesan cheese, grated
- 2 garlic cloves, peeled

- 1 tablespoon almond meal

For the salad

- 1 cup arugula

- 8 small radishes, thinly sliced

- ⅓ cucumber, thinly sliced

- Juice of ½ lemon

- 2 tablespoons extra-virgin olive oil

- Salt

- Freshly ground black pepper

Directions

To make the salmon

522.   Preheat the broiler to 425°F.

523.   To make the salmon, take the fillets out of the refrigerator to allow them to come up to room temperature while you make the pesto. Put the walnuts, basil, olive oil, and Parmesan in a blender. Grate in the garlic cloves and blend until you have a rough pesto consistency.

524.   Warm a nonstick sauté pan or skillet over medium heat. Place the salmon skin-side down in the pan and spoon the pesto mixture on top. Sprinkle the almond meal over the pesto. Cook for 3 minutes.

525.   Transfer the salmon to an oven-safe dish and place it under the broiler for 1 to 2 minutes to add color to the topping and finish cooking the fish.

To make the salad

526.   In a medium bowl, toss the arugula, radishes, and cucumber.

527.   In a small bowl, whisk the lemon juice and olive oil with some salt and pepper to taste for your salad dressing. Pour over the salad. Serve with the salmon fillets.

Recipe 91: <u>Salmon Chowder</u>

This excellent recipe can fill you right up.

Calories: 285

Prep Time: 5 minutes

Cook Time: 20 minutes

Serving Size: 1

Ingredients:

- 1 fennel bulb.
- ¾ lb. of thinly sliced baby potatoes
- 2–3 tbsp. of butter or olive oil
- 1 cup of sliced celery
- ½ tsp. of smoked paprika
- 2–4 rough chopped garlic cloves,
- 2 cups of whole milk
- 1 tsp. of fennel seeds
- 1 diced onion
- 3 cups of chicken or fish stock
- ½ tsp. of thyme
- 1/3 cup of vermouth
- 1 lb. of skinless salmon
- 1 tsp. of salt
- Garnish:

- Lemon wedges
- Bay leaf

Directions:

528.   Warm oil on medium heat, fry the fennel, onion, and celery for 5-6 minutes until fragrant. Put the garlic, thyme, fennel seeds, and sauté, swirling for about 2 minutes. Stir in the dried paprika.

529.   Put vermouth, and simmer for 1-2 minutes. Put some salt, thyme, stock, and bay, over high temperature, and bring to boil. Stir and add potatoes. Carry to a boil, put a lid, and cook over medium-low heat until soft, around 8-10 minutes (see at 7 minutes, be cautious not to cook too much). Get the salmon ready as this is frying.

530.   Slice salmon into parts of 2 inches and cut all of the fat and bones. Then dust with salt gently.

531.   When the potatoes are only a fork-tender, put some milk and get to a low simmer (do not boil) and put the salmon, poaching it gently in the soup for 2 minutes only. Switch off the fire. Fish continues being cooked. If you keep simmering the soup for longer, it may induce a mild curdling. (Don't bother, it's still tasty, just not as nice.) Chip the fish apart, in bits of bite-size, using a fork.

532.   Change seasonings to meet your needs and serve instantly.

533.   Sprinkle with lemon wedges or tarragon.

Recipe 92: Seared White Fish with Pan-Fried Vegetables

This is the ultimate clean eating recipe. The flavors of this dish are subtle, delicate, and light. You'll feel satisfied but clean after enjoying this fresh summery meal. Add some fresh dill on top, if you have it.

Calories: 288

Prep Time: 15 minutes

Cook Time: 15 minutes

Serving Size: 2

Ingredients:

- 2 teaspoons extra-virgin olive oil or high-oleic sunflower, safflower, or canola oil, divided

- 1 small onion, finely diced (about ½ cup)

- 1 carrot, finely diced (about ½ cup)

- 1 Roma tomato, finely diced (about ½ cup)

- 1 celery stalk, finely diced (about ¼ cup)

- Salt

- Freshly ground black pepper

- 1 pound halibut, cod, or another firm white fish

- Fresh dill, for garnish (optional)

Directions:

534.   1 teaspoon oil, heated in a skillet over medium-high heat, and swirled to coat the skillet

535.   Combine the onion, carrot, tomato, and celery in a large mixing bowl. To taste, season with salt and pepper. Cook for 10 to 12 minutes, or until the veggies are tender and the juices have come to the surface.

536.   Rinse the fish and pat it dry. Season the fish all over with salt and pepper and place the fish in the skillet. Let the fish sear for about 5 minutes. Flip the fish and sear the other side for about 5 minutes. Check that the fish is cooked through. It will no longer appear glassy and the flesh will flake easily with a fork.

537.   Plate the fish and top with the pan-fried vegetables. Garnish with fresh dill (if using).

Recipe 93: <u>Sichuan Chili Tofu</u>

A great recipe if you want to try something new.

Calories: 310

Prep Time: 15 minutes

Cook Time: minutes

Serving Size: 4

Ingredients:

- Sichuan Chilli bean paste – 2 tbsp
- fermented black beans, rinsed – 1 ½ tsp
- ginger, peeled and finely diced – 2 cm piece
- pork mince – 100 g
- groundnut oil – 3 tbsp
- tofu – 450 g
- garlic, chopped – 3 cloves
- corn flour, combined with 1 tbsp of water – 1 tsp
- Sichuan Chilli oil – 1 tbsp
- Sichuan peppercorns, ground – ½ tsp
- light chicken stock or water – 200 ml
- Spring onions, chopped - 6

Directions:

538.   Cut The tofu into 1.5cm cubes after removing its moisture. To remove its moisture, lightly press it

with a towel. Place it in a bowl and cover it with very hot water and set it aside.

539.   Pour the oil in a heated wok and when the oil is very hot, fry the pork to make it crispy. Take it out with a slotted spoon and drain the oil from it.

540.   Stir and cook the bean paste in the wok until it's fragrant which will take a few minutes. Then, mix in the ginger, garlic, and black beans. Cook them for 1 minute and then add the stock/water and allow it to bubble away.

541.   In the wok, combine the cornflour and water with the sauce. Drain (to remove moisture) the tofu and stir it in with spring onions and the mince.

542.   Add the Chilli oil to the sauce, drizzle the peppercorns and serve with steamed white rice.

Recipe 94: Smoked-Paprika Cod with Spanish Green Beans

This dish uses beautiful ingredients simply cooked with authentic Spanish flavors to showcase the delicate texture of the fish and the crunch of fresh green beans. Vegetarian? No problem. Swap the cod for pan-fried halloumi with an oregano and flaxseed crust and add an extra side of  vegetables such as roasted beets with a splash of balsamic vinegar, if your carb allowance permits.

Calories: 509

Prep time: 10 minutes

Cook time: 20 minutes

Serving Size: 2

Ingredients

For the green beans

- 2 tablespoons extra-virgin olive oil, divided
- 6 ounces green beans, trimmed
- 4 garlic cloves, minced
- 1 (14-ounce) can chopped Italian tomatoes
- 1 teaspoon dried oregano
- Salt
- Freshly ground black pepper

- 3 tablespoons chopped pine nuts or hazelnuts, lightly toasted

- Juice of ½ lemon

For the fish

- 1 teaspoon extra-virgin olive oil

- 2 (6-ounce) cod fillets, skin on

- ½ teaspoon smoked paprika

- 1 tablespoon unsalted butter

Directions

To make the green beans

543.   Heat 1 tablespoon of the olive oil in a large saucepan over medium heat. Add your garlic and green beans to the saucepan. Stir and sauté for about 2 minutes, making sure not to brown the garlic.

544.   Add the tomatoes with their juice and the oregano to the same pan and stir with the green beans. Season with salt and pepper.

545.   Cover the pan and bring to a simmer. Turn the heat down from medium to low and then gently cook for 15 minutes.

To make the fish and serve

546.   After the beans have been cooking for 5 minutes, get started on the fish by adding the remaining olive oil to a sauté pan or skillet over medium heat. Place the cod fillets in the pan skin-side down and sprinkle the paprika over the top. Leave to cool for 2 minutes.

547. Add the butter to the fish pan. When the butter is melted, tip the pan to one side, and using a spoon, repeatedly pour the melted butter over the top of the fillets for a minute or so or until the top of the fish is cooked. Take it from the heat and let rest for a few minutes.

548. Adjust salt in the green beans as needed. Transfer the green beans to two plates, and sprinkle on the pine nuts, add a squeeze of lemon juice, and drizzle the rest of the olive oil over the top. Add the cod fillets to the plates and serve immediately.

Recipe 95: Spicy Keto Chicken Tenders with Parmesan Mayo

These chicken tenders might look like kid's food, but the chipotle chile powder elevates this dish for the adult palate. Almond flour helps keep the carb level down and adds calcium and vitamin E.

Calories: 607

Prep Time: 20 minutes

Cook Time: 20 minutes

Serving Size: 4

Ingredients:

For the chicken

- 1 large egg

- 1 tablespoon heavy (whipping) cream

- ⅔ cup superfine almond flour (without almond skins)

- ¼ cup full-fat grated Parmesan cheese

- 1 teaspoon freshly ground black pepper

- 1 teaspoon chipotle chile powder

- 12 ounces boneless, skinless chicken breast, cut into strips

- 1 cup high-oleic sunflower oil, safflower oil, or canola oil

For the Parmesan mayo

- ¼ cup full-fat mayonnaise

- 1 tablespoon full-fat grated Parmesan cheese

- ¼ teaspoon garlic powder

- ¼ teaspoon onion flakes

Directions:

To make the chicken

549.   In a small bowl, whisk together the egg and heavy cream. Set aside.

550.   In another small bowl, stir together the almond flour, Parmesan cheese, black pepper, and chipotle powder to combine.

551.   Working with one piece at a time, dip the chicken into the flour dredge, then the egg mixture, and into the flour dredge again.

552.   In an electric skillet set to 350°F or in a skillet over medium-high heat on the stovetop, heat the oil. To test that the oil is hot enough, dip the handle of a wooden spoon in it; if the oil bubbles around the spoon, it's ready.

553.   Working in batches, carefully add the battered chicken to the hot oil. Cook for about 4 minutes until golden brown. Flip and cook for about 4 minutes more, until golden on the other side.

To make the Parmesan mayo

554.   While the chicken cooks, in a small bowl, stir together the mayonnaise, Parmesan cheese, garlic powder, and onion flakes. Set aside.

555.   Serve the fried chicken with Parmesan mayo.

Recipe 96: Spicy Pork Lettuce Wraps

Who needs tortillas and pita bread when you have fresh lettuce? Lettuce wraps are popular as a snack or an appetizer, but you can also create the main course wraps with nutritious fillings. In this recipe, the spicy pork and vegetable combination contains enough calories to make a full meal.

Calories: 383

Prep Time: 15 minutes

Cook Time: 20 minutes

Serving Size: 4

Ingredients:

FOR THE SAUCE

- 2 tablespoons coconut oil

- 1 tablespoon rice vinegar

- 1 tablespoon granulated erythritol

- 1 tablespoon fish sauce

- 1 tablespoon almond flour

- 1 teaspoon coconut amino

FOR THE WRAPS

- 2 tablespoons sesame oil, divided

- 1 pound ground pork

- 1 teaspoon minced garlic

- 1 teaspoon peeled grated fresh ginger

- 1, seeded and thinly sliced, red bell pepper

- 1 carrot, peeled and grated

- 1, thinly sliced, scallion of white and green parts,

- 8 large romaine or Boston lettuce leaves

Directions:

TO MAKE THE SAUCE

556.   Whisk together the coconut oil, rice vinegar, erythritol, fish sauce, almond flour, and coconut amino in a small bowl. Set aside.

TO MAKE THE WRAPS

557.   Heat 1 tablespoon of sesame oil in a large skillet over medium-high heat and sauté the pork until cooked through about 8 minutes.

558.   Add the sauce and stir until it is thickened about 4 minutes.

559.   With a slotted spoon, remove the pork to a plate and set it aside.

560.   Wipe the skillet with a paper towel and heat the remaining 1 tablespoon of oil over medium-high heat.

561.   Sauté the garlic and ginger until softened, about 3 minutes.

562.	Add the bell pepper, carrot, and scallion and sauté until they are softened for about 5 minutes.

563.	Return the pork to the skillet with any sauce on the plate, stirring to combine.

564.	Spoon the hot pork filling into the lettuce leaves and serve.

Recipe 97: Thai Cashew Nut Curry

This warming and fragrant curry is cozier than a warm blanket and is a dish everyone will enjoy. Add a side of cauliflower rice or basmati rice depending on your carbohydrate allowance. For carnivores, leftover roasted meat makes a delicious addition.

Calories: 876

Prep time: 5 minutes

Cook time: 15 minutes

Serving Size: 2

Ingredients

- 2 ounces cashew nuts, whole

- 1 tablespoon coconut oil

- 1 medium zucchini, chopped

- 1 red bell pepper, chopped

- 4, chopped, scallions of white and light green parts

- 1 tablespoon red Thai curry paste

- 10 cherry tomatoes, halved

- 1 cup broccoli florets

- 1 (14-ounce) can coconut milk

- 3 tablespoons smooth peanut butter with no added sugar

- 1 tablespoon tamari or soy sauce

- Juice from ½ lime

Directions

565.   Heat a wok or other large sauté pan or skillet over medium heat. Add the cashew nuts and dry toast them for about 2 minutes. Tip the nuts onto a plate and set them aside.

566.   Turn the heat up to high and add the coconut oil to the pan to melt. Add the zucchini, pepper, and scallions to the pan and sauté for about 2 minutes, stirring constantly.

567.   Add the curry paste and stir to coat the ingredients in the pan roughly.

568.   Add the cherry tomatoes, broccoli florets, coconut milk, and peanut butter to the pan. Stir well to combine and turn the heat down to medium.

569.   Let the curry simmer for 3 to 4 minutes or until the vegetables are al dente. Turn off the heat, and stir in the tamari, lime juice, and toasted cashew nuts. Ladle into serving bowls and enjoy hot on its own or with a side of rice or cauliflower rice.

Recipe 98: <u>Vegetarian Chili with Cranberries</u>

The pizzazz with this chili is the cranberries. Everyone who tastes it tells me what a great addition they are. I use frozen cranberries and they thaw quickly after just a couple of minutes in the hot chili. This tart fruit has more than 10 percent of your daily requirement for vitamin C, manganese, and fiber in a 3½-ounce serving.

Calories: 138

Prep Time: 10 minutes

Cook Time: 30 minutes

Serving Size: 6

Ingredients:

- 1 tablespoon extra-virgin olive oil, high-oleic sunflower oil, safflower oil, or canola oil

- 1 small onion, chopped

- 1 celery stalk, chopped

- 1 carrot, chopped

- 1 garlic clove, minced

- 1 can (14 oz.) rinsed and drained red kidney beans,

- 2 tablespoons chili powder

- 1 teaspoon red pepper flakes

- 1 (28-ounce) can stewed tomatoes, with liquid

- 1 cup fresh or frozen cranberries

- 2 tablespoons chopped fresh parsley

Directions:

570.   Heat the oil in a big pot over medium. Combine the onion, celery, and carrot in a large mixing bowl. Cook, stirring occasionally, for about 8 minutes, or until the vegetables are soft.

571.   Combine the garlic, chili powder, and red pepper flakes in a large mixing bowl. To soften the garlic, reduce the heat to medium-low and cook for about 3 minutes.

572.   Fill the pot with the juice from the tomatoes. Cut through the tomato chunks in the can with an immersion blender, leaving some texture if preferred. Toss the tomatoes and kidney beans into the pot. Raise the heat to medium-low and let the chili simmer. Cook for 15 minutes to allow the flavors to meld.

573.   Stir in the cranberries and cook for 2 to 3 minutes to incorporate the flavors.

574.   Sprinkle with fresh parsley just before serving.

Chapter 7: The 7-Day Meal Plan

This meal plan follows the 16/8 period of intermittent fasting. In this particular meal plan, you will skip breakfast and eat your lunch and dinner in the eight-hour eating period.

If you'd rather skip dinner, you can make some adjustments or even customize the meal plan according to your liking. Just remember to follow the 16-hour fasting and 8 hour eating period.

DAY 1

[Fast for 16 hours]   **Breakfast:** <Skip>

[Begin at 12 PM]   **Lunch:** Bacon and Egg Salad (314 kcal)

Snacks (Optional): Baked Fennel (75 kcal)

[Finish until 8 PM]   **Dinner:** Chicken Tenders with Creamy Almond Sauce (555 kcal)

(Total Calories:944 kcal)

DAY 2

[Fast for 16 hours]   **Breakfast:** <Skip>

[Begin at 12 PM]   **Lunch:** Kale and Chard Shakshuka (408 kcal)

Snacks (Optional: Baked Fennel (75 kcal)

[Finish until 8 PM]   **Dinner:** Spicy Pork Lettuce Wraps (383 kcal)

(Total Calories:866 kcal)

DAY 3

[Fast for 16 hours] **Breakfast:** <Skip>

[Begin at 12 PM] **Lunch:** Coconut Noodle Crab Salad (314 kcal)

Snacks (Optional): Lemon-Lavender Muffins (129 kcal)

[Finish until 8 PM] **Dinner:** Pasta Carbonara (329 kcal)

(Total Calories:772 kcal)

DAY 4

[Fast for 16 hours]   **Breakfast:** \<Skip\>

[Begin at 12 PM]   **Lunch:** Keto Meatballs with Zucchini Pasta in Tomato Cream Sauce

(649 kcal)

Snacks (Optional): Cabbage Chips (35 kcal)

[Finish until 8 PM]   **Dinner:** Fried Shrimp Rice (205 kcal)

(Total Calories: 889 kcal)

DAY 5

[Fast for 16 hours]   **Breakfast:** \<Skip\>

[Begin at 12 PM]   **Lunch:** Greek Village Salad (207 kcal)

Snacks (Optional): Cheesy Breadsticks (399 kcal)

[Finish until 8 PM]   **Dinner:** Jerk Pork Tenderloin (287 kcal)

(Total Calories: 893 kcal)

DAY 6

[Fast for 16 hours]   **Breakfast:** \<Skip\>

[Begin at 12 PM]   **Lunch:** Chicken Chow Mein (406 kcal)

Snacks (Optional): Dijon Mustard Deviled Eggs (84 kcal)

[Finish until 8 PM]   **Dinner:** Sichuan Chili Tofu (310 kcal)

(Total Calories: 800 kcal)

DAY 7

[Fast for 16 hours]   **Breakfast:** <Skip>

[Begin at 12 PM]   **Lunch:** Kale and Chard Shakshuka (407 kcal)

Snacks (Optional): Creamy and Crunchy Egg Balls (67 kcal)

[Finish until 8 PM]   **Dinner:** Cream-Poached Trout (499 kcal)

(Total Calories: 973 kcal)

Conclusion

Thank you for making it through to the end of *Intermittent Fasting for Women*, let's hope it was informative and able to provide you with all of the tools you need to achieve your goals whatever they may be.

The next step is to take action that will usher you into a new level of wellness. If you still need help getting started, you are likely to get better results by evaluating your current schedule before you can select an appropriate intermittent fasting plan that is realistic, to begin with. Remember, you'll not be doing this to please anyone but for your own benefit.

Intermittent fasting is a great concept of scheduling your meal times, not just for weight loss but also living holistically because it gives you access to numerous health benefits. What's more? Unlike many weight loss diets that are restrictive, expensive, and offer minimal results, intermittent fasting is free and easy to follow through. You simply need to change your eating pattern so that you have periods of fasting followed by periods of feasting.

This book is especially a great resource that will help you through your journey in carving a new lifestyle. Remember, you don't have to change your way of living but instead embrace the new way of feeding to suit your way of living. In fact, you can still carry on with your exercise routine even though you may have to tailor it to your current situation in terms of when you eat and how intense your workout is.

What are you waiting for? Go ahead and start preparing for your intermittent fasting experience to tap into its benefits. Use the information you have acquired in this book as a springboard to prepare and transform your life.